ONE
MINUTE
BIBLE

FOR STUDENTS

ONE MINUTE BIBLE
FOR STUDENTS

365 DAILY DEVOTIONS

DOUG FIELDS: GENERAL EDITOR

CSB
CHRISTIAN STANDARD BIBLE®

HOLMAN®
BIBLES

TABLE OF CONTENTS

INTRODUCTION

The Bible is the greatest of all books ... ever! Actually, it's much more than a book, it is a collection of sixty-six books written over the span of sixteen centuries by kings, peasants, poets ,and prophets. These sixty-six can be divided into several categories, like ...

The Books of the Law. Genesis through Deuteronomy recount the early history of humanity. It is the history of God's beginnings on earth and reveals the great covenant at Mount Sinai where the living God of the universe bound himself to the nation of Israel (the Israelites).

The Historical Books of Joshua through Esther highlight the history of Israel, noting Israel's successes and failures as well as God's patience, love, and grace.

The Books of Poetry and Wisdom. Job through Song of Songs celebrate the God of Israel for his goodness, his holiness, and his accessibility to all who approach him on his terms. Wisdom offers timeless principles for living a successful life in relation to God and others.

The Prophets. Isaiah through Malachi were the preachers of old. They proclaimed to the Israelites their failure to honor their obligations to their God, warned them of his impending righteous judgment, and offered hope to all nations of his coming salvation.

The Gospels and Acts. Matthew through John tell of the life and the teaching of Jesus the Messiah, the promised Savior of Israel and all the nations. Acts recounts the early history of the Christian church as the followers of Jesus take his message to the farthest corners of the globe.

The Letters and Revelation. Romans through Jude were written by the first leaders of the church to offer encouragement, discipline, teaching, and hope. The book of Revelation tells of the end of this present world and of the establishment of the new heavens and new earth in which God will live with his people forever.

Our prayer is that what you are holding in your hands will offer you a taste of God's Word that will trigger a deeper hunger beyond these 365 bite-sized samplings. We hope you'll be inspired to read daily from a full-text Bible—as it is God's personal revelation to you and the only book that will provide accurate information about the love and character of God and how he wants to meet your deepest needs.

A NOTE TO STUDENTS

There's not a week that goes by that I don't speak to a teenager about their thoughts, concerns, doubts, and questions about life, faith, God, and the Bible. As a result of these conversations, I've tried to provide some clarity to many of the reoccurring questions and topics I hear from your peers.

You'll notice that on every day's reading, there will be a Scripture passage on one side of the page and then a quick thought or two from me on the other side of the page. Take your time. Read the portion from God's Word first. Then, read what I've written. Finally, feel free to write your thoughts or questions in the space provided. Also, we've supplied you with some additional sections of Scripture that you may want to read for greater insight into God's Word. Each day, when you're done with the reading, check the small box provided at the top of the page. This will remind you of your progress.

One of the challenges I'll often repeat to my students is this: *Don't give up* if you don't understand something. Some parts of the Bible are very difficult to understand. Don't give up! *Keep reading!* Write down your questions that you want to be sure to ask someone about—questions will lead to your spiritual growth, and chances are real high that someone has an answer for you. As you read, ask God to help you better understand the words in this love letter that he put together for you. Keep going . . . *you can do it!*

I applaud you for digging in and making a daily commitment to learn about God and his ways. My prayer is that your faith will deepen as you consume regular doses of God's Word.

I believe in you!
Doug Fields

A NOTE TO PARENTS

As a parent of three grown children, I know how important it is to help them experience, understand, and fall in love with God's Word. This book will help! Honestly, I know of no better resource to help teenagers, or anyone for that matter, develop the habit of reading God's Word. If your son or daughter has no Bible background, this will serve as a perfect introductory tool! I've discovered the simple truth that almost anyone will give one minute a day to the *greatest book* ever written. Or, if your child has grown up in the church and has a developing and mature faith, The *One-Minute Bible for Students* will be a powerful devotional resource that can encourage a daily habit. The breakdown of the content is intended to help develop the spiritual habit of reading the Bible while fostering and encouraging *spiritual maturity*.

Put this book in your child's hands, comment on the *ease* of the reading plan, and leave him or her alone to discover the power of life-giving transformation from God's Word. Over the years I've had so many parents enthusiastically tell me, "This is the only book my kid will read." I've also had parents admit that they bought an extra copy for themselves to track along with the readings and quickly find themselves being "hooked" on the ease of reading, the systematic order of Scriptures, and the relevancy of the additional notes. I'm never surprised by the power of God's Word, but I always smile when I meet a parent who has fallen in love with God's Word because of this devotional.

My prayer is that this book will *ignite a desire* within your entire family to consume more of God's love letter.

I'm cheering you on!
Doug Fields

A NOTE TO YOUTH WORKERS

As a *youth pastor* for more than thirty years and author of many books, I can't think of any other book, aside from the Bible itself, that I'd rather teenagers read than this one. This book not only helps students understand the Bible, but it emphasizes God's passionate and unconditional love for them and will challenge them to respond. Every day I've written an additional note to get them thinking and putting God's Word into action.

Youth ministry is tough in today's world! As you know, most teenagers, and their parents, are not reading the Bible. You and I are ministering to a biblically illiterate generation. I really believe they want to know God's ways, but they need tools to guide them to discover and discern God's Word. This is a tool that will do just that! My guess is that you'll see your teenagers begin to ask you more Bible questions simply because they are reading the Bible. That's definitely one of the signs of people reading the Bible—they have questions.

My prayer is that the *One-Minute Bible for Students* will assist you in your discipleship efforts and ministry to students. If it's helpful, I've written a supplemental fifty-two week teaching and small group curriculum that accompanies their daily reading and can help you have more focused content that connects to their daily life. It can be used for Sunday School or a midweek meeting or even for parents to discuss at home. If you're interested, it's available at downloadyouthministry.com (search: one minute Bible).

Thanks for doing what you do to guide students to become devoted followers of Jesus. You may not get the thanks you deserve from teenagers, their parents, or even your church . . . but you are appreciated. As a brother in Christ who knows what you're doing on a weekly basis may I say thank you!

I'm honored to share in the same ministry as you,
Doug

Doug Fields
www.dougfields.com

ANSWERS TO SOME COMMON QUESTIONS

WHERE DO I BEGIN?
The *One-Minute Bible for Students* offers 365 daily one-minute readings from the world's greatest literary treasure . . . the Bible. One reading for each day of the year.

IS THIS THE ENTIRE BIBLE?
Although every day contains selections from the Bible, the *One-Minute Bible for Students* isn't a complete Bible. Reading one minute a day will allow you to survey the heart of the Bible in one year. If you want more, we've provided related texts at the bottom of each day's devotion to direct you to nearly eighteen-hundred passages of Scripture that will further your understanding of what you read that day.

HOW MUCH OF THE BIBLE IS COVERED?
The *One-Minute Bible for Students* begins with the first verse of Genesis and ends with the last verse of Revelation. Readings follow the general flow of biblical history, interspersed with several topical series for dated occasions (like Easter, Mother's Day, Christmas, etc.). The seven-hundred selected Scriptures and eighteen-hundred related texts present the key themes of the Bible and draw from all sixty-six books within the Bible. Great care was taken to ensure that each text has the same meaning in the *One-Minute Bible for Students* as it does in its larger context in the Bible.

WHAT HAPPENS IF I DON'T READ EVERY DAY?
If you fall behind in your goal to read daily, don't worry! You can either resume where you left off—be sure to check the box at the top of the page—or if you desire to read the entire book in a year, you can make up one week's worth of reading in seven minutes. The point isn't to fault you when you miss, but to make it easy for you to develop a habit that will stick with you for the rest of your life. Don't feel guilty for missing a day . . . if you get behind, simply jump back in where you left off and . . .

"Just read it!"

I n the beginning God created the heavens and the earth.

Now the earth was formless and empty, darkness covered the surface of the watery depths, and the Spirit of God was hovering over the surface of the waters.

–Genesis 1:1–2

In the beginning was the Word, and the Word was with God, and the Word was God. He was with God in the beginning. All things were created through him, and apart from him not one thing was created that has been created. In him was life, and that life was the light of men. That light shines in the darkness, and yet the darkness did not overcome it.

–John 1:1–5

Hallelujah!
Praise the Lord from the heavens;
praise him in the heights.
Praise him, all his angels;
praise him, all
    his heavenly armies.
Praise him, sun and moon;
praise him, all you shining stars.
Praise him, highest heavens,
and you waters above the heavens.
Let them praise the name
    of the Lord,
for he commanded,
    and they were created.
He set them in position
    forever and ever;
he gave an order that will never
    pass away.

–Psalm 148:1–6

HERE'S THE DEAL

These few verses sure cause big debates in science class. Unfortunately, there are no quick or easy answers in the creation and evolution controversy. Believers in evolution claim the world suddenly exploded into existence billions of years ago—pits of slime somehow sprouted legs and started growing chest hair. It's a compelling story for those who don't believe in God or the Bible. The Bible teaches that God created the earth, and through him all things were made—including you.

Actually, it takes less faith to believe God created this world and you than it does to believe your complex minds and bodies evolved from a "big bang" and a drop of ooze.

God created you in his image. Spend time thinking about that truth and thank God that your uniqueness is no accident!

Related Texts: Psalms 102:25–28; 139:13–18; Proverbs 8; Isaiah 40:12– 31; 45:18–25; Hebrews 11:1–3

Then God said, "Let there be light," and there was light. God saw that the light was good, and God separated the light from the darkness. God called the light "day," and the darkness he called "night." There was an evening, and there was a morning: one day.

—Genesis 1:3–5

LORD, you are my lamp; the LORD illuminates my darkness.

—2 Samuel 22:29

The LORD is my light and my salvation — whom should I fear? The LORD is the stronghold of my life — whom should I dread?

—Psalm 27:1

Jesus spoke to them again: "I am the light of the world. Anyone who follows me will never walk in the darkness but will have the light of life."

—John 8:12

And there will no longer be any curse. The throne of God and of the Lamb will be in the city, and his servants will worship him. They will see his face, and his name will be on their foreheads. Night will be no more; people will not need the light of a lamp or the light of the sun, because the Lord God will give them light, and they will reign forever and ever.

—Revelation 22:3–5

DIG DEEPER

The Bible uses the term light on many different occasions. In Matthew 5:14–16 Jesus used the illustration of light to challenge and remind Christians that their lives are open books for everyone to read. Jesus said, "You are the light of the world. . . . Let your light shine before others, so that they may see your good works and give glory to your Father in heaven."

Being a light to the world is a big deal and a high calling from God! It's pretty wild to realize that you may be the only Christian some of your friends will ever meet.

So, here's a question: Are you "shining brightly" as a light? If not, what needs to change for you to become a brighter light for God?

Related Texts: Leviticus 24:1–4; Job 24:13–17; 38:8–20; John 3:19–21; 1 John 1:5–8

Then God said, "Let there be an expanse between the waters, separating water from water." So God made the expanse and separated the water under the expanse from the water above the expanse. And it was so. God called the expanse "sky." Evening came and then morning: the second day.

—Genesis 1:6–8

The heavens declare the glory
    of God,
and the expanse proclaims
    the work of his hands.
Day after day
    they pour out speech;
night after night
    they communicate knowledge.
There is no speech; there are
    no words;
their voice is not heard.

—Psalm 19:1–3

I will praise you, Lord,
    among the peoples;
I will sing praises to you
    among the nations.
For your faithful love is as high as
    the heavens;
your faithfulness reaches
    the clouds.
God, be exalted above the heavens;
let your glory be
    over the whole earth.

—Psalm 57:9–11

He made the earth by his power,
established the world
    by his wisdom,
and spread out the heavens
    by his understanding.
When he thunders,
the waters in the heavens
    are in turmoil,
and he causes the clouds to rise
from the ends of the earth.
He makes lightning for the rain
and brings the wind
    from his storehouses.

—Jeremiah 10:12–13

JUST A THOUGHT

If God is powerful enough to create this huge playground called "earth", don't you think he's mighty enough to have created you exactly as he intended?

Related Texts: 1 Chronicles 16:23–31; Job 38:22–38; Psalm 102:25–28; Acts 1:1–12

Then God said, "Let the water under the sky be gathered into one place, and let the dry land appear." And it was so. God called the dry land "earth," and the gathering of the water he called "seas." And God saw that it was good. Then God said, "Let the earth produce vegetation: seed-bearing plants and fruit trees on the earth bearing fruit with seed in it according to their kinds." And it was so. The earth produced vegetation: seed-bearing plants according to their kinds and trees bearing fruit with seed in it according to their kinds. And God saw that it was good. Evening came and then morning: the third day.

−Genesis 1:9−13

Do you not fear me?
   This is the LORD's declaration.
Do you not tremble before me,
the one who set the sand
   as the boundary of the sea,
an enduring barrier that
   it cannot cross?
The waves surge, but they
   cannot prevail.
They roar but cannot pass over it.
−Jeremiah 5:22

He causes grass to grow
   for the livestock
and provides crops for man
   to cultivate,
producing food from the earth,
wine that makes
   human hearts glad —
making his face shine with oil —
and bread that sustains
   human hearts.
−Psalm 104:14−15

IN OTHER WORDS

FEAR: To fear God doesn't mean to be afraid of him or fear some type of unknown punishment or terror.

To fear God means to respect him, to honor him, to be amazed by his greatness, and to admire all he has done for you and this world. You will know that you fear God when you have nothing to say but "Wow!" when trying to describe him. Developing an attitude of fear and awe is pleasing to God and one of the first steps toward gaining wisdom.

When you're done reading today, take a minute to think about all the "Wow!" that God has done for you.

Related Texts: Job 12:7−12; 38:8−11; Psalm 104; Revelation 20:11− 21:4; 22:13

T hen God said, "Let there be lights in the expanse of the sky to separate the day from the night. They will serve as signs for seasons and for days and years. They will be lights in the expanse of the sky to provide light on the earth." And it was so. God made the two great lights — the greater light to rule over the day and the lesser light to rule over the night — as well as the stars. God placed them in the expanse of the sky to provide light on the earth, to rule the day and the night, and to separate light from darkness. And God saw that it was good. Evening came and then morning: the fourth day.

—Genesis 1:14–19

I did not see a temple in it, because the Lord God the Almighty and the Lamb are its temple. The city does not need the sun or the moon to shine on it, because the glory of God illuminates it, and its lamp is the Lamb. The nations will walk by its light, and the kings of the earth will bring their glory into it. Its gates will never close by day because it will never be night there. They will bring the glory and honor of the nations into it. Nothing unclean will ever enter it, nor anyone who does what is detestable or false, but only those written in the Lamb's book of life.

—Revelation 21:22–27

WEIRD OR WHAT?

The word *lamb* is used in the Bible 138 times—93 of those refer to Jesus. A lamb was one of the main animals used for sacrifices. Jesus received the title "Lamb" because of his ultimate sacrifice on the cross—death. Do you feel like you understand what that means? It's a biggie! Jesus sacrificed his life so that you can share all of eternity with him and other believers. His sacrifice paved the way to heaven and made it available to you.

Related Texts: Nehemiah 9:5–6; Job 9:1–9; Psalms 19:1–6; 104:19–23; Proverbs 4:18–19; Ephesians 5:8–16

Then God said, "Let the water swarm with living creatures, and let birds fly above the earth across the expanse of the sky." So God created the large sea-creatures and every living creature that moves and swarms in the water, according to their kinds. He also created every winged creature according to its kind. And God saw that it was good. God blessed them: "Be fruitful, multiply, and fill the waters of the seas, and let the birds multiply on the earth." Evening came and then morning: the fifth day.

—Genesis 1:20–23

How countless are
    your works, LORD!
In wisdom
    you have made them all;
the earth is full of your creatures.
Here is the sea, vast and wide,
teeming with creatures
    beyond number —
living things both large and small.
There the ships move about,
and Leviathan, which you formed
    to play there.

All of them wait for you
to give them their food
    at the right time.
When you give it to them,
they gather it;
when you open your hand,
they are satisfied
    with good things.

—Psalm 104:24–28

DIG DEEPER

It's great to know that God not only created animals, but he cares about them as well. What's even more incredible is the truth that God cares more about you than animals—you are more valuable. Jesus said that not even a sparrow "falls to the ground without your Father's consent. But even the hairs of your head have all been counted. So don't be afraid; you are worth more than many sparrows" (Mt 10:29–31).

You are God's unique creation! You are so special and so known by God that the number of hairs on your head is not a secret to God. You might even say, "Not one hair can fall into the bathroom sink without God knowing about it." Wow . . . that's incredible and a great image of God's concern for you!

Related Texts: Psalms 104;11–18; 148:7–12; Matthew 6:25–33; 10:29–31; Revelation 5:11–13

T hen God said, "Let the earth produce living creatures according to their kinds: livestock, creatures that crawl, and the wildlife of the earth according to their kinds." And it was so. So God made the wildlife of the earth according to their kinds, the livestock according to their kinds, and all the creatures that crawl on the ground according to their kinds. And God saw that it was good.

–Genesis 1:24–25

I do not rebuke you
    for your sacrifices
or for your burnt offerings,
which are continually before me.
I will not take a bull
    from your household
or male goats from your pens,
for every animal of the forest
    is mine,
the cattle on a thousand hills.
I know every bird
    of the mountains,
and the creatures of the field
    are mine.
If I were hungry, I would not
    tell you,
for the world and everything in it
    is mine.
Do I eat the flesh of bulls
or drink the blood of goats?
Offer a thanksgiving sacrifice
    to God,
and pay your vows
    to the Most High.
Call on me in a day of trouble;
I will rescue you,
    and you will honor me."

–Psalm 50:8–15

IN OTHER WORDS

Sacrifice: Several types of animal sacrifices are mentioned throughout the Bible. People made sacrifices when they wanted to get right with God. In the Old Testament, God instructed a person to sacrifice (kill) an animal as a type of payment. This "payment" was made to God for their sin and it resulted in forgiveness. Thankfully, when Jesus died on the cross, he became the "ultimate payment." Once and for all, Jesus's death paid the penalty and debt for your sin.

Related Texts: Genesis 9:1–3; Psalm 8; Proverbs 12:10; Isaiah 11:1–10; 65:17–25

Then God said, "Let us make man in our image, according to our likeness. They will rule the fish of the sea, the birds of the sky, the livestock, the whole earth, and the creatures that crawl on the earth."

So God created man
in his own image;
he created him in the image
of God;
he created them male
and female.

God blessed them, and God said to them, "Be fruitful, multiply, fill the earth, and subdue it. Rule the fish of the sea, the birds of the sky, and every creature that crawls on the earth." God also said, "Look, I have given you every seed-bearing plant on the surface of the entire earth and every tree whose fruit contains seed. This will be food for you, for all the wildlife of the earth, for every bird of the sky, and for every creature that crawls on the earth — everything having the breath of life in it — I have given every green plant for food." And it was so. God saw all that he had made, and it was very good indeed. Evening came and then morning: the sixth day.

—Genesis 1:26–31

HERE'S THE DEAL

These verses are awesome! God created you in his image and views his creation as very good. Not average. Not weird. Not ugly. But very good! If that truth doesn't get you excited, you'd better check your pulse; you might already be dead.

Take a minute and thank God for your image that God created. Rest in the truth that no matter what you think of yourself and your body, God sees you as good. No, *very* good.

Related Texts: Genesis 2:4–25; 9:6–7; Psalm 8; 1 Corinthians 6:1–4; 2 Corinthians 4:4–6; Colossians 1:9– 20; 3:5–10

So the heavens and the earth and everything in them were completed. On the seventh day God had completed his work that he had done, and he rested on the seventh day from all his work that he had done. God blessed the seventh day and declared it holy, for on it he rested from all his work of creation.

−Genesis 2:1−3

Remember the Sabbath day, to keep it holy. . . . For the Lord made the heavens and the earth, the sea, and everything in them in six days; then he rested on the seventh day. Therefore the Lord blessed the Sabbath day and declared it holy.

−Exodus 20:8,11

On the Sabbath he was going through the grainfields, and his disciples began to make their way, picking some heads of grain. The Pharisees said to him, "Look, why are they doing what is not lawful on the Sabbath?"

He said to them, "Have you never read what David and those who were with him did when he was in need and hungry — how he entered the house of God in the time of Abiathar the high priest and ate the bread of the Presence — which is not lawful for anyone to eat except the priests — and also gave some to his companions?" Then he told them, "The Sabbath was made for man and not man for the Sabbath. So then, the Son of Man is Lord even of the Sabbath."

−Mark 2:23−28

JUST A THOUGHT

Don't you think that if God found the time to rest after all he did, you can spend some time enjoying his good work?

Related Texts: Exodus 16:11−30; Psalm 62:1−5; Matthew 11:25−30; Mark 6:30−32; Hebrews 4:1−4

Then the LORD God formed the man out of the dust from the ground and breathed the breath of life into his nostrils, and the man became a living being. . . .

The LORD God took the man and placed him in the garden of Eden to work it and watch over it. And the LORD God commanded the man, "You are free to eat from any tree of the garden, but you must not eat from the tree of the knowledge of good and evil, for on the day you eat from it, you will certainly die." Then the LORD God said, "It is not good for the man to be alone. I will make a helper corresponding to him."

So the LORD God caused a deep sleep to come over the man, and he slept. God took one of his ribs and closed the flesh at that place. Then the LORD God made the rib he had taken from the man into a woman and brought her to the man. And the man said:

This one, at last, is bone
    of my bone
and flesh of my flesh;
this one will be called "woman,"
for she was taken from man.

This is why a man leaves his father and mother and bonds with his wife, and they become one flesh. Both the man and his wife were naked, yet felt no shame.

—*Genesis 2:7,15–18,21–25*

BIG TIME WORD

Bonds is a very important word to understand (Gn 2:24) because it's a graphic description of sex. That's right—sex! Sex wasn't invented by a group of scientists or a guy named Bob during the middle ages. Sex was God's idea. He designed it! But from the very beginning, God set a standard for sex to bond husband and wife into "one flesh." It's sort of reverse arithmetic: two become one. God wants you to become one flesh with only one other person—it's his design and it's his standard. Just like Adam and Eve, that one other person is to be your spouse. What a beautiful gift from God! It's a design worth waiting for!

Related Texts: Genesis 1:26–29; Matthew 19:1–12; Mark 10:1–12; 1 Corinthians 6:15–7:40

L ORD, our Lord,
how magnificent is your name
throughout the earth!

You have covered the heavens
with your majesty.
From the mouths of infants and
nursing babies,
you have established a stronghold
on account of your adversaries
in order to silence the enemy
and the avenger.

When I observe your heavens,
the work of your fingers,
the moon and the stars,
which you set in place,
what is a human being
that you remember him,
a son of man that you look
after him?
You made him little less than God
and crowned him with glory
and honor.
You made him ruler
over the works of your hands;
you put everything under his feet:
all the sheep and oxen,
as well as the animals in the wild,
the birds of the sky,
and the fish of the sea
that pass through the currents
of the seas.

LORD, our Lord,
how magnificent is your name
throughout the earth!
—Psalm 8

TAKE A SHOT

This psalm was written to express
thankfulness for all God has done.
What are three things for which you
are thankful?

1.

2.

3.

Related Texts: Genesis 1–2;
Matthew 21:16; Hebrews 2:5–9

Now the serpent was the most cunning of all the wild animals that the LORD God had made. He said to the woman, "Did God really say, 'You can't eat from any tree in the garden'?"

The woman said to the serpent, "We may eat the fruit from the trees in the garden. But about the fruit of the tree in the middle of the garden, God said, 'You must not eat it or touch it, or you will die.'"

"No! You will certainly not die," the serpent said to the woman. "In fact, God knows that when you eat it your eyes will be opened and you will be like God, knowing good and evil." The woman saw that the tree was good for food and delightful to look at, and that it was desirable for obtaining wisdom. So she took some of its fruit and ate it; she also gave some to her husband, who was with her, and he ate it. Then the eyes of both of them were opened, and they knew they were naked; so they sewed fig leaves together and made coverings for themselves.

Then the man and his wife heard the sound of the LORD God walking in the garden at the time of the evening breeze, and they hid from the LORD God among the trees of the garden.

—Genesis 3:1–8

IN OTHER WORDS

Satan is not a make-believe character created to scare you. Satan is real. The Bible refers to Satan several times and gives him very descriptive names: Evil One, Serpent or Snake, Murderer, Roaring Lion, Liar, Tempter, Dragon, and the Devil. Not the types of name that describe love, huh?

Satan's role started when he tempted Adam and Eve to disobey God. He did a good job! Their act of disobedience or rebellion is known as the first or "original" sin. Their sin led the way for the entire world to follow.

Since then, this world has gotten pretty bad. Death, violence, pain, terrorism, and wickedness are everywhere. But there's hope in the midst of this chaos! If you read to the end of this book, you'll see how God has his way with Satan. It's good to be on God's side since he wins in the end!

Related Texts: Ezekiel 28:13–19; Romans 5:12–19; 1 Tim 2:11–15; James 1:12–15

So the LORD God called out to the man and said to him, "Where are you?"

And he said, "I heard you in the garden, and I was afraid because I was naked, so I hid."

Then he asked, "Who told you that you were naked? Did you eat from the tree that I commanded you not to eat from?"

The man replied, "The woman you gave to be with me — she gave me some fruit from the tree, and I ate."

So the LORD God asked the woman, "What have you done?"

And the woman said, "The serpent deceived me, and I ate."

So the LORD God said to the serpent:

Because you have done this,
you are cursed more than
    any livestock
and more than any wild animal.
You will move on your belly
and eat dust all the days
    of your life.
I will put hostility between you
    and the woman,
and between your offspring
    and her offspring.
He will strike your head,
and you will strike his heel.

He said to the woman:
I will intensify your labor pains;
you will bear children
    with painful effort.
Your desire will be
    for your husband,
yet he will rule over you.

—Genesis 3:9–16

ONE MINUTE MEMORY

"Therefore, there is now no condemnation for those in Christ Jesus" (Rm 8:1).

Related Texts: Deuteronomy 32:1–6; Romans 3:9–18; Revelation 12:9; 20:1–3,7–15; 22:1–3

And he said to the man, "Because you listened to your wife and ate from the tree about which I commanded you, 'Do not eat from it':

The ground is cursed
    because of you.
You will eat from it by means of
    painful labor
all the days of your life.
It will produce thorns
    and thistles for you,
and you will eat the plants
    of the field.
You will eat bread by the sweat
    of your brow
until you return to the ground,
since you were taken from it.
For you are dust,
    and you will return to dust."

The man named his wife Eve because she was the mother of all the living. The LORD God made clothing from skins for the man and his wife, and he clothed them.

The LORD God said, "Since the man has become like one of us, knowing good and evil, he must not reach out, take from the tree of life, eat, and live forever." So the LORD God sent him away from the garden of Eden to work the ground from which he was taken. He drove the man out and stationed the cherubim and the flaming, whirling sword east of the garden of Eden to guard the way to the tree of life.

—Genesis 3:17–24

For just as in Adam all die, so also in Christ all will be made alive.

—1 Corinthians 15:22

DIG DEEPER

It sounds depressing to read that you will die because of your disobedience. You may even be thinking, "What did I do wrong?" It's a good and fair question! The answer is that just like everyone else, you were born into a sinful world where death goes along with living.

It's good news to know that your future is in God's hands and it's one filled with hope. One day God will get rid of sin and death. The Bible teaches that all creation anticipates the day when it will join God's children in glorious freedom from death and decay (Rm 8:21). If you are one of God's children, get ready to celebrate! If not . . . well, let's just say it doesn't look good.

Related Texts: Genesis 18:16–33; Psalm 50; Romans 8:18–25; Revelation 22

Therefore, just as sin entered the world through one man, and death through sin, in this way death spread to all people, because all sinned. In fact, sin was in the world before the law, but sin is not charged to a person's account when there is no law. Nevertheless, death reigned from Adam to Moses, even over those who did not sin in the likeness of Adam's transgression. He is a type of the Coming One.

But the gift is not like the trespass. For if by the one man's trespass the many died, how much more have the grace of God and the gift which comes through the grace of the one man Jesus Christ overflowed to the many. And the gift is not like the one man's sin, because from one sin came the judgment, resulting in condemnation, but from many trespasses came the gift, resulting in justification. If by the one man's trespass, death reigned through that one man, how much more will those who receive the overflow of grace and the gift of righteousness reign in life through the one man, Jesus Christ.
—*Romans 5:12–17*

For the wages of sin is death, but the gift of God is eternal life in Christ Jesus our Lord.
—*Romans 6:23*

ONE MINUTE MEMORY

"For the wages of sin is death, but the gift of God is eternal life in Christ Jesus our Lord" (Rm 6:23).

Related Texts: Genesis 3; Romans 5:18–6:23; Ephesians 2:1–10; Colossians 3:1–17

The man was intimate with his wife Eve, and she conceived and gave birth to Cain. She said, "I have had a male child with the LORD's help." She also gave birth to his brother Abel. Now Abel became a shepherd of flocks, but Cain worked the ground. In the course of time Cain presented some of the land's produce as an offering to the LORD. And Abel also presented an offering — some of the firstborn of his flock and their fat portions. The LORD had regard for Abel and his offering, but he did not have regard for Cain and his offering. Cain was furious, and he looked despondent.

Then the LORD said to Cain, "Why are you furious? And why do you look despondent? If you do what is right, won't you be accepted? But if you do not do what is right, sin is crouching at the door. Its desire is for you, but you must rule over it."

Cain said to his brother Abel, "Let's go out to the field." And while they were in the field, Cain attacked his brother Abel and killed him.

Then the LORD said to Cain, "Where is your brother Abel?"

"I don't know," he replied. "Am I my brother's guardian?"

Then he said, "What have you done? Your brother's blood cries out to me from the ground! So now you are cursed, alienated from the ground that opened its mouth to receive your brother's blood you have shed. If you work the ground, it will never again give you its yield. You will be a restless wanderer on the earth."

—Genesis 4:1–12

HERE'S THE DEAL

It doesn't take the IQ of a genius to recognize Cain's jealousy. He compared his gift with Abel's, and by all comparison, he lost. Instead of attacking his own problem of jealousy, he attacked his brother and killed him. Not exactly a fairy-tale ending, right?

Jealous people are typically not happy with who they are. They spend too much time comparing themselves to others and trying to conform to another's style, personality, or look. This comparison game can leave you feeling like a loser because you'll always find someone stronger, smarter, more athletic, or better looking than you.

Fortunately, God doesn't play the comparison game. He doesn't care if you are tan, fat, thin, athletic, or smart. God is interested in your heart. If you can understand this truth, jealousy can disappear. He loves you just the way you are; so thank him and celebrate your creation.

Related Texts: Exodus 20:13; Matthew 5:21–26; Hebrews 11:4; 1 John 3:11–12

These are the family records of Noah. Noah was a righteous man, blameless among his contemporaries; Noah walked with God. And Noah fathered three sons: Shem, Ham, and Japheth.

Now the earth was corrupt in God's sight, and the earth was filled with wickedness. God saw how corrupt the earth was, for every creature had corrupted its way on the earth. Then God said to Noah, "I have decided to put an end to every creature, for the earth is filled with wickedness because of them; therefore I am going to destroy them along with the earth.

"Make yourself an ark of gopher wood. Make rooms in the ark, and cover it with pitch inside and outside....

"Understand that I am bringing a flood — floodwaters on the earth to destroy every creature under heaven with the breath of life in it. Everything on earth will perish. But I will establish my covenant with you, and you will enter the ark with your sons, your wife, and your sons' wives. You are also to bring into the ark two of all the living creatures, male and female, to keep them alive with you.... Take with you every kind of food that is eaten; gather it as food for you and for them." And Noah did this. He did everything that God had commanded him.

–Genesis 6:9–14,17–19,21–22

PERSONALITY PLUS

Many seem to know the connection between Noah and his ark, but as important as the ark is the fact that Noah was a man who walked with God. Noah lived during a difficult time period when sin was everywhere, people were wicked, and the world was losing control to evil. Noah is heroic because he remained faithful to God, and God was faithful to him and honored him by choosing him and his family to repopulate the world.

Wouldn't you love to be described as a person who "walked with God"? Are you currently open to God's using you to do great things? Faithfulness is good preparation for being used by God. You too can be a spiritual hero through faithfulness.

Related Texts: Psalms 29; 36; Hebrews 11:1–7; 1 Peter 3:18–22

Noah was six hundred years old when the flood came and water covered the earth. So Noah, his sons, his wife, and his sons' wives entered the ark because of the floodwaters. From the animals that are clean, and from the animals that are not clean, and from the birds and every creature that crawls on the ground, two of each, male and female, came to Noah and entered the ark, just as God had commanded him. Seven days later the floodwaters came on the earth.

The flood continued for forty days on the earth; the water increased and lifted up the ark so that it rose above the earth. The water surged and increased greatly on the earth, and the ark floated on the surface of the water. Then the water surged even higher on the earth, and all the high mountains under the whole sky were covered. . . . He wiped out every living thing that was on the face of the earth, from mankind to livestock, to creatures that crawl, to the birds of the sky, and they were wiped off the earth. Only Noah was left, and those that were with him in the ark. And the water surged on the earth 150 days.
        —*Genesis 7:6–10,17–19,23–24*

By faith Noah, after he was warned about what was not yet seen and motivated by godly fear, built an ark to deliver his family. By faith he condemned the world and became an heir of the righteousness that comes by faith.
        —*Hebrews 11:7*

WEIRD OR WHAT?

It's not exactly clear what Noah's ark looked like . . . just a bunch of educated guesses based on dimensions. It was 300 cubits in length, 50 cubits in width, and 30 cubits in height. If that doesn't help you any, you can figure out the size of the boat by multiplying 21 inches per cubit. If you don't want the math challenge but want to use the answers to stump a friend, turn this upside down for the dimensions.

[It's 525 feet long, 87 feet 6 inches wide, and 52 feet 6 inches high.]

Related Texts: Psalm 93; Nahum 1:1–8; Matthew 24:36–42; Luke 17:26–36; 2 Peter 2:4–9

God remembered Noah, as well as all the wildlife and all the livestock that were with him in the ark. God caused a wind to pass over the earth, and the water began to subside. . . .

After forty days Noah opened the window of the ark that he had made, and he sent out a raven. It went back and forth until the water had dried up from the earth. Then he sent out a dove to see whether the water on the earth's surface had gone down, but the dove found no resting place for its foot. It returned to him in the ark because water covered the surface of the whole earth. He reached out and brought it into the ark to himself. So Noah waited seven more days and sent out the dove from the ark again. When the dove came to him at evening, there was a plucked olive leaf in its beak. So Noah knew that the water on the earth's surface had gone down. . . .

So Noah, along with his sons, his wife, and his sons' wives, came out. . . .

When the LORD smelled the pleasing aroma, he said to himself, "I will never again curse the ground because of human beings, even though the inclination of the human heart is evil from youth onward. And I will never again strike down every living thing as I have done."
—*Genesis 8:1,6–11,18,21*

IN OTHER WORDS

These last two verses are referred to as the "Noahic Covenant." A covenant is an oath or a promise made by God. The Noahic Covenant is the promise God made to Noah—and to everyone who would be alive in the future—that he would never again destroy the earth by flooding. Remember that truth during the next heavy rain.

As you read the Bible, you can always look to God's covenants with confidence that he will keep his promises—he always has.

Related Texts: Genesis 9; 2 Peter 3:1–14; Revelation 21:1–4

The Lord said to Abram:
Go from your land,
your relatives,
and your father's house
to the land that I will show you.
I will make you
into a great nation,
I will bless you,
I will make your name great,
and you will be a blessing.
I will bless those who bless you,
I will curse anyone
who treats you
with contempt,
and all the peoples on earth
will be blessed through you.

So Abram went, as the Lord had told him, and Lot went with him. Abram was seventy-five years old when he left Haran. He took his wife, Sarai, his nephew Lot, all the possessions they had accumulated, and the people they had acquired in Haran, and they set out for the land of Canaan. When they came to the land of Canaan, Abram passed through the land to the site of Shechem, at the oak of Moreh. (At that time the Canaanites were in the land.) The Lord appeared to Abram and said, "To your offspring I will give this land." So he built an altar there to the Lord who had appeared to him.

—Genesis 12:1–7

BIBLICAL BIO

Abraham is one of the most popular people in the Bible. He is known as the "father of the faithful." Like Noah, Abraham was a faithful person who put God first in his life. His faith was tested when he had to leave his country and family and travel to an unknown land. He had so much confidence in God that he was willing to offer his only child, Isaac, as a sacrifice to prove this faithfulness. Thankfully, God rewarded his faithfulness and Isaac was spared.

As you read about Abraham, think about how your life reveals faithfulness. God has a vision for your life. Are you ready? Available? Faithful? Willing? How about today?

Related Texts: Psalm 67; Acts 7:2–5; Hebrews 6:13–16; 11:8–10

After these events, the word of the LORD came to Abram in a vision:

Do not be afraid, Abram.
I am your shield;
your reward will be very great.

But Abram said, "Lord GOD, what can you give me, since I am childless and the heir of my house is Eliezer of Damascus?" Abram continued, "Look, you have given me no offspring, so a slave born in my house will be my heir."

Now the word of the LORD came to him: "This one will not be your heir; instead, one who comes from your own body will be your heir." He took him outside and said, "Look at the sky and count the stars, if you are able to count them." Then he said to him, "Your offspring will be that numerous."

Abram believed the LORD, and he credited it to him as righteousness.

–Genesis 15:1–6

Now **it was credited to him** was not written for Abraham alone, but also for us. It will be credited to us who believe in him who raised Jesus our Lord from the dead. He was delivered up for our trespasses and raised for our justification.

–Romans 4:23–25

IN OTHER WORDS

Righteous — The words *righteous* and *righteousness* are used many times in the Bible. A righteous person is someone who has an intimate relationship with God and constantly lives to please him and do what's right.

In the Old Testament a righteous person is someone who "fears" God and lives his life by keeping God's commandments (see also Day 4 on "fear").

In the New Testament, Jesus went beyond the definition of doing right and focused more on being right. He placed priority on a person's heart (being) than his behavior (doing). A person with a good heart will automatically want to do what's right. How's your heart today?

Related Texts: Genesis 21:1–5; Romans 4; Galatians 3:1–9

Abram's wife, Sarai, had not borne any children for him, but she owned an Egyptian slave named Hagar. Sarai said to Abram, "Since the LORD has prevented me from bearing children, go to my slave; perhaps through her I can build a family." And Abram agreed to what Sarai said. So Abram's wife, Sarai, took Hagar, her Egyptian slave, and gave her to her husband, Abram, as a wife for him. This happened after Abram had lived in the land of Canaan ten years. He slept with Hagar, and she became pregnant. When she saw that she was pregnant, her mistress became contemptible to her. . . .

So Hagar gave birth to Abram's son, and Abram named his son (whom Hagar bore) Ishmael. Abram was eighty-six years old when Hagar bore Ishmael to him. . . .

The LORD came to Sarah as he had said, and the LORD did for Sarah what he had promised. Sarah became pregnant and bore a son to Abraham in his old age, at the appointed time God had told him. Abraham named his son who was born to him — the one Sarah bore to him — Isaac. When his son Isaac was eight days old, Abraham circumcised him, as God had commanded him. Abraham was a hundred years old when his son Isaac was born to him.

—Genesis 16:1–4,15–16; 21:1–5

By faith even Sarah herself, when she was unable to have children, received power to conceive offspring, even though she was past the age, since she considered that the one who had promised was faithful.

—Hebrews 11:11

JUST A THOUGHT

God's ability to perform miracles in your life and answer your prayers doesn't depend on how young or old you are.

Fortunately, God isn't confined to your limited way of thinking—remember, he's God!

Related Texts: Genesis 21:6–21; Acts 7:1–8; Romans 4; Galatians 4:22–31

A fter these things God tested Abraham and said to him, "Abraham!"

"Here I am," he answered.

"Take your son," he said, "your only son Isaac, whom you love, go to the land of Moriah, and offer him there as a burnt offering on one of the mountains I will tell you about."

When they arrived at the place that God had told him about, Abraham built the altar there and arranged the wood. He bound his son Isaac and placed him on the altar on top of the wood. Then Abraham reached out and took the knife to slaughter his son.

But the angel of the LORD called to him from heaven and said, "Abraham, Abraham!"

He replied, "Here I am."

Then he said, "Do not lay a hand on the boy or do anything to him. For now I know that you fear God, since you have not withheld your only son from me." Abraham looked up and saw a ram caught in the thicket by its horns. So Abraham went and took the ram and offered it as a burnt offering in place of his son. And Abraham named that place The LORD Will Provide, so today it is said, "It will be provided on the LORD's mountain."

—Genesis 22:1–2,9–14

Love consists in this: not that we loved God, but that he loved us and sent his Son to be the atoning sacrifice for our sins.

—1 John 4:10

TAKE A SHOT

God tested Abraham's faith and in doing so pushed him into an uncomfortable situation. What is something or who is someone you love more than anything else? Write the answer in the blank space below:

"For now I know that you fear God, since you have not withheld your _____ from me" (Gn 22:12).

Would this be true of you if God asked you to make a sacrifice? Yes or No (circle one)

If "No," what might you need to consider in order for God to have the highest priority in your life?

Related Texts: Genesis 22:15–19; John 3:16; Romans 8:31–39; Hebrews 11:17–19

These are the family records of Isaac son of Abraham. Abraham fathered Isaac. Isaac was forty years old when he took as his wife Rebekah daughter of Bethuel the Aramean from Paddan-aram and sister of Laban the Aramean. Isaac prayed to the LORD on behalf of his wife because she was childless. The LORD was receptive to his prayer, and his wife Rebekah conceived. But the children inside her struggled with each other, and she said, "Why is this happening to me?" So she went to inquire of the LORD. And the LORD said to her:

Two nations are in your womb;
    two peoples will come from you
        and be separated.
One people will be stronger
        than the other,
    and the older will serve
        the younger.

When her time came to give birth, there were indeed twins in her womb. The first one came out red-looking, covered with hair like a fur coat, and they named him Esau. After this, his brother came out grasping Esau's heel with his hand. So he was named Jacob. Isaac was sixty years old when they were born.

When the boys grew up, Esau became an expert hunter, an outdoorsman, but Jacob was a quiet man who stayed at home. Isaac loved Esau because he had a taste for wild game, but Rebekah loved Jacob.

—*Genesis 25:19–28*

JUST A THOUGHT

Everyone is a favorite creation to God! God's love for you has nothing to do with your background, skin color, financial situation, family condition, IQ, neighborhood, or even your grades. Take a look at yourself—you're one of God's favorite creations.

Related Texts: 1 Samuel 1;
Malachi 1:1–5; Romans 9

O nce when Jacob was cooking a stew, Esau came in from the field exhausted. He said to Jacob, "Let me eat some of that red stuff, because I'm exhausted." That is why he was also named Edom.

Jacob replied, "First sell me your birthright."

"Look," said Esau, "I'm about to die, so what good is a birthright to me?"

Jacob said, "Swear to me first." So he swore to Jacob and sold his birthright to him. Then Jacob gave bread and lentil stew to Esau; he ate, drank, got up, and went away. So Esau despised his birthright.

—Genesis 25:29–34

"I have loved you," says the LORD.

Yet you ask, "How have you loved us?"

"Wasn't Esau Jacob's brother?" This is the LORD's declaration. "Even so, I loved Jacob, but I hated Esau. I turned his mountains into a wasteland, and gave his inheritance to the desert jackals."

—Malachi 1:2–3

And make sure that there isn't any immoral or irreverent person like Esau, who sold his birthright in exchange for a single meal. For you know that later, when he wanted to inherit the blessing, he was rejected, even though he sought it with tears, because he didn't find any opportunity for repentance.

—Hebrews 12:16–17

IN OTHER WORDS

Birthright—A birthright was a special privilege given to the oldest son. The child who had the birthright received the blessing of the father as well as all the father had built and accomplished. In the case of Esau and Jacob, it was more than gaining dad's money, it was about receiving God's special blessing.

Today you have the opportunity to receive the birthright that God intended for Jesus. Jesus is both the only Son of God and the firstborn of God. By having a relationship with Jesus, you can share in the blessings intended for him. The Bible says, "For all those led by God's Spirit are God's sons. . . . The Spirit himself testifies together with our spirit that we are God's children, and if children, also heirs—heirs of God and coheirs with Christ" (Rm 8:14,16–17).

Congratulations!

Related Texts: Genesis 27–36; Psalm 60; Obadiah

At seventeen years of age, Joseph tended sheep with his brothers. The young man was working with the sons of Bilhah and Zilpah, his father's wives, and he brought a bad report about them to their father.

Now Israel loved Joseph more than his other sons because Joseph was a son born to him in his old age, and he made a long-sleeved robe for him. When his brothers saw that their father loved him more than all his brothers, they hated him and could not bring themselves to speak peaceably to him.

Then Joseph had a dream. When he told it to his brothers, they hated him even more. He said to them, "Listen to this dream I had: There we were, binding sheaves of grain in the field. Suddenly my sheaf stood up, and your sheaves gathered around it and bowed down to my sheaf."

Then he had another dream and told it to his brothers. "Look," he said, "I had another dream, and this time the sun, moon, and eleven stars were bowing down to me."

He told his father and brothers, and his father rebuked him. "What kind of dream is this that you have had?" he said. "Am I and your mother and your brothers really going to come and bow down to the ground before you?" His brothers were jealous of him, but his father kept the matter in mind.

—Genesis 37:2–7, 9–11

BIBLICAL BIO

Joseph is a great example of good things happening to those who are faithful.

Joseph was sold into slavery by his brothers. As odd as it sounds, God never left him during his darkest hours. Joseph's life illustrates this truth: When you are obedient to God, you can conquer any obstacle put in your way. Joseph's statement supports this, "Don't be grieved or angry with yourselves for selling me here, because God sent me ahead of you to preserve life" (Gn 45:5).

Joseph believed that no matter what harm his enemies might inflict upon him, God would remain faithful and reward him. Be faithful today and know God sees and rewards your faithfulness.

Related Texts: Genesis 28:10–19; 41:1–45; Joel 2:28–32; Matthew 1:18–2:22

A nd so he gave Abraham the covenant of circumcision. After this, he fathered Isaac and circumcised him on the eighth day. Isaac became the father of Jacob, and Jacob became the father of the twelve patriarchs.

"The patriarchs became jealous of Joseph and sold him into Egypt, but God was with him and rescued him out of all his troubles. He gave him favor and wisdom in the sight of Pharaoh, king of Egypt, who appointed him ruler over Egypt and over his whole household. Now a famine and great suffering came over all of Egypt and Canaan, and our ancestors could find no food. When Jacob heard there was grain in Egypt, he sent our ancestors there the first time. The second time, Joseph revealed himself to his brothers, and Joseph's family became known to Pharaoh. Joseph invited his father Jacob and all his relatives, seventy-five people in all, and Jacob went down to Egypt. He and our ancestors died there."

—Acts 7:8–15

Now Jacob lived in the land of Egypt 17 years, and his life span was 147 years.

—Genesis 47:28

BIG TIME WORD

Delivered—Joseph is one of many examples of God delivering someone from evil, pain, or a specific situation. Other words that could be used to help define "delivered" are "rescued," "saved," or "escaped." God's power to deliver can give you hope every single day. Jesus taught his followers to pray using words like these: "Do not bring us into temptation, but deliver us from the evil one" (Mt 6:13).

What's an area in your life from which you need to be rescued? Ask God to deliver you. He's done it millions of times. He has all the power in the world to do it for you too.

Related Texts: Genesis 37–50; Psalm 46; Matthew 8:5–13; Mark 12:24–27

When Joseph's brothers saw that their father was dead, they said to one another, "If Joseph is holding a grudge against us, he will certainly repay us for all the suffering we caused him."

So they sent this message to Joseph, "Before he died your father gave a command: 'Say this to Joseph: Please forgive your brothers' transgression and their sin — the suffering they caused you.' Therefore, please forgive the transgression of the servants of the God of your father." Joseph wept when their message came to him. His brothers also came to him, bowed down before him, and said, "We are your slaves!"

But Joseph said to them, "Don't be afraid. Am I in the place of God? You planned evil against me; God planned it for good to bring about the present result — the survival of many people. Therefore don't be afraid. I will take care of you and your children." And he comforted them and spoke kindly to them...

Joseph said to his brothers, "I am about to die, but God will certainly come to your aid and bring you up from this land to the land he swore to give to Abraham, Isaac, and Jacob."

—Genesis 50:15–21,24

We know that all things work together for the good of those who love God, who are called according to his purpose.

—Romans 8:28

ONE MINUTE MEMORY

"We know that all things work together for the good of those who love God, who are called according to his purpose" (Rm 8:28).

Related Texts: Genesis 37–50; Exodus 1; 12:17–19; Joshua 24:32; Psalm 105:7–25; Hebrews 11:21–22

There was a man in the country of Uz named Job. He was a man of complete integrity, who feared God and turned away from evil. He had seven sons and three daughters. His estate included seven thousand sheep and goats, three thousand camels, five hundred yoke of oxen, five hundred female donkeys, and a very large number of servants. Job was the greatest man among all the people of the east. . . .

One day the sons of God came to present themselves before the LORD, and Satan also came with them. The LORD asked Satan, "Where have you come from?"

"From roaming through the earth," Satan answered him, "and walking around on it."

Then the LORD said to Satan, "Have you considered my servant Job? No one else on earth is like him, a man of perfect integrity, who fears God and turns away from evil."

Satan answered the LORD, "Does Job fear God for nothing? Haven't you placed a hedge around him, his household, and everything he owns? You have blessed the work of his hands, and his possessions have increased in the land. But stretch out your hand and strike everything he owns, and he will surely curse you to your face."

"Very well," the LORD told Satan, "everything he owns is in your power. However, do not lay a hand on Job himself." So Satan left the LORD's presence.

—Job 1:1–3,6–12

BIBLICAL BIO

Job was one of the richest, most God-loving, most well-known, most respected people in his world. There was no wrong found in him. But Job suffered tragically. His pain was unbelievable!

Shockingly, no matter how incredible the pain, Job was able to keep his faith. He never blamed God. Job is proof that it's possible to endure incredible pain and still remain confident in God.

Job's life is a reminder that God remains God no matter how happy and wealthy or sad and poor you might be. His statement sums this up: "The LORD gives, and the LORD takes away. Blessed be the name of the LORD" (Jb 1:21).

Related Texts: Job 28; Proverbs 1:7;
8:13; 9:10; Philippians 2:14–15;
1 Peter 5:8–11

One day when Job's sons and daughters were eating and drinking wine in their oldest brother's house, a messenger came to Job and reported, "While the oxen were plowing and the donkeys grazing nearby, the Sabeans swooped down and took them away. They struck down the servants with the sword, and I alone have escaped to tell you!"

He was still speaking when another messenger came and reported, "God's fire fell from heaven. It burned the sheep and the servants and devoured them, and I alone have escaped to tell you!"

That messenger was still speaking when yet another came and reported, "The Chaldeans formed three bands, made a raid on the camels, and took them away. They struck down the servants with the sword, and I alone have escaped to tell you!"

He was still speaking when another messenger came and reported, "Your sons and daughters were eating and drinking wine in their oldest brother's house. Suddenly a powerful wind swept in from the desert and struck the four corners of the house. It collapsed on the young people so that they died, and I alone have escaped to tell you!"

Then Job stood up, tore his robe, and shaved his head. He fell to the ground and worshiped.

Throughout all this Job did not sin or blame God for anything.

—Job 1:13–20,22

HERE'S THE DEAL

No one wakes up in the morning and hopes for a lousy day. Crummy days just seem to happen without any warning. It would be great if someone called ahead to warn you about potentially dreadful days. You wouldn't even have to get out of bed. Just sleep the bad day away, right? Dream on! That's not going to happen because bad days happen.

Next time you have a terrible day, realize you're not alone. People have been having them for thousands of years, and you're going to record several more onto your life's scroll before it's over.

Consider yourself lucky you weren't created to be Job. He's the poster-child for a lousy day. But, it's amazing to see that Job didn't blame God for his pain. When it seemed like it would have been so easy to blame God, Job chose a different response.

If today or tomorrow screams "lousy," remember Job's example.

Related Texts: Habakkuk 3:17–19; 1 Thessalonians 5:16–18; Revelation 7:13–17

One day the sons of God came again to present themselves before the LORD, and Satan also came with them to present himself before the LORD. . . .

Then the LORD said to Satan, "Have you considered my servant Job? No one else on earth is like him, a man of perfect integrity, who fears God and turns away from evil. He still retains his integrity, even though you incited me against him, to destroy him for no good reason."

"Skin for skin!" Satan answered the LORD. "A man will give up everything he owns in exchange for his life. But stretch out your hand and strike his flesh and bones, and he will surely curse you to your face."

"Very well," the LORD told Satan, "he is in your power; only spare his life." So Satan left the LORD's presence and infected Job with terrible boils from the soles of his feet to the top of his head. Then Job took a piece of broken pottery to scrape himself while he sat among the ashes.

His wife said to him, "Are you still holding on to your integrity? Curse God and die!"

"You speak as a foolish woman speaks," he told her. "Should we accept only good from God and not adversity?" Throughout all this Job did not sin in what he said.

—Job 2:1,3–10

TAKE A SHOT

Even when life is going well, it's usually easier to focus on the negative things than the positive. Then, when pain is added in, it's even more difficult to recognize anything good about life.

Write down two good things that happened to you this month:

1.

2.

Write down three good things you'd love to see happen next month:

1.

2.

3.

Related Texts: Job 19:25–27; Proverbs 11:2–6; Philippians 3:7–11

Now when Job's three friends — Eliphaz the Temanite, Bildad the Shuhite, and Zophar the Naamathite — heard about all this adversity that had happened to him, each of them came from his home. They met together to go and sympathize with him and comfort him. When they looked from a distance, they could barely recognize him. They wept aloud, and each man tore his robe and threw dust into the air and on his head. Then they sat on the ground with him seven days and nights, but no one spoke a word to him because they saw that his suffering was very intense. . . .

Then Eliphaz the Temanite replied:

Consider: Who has perished
   when he was innocent?
Where have the honest
   been destroyed?
In my experience,
   those who plow injustice
and those who sow trouble reap
   the same.
They perish at a single blast
   from God
and come to an end by the breath
   of his nostrils. . . .

However, if I were you,
   I would appeal to God
and would present my case to him.

See how happy is
   the person whom God corrects;
so do not reject the discipline
   of the Almighty.
For he wounds but he also
   bandages;

he strikes, but his hands
   also heal. . . .
    −Job 2:11−13; 4:1,7−9; 5:8,17−18

BIG TIME WORD

Comfort + Sympathy = Empathy. Empathy is possessing and showing genuine interest and concern in what is happening with another person. Empathy means that you can actually feel another person's pain. If you feel and express empathy you don't need to know what to say, how to act, or have a Bible verse to share.

People are experiencing tragedies on a daily basis and they're all around you. Expressing empathy will reveal God's love. Where there is empathy, there is support; where there is support, there is encouragement; and where there is encouragement, there is love.

Next time a friend is hurting and you don't know what to say, don't worry . . . empathy communicates the right words: "I care!"

Related Texts: Job 4−5; 8; 11; 15; 18; 20; 22; 25; 32−37; Hebrews 12:5−11

Then Job answered:
How long will you torment me
and crush me with words?
You have humiliated me
ten times now,
and you mistreat me
without shame.
Even if it is true that
I have sinned,
my mistake concerns only me.
If you really want to appear
superior to me
and would use my disgrace
as evidence against me,
then understand that it is God
who has wronged me
and caught me in his net.

I cry out, "Violence!"
but get no response;
I call for help, but there is
no justice.
—Job 19:1–7

Job continued his discourse,
saying:
As God lives, who has
deprived me of justice,
and the Almighty who has
made me bitter,
as long as my breath is still
in me
and the breath from God
remains in my nostrils,
my lips will not speak unjustly,
and my tongue will not
utter deceit.
I will never affirm that you
are right.
I will maintain my integrity
until I die.
I will cling to my righteousness
and never let it go.
My conscience will not
accuse me as long as I live!
—Job 27:1–6

DIG DEEPER

God heard the prayers of Job thousands of years ago, and he hears your prayers today! While God doesn't always choose to answer them the way you want them answered, you can be confident that God is not hard of hearing, and he always hears them.

In Luke 18:1–11 Jesus explained the need to pray consistently and to keep praying until an answer comes. In verses 7–8 Jesus said, "Will not God grant justice to his elect who cry out to him day and night? Will he delay helping them? I tell you that he will swiftly grant them justice. Nevertheless, when the Son of Man comes, will he find that faith on earth?"

Next time you get the urge to worry, try replacing your worry with a prayer. How about a prayer of worship? Worrying won't help you at all, but worshiping the one who can make things happen is a good idea.

Related Texts: Job 3; 6–7; 9–10; 12–14; 16–17; 19; 21; 23–24; 26–31; Psalm 7; Luke 18:1–8

Then the LORD answered Job
from the whirlwind. He said:
Who is this who obscures
   my counsel
with ignorant words?
Get ready to answer me
   like a man;
when I question you,
   you will inform me.
Where were you
   when I established the earth?
Tell me, if you have
   understanding.
Who fixed its dimensions?
   Certainly you know!
Who stretched a measuring line
   across it?
What supports its foundations?
                    —Job 38:1–6

The LORD answered Job:
Will the one who contends
   with the Almighty
   correct him?
Let him who argues with God
   give an answer.

Then Job answered the LORD:
I am so insignificant. How can I
   answer you?
I place my hand over my mouth.
I have spoken once,
   and I will not reply;
twice, but now I can add nothing.

Then the LORD answered Job from
the whirlwind:
Get ready to answer me
   like a man;
When I question you, you will
   inform me.
Would you really challenge
   my justice?
Would you declare me guilty
   to justify yourself?
                    —Job 40:1–8

WEIRD OR WHAT?

Job screamed out because of his pain, anguish, and torment. No one can blame him. But what's totally unexpected is God's response to Job. Instead of answering Job's cry and explaining why a good person can suffer, God reminds Job of his greatness. God pointed to the fact that he is awesome. Job listened and did the only thing he could do in God's presence—he shut his mouth.

Be reminded today that God is much bigger than your ability to understand him. If you understood everything about God he wouldn't be big enough. Consider his greatness today and you may end up speechless too!

Related Texts: Job 38–41; Psalm 30; Habakkuk 1:1–2:1; Romans 9–10

Then Job replied to the Lord:
I know that you can do
anything
and no plan of yours
can be thwarted.
You asked, "Who is this
who conceals my counsel
with ignorance?"
Surely I spoke about things
I did not understand,
things too wondrous for me
to know.
You said, "Listen now,
and I will speak.
When I question you, you will
inform me."
I had heard reports about you,
but now my eyes have seen you.
Therefore, I reject my words
and am sorry for them;
I am dust and ashes.

After the Lord had finished
speaking to Job, he said to Eliphaz
the Temanite, "I am angry with
you and your two friends, for you
have not spoken the truth about
me, as my servant Job has. Now
take seven bulls and seven rams,
go to my servant Job, and offer
a burnt offering for yourselves.
Then my servant Job will pray
for you. I will surely accept his
prayer and not deal with you as
your folly deserves. For you have
not spoken the truth about me, as
my servant Job has." Then Eliphaz
the Temanite, Bildad the Shuhite,
and Zophar the Naamathite went
and did as the Lord had told
them, and the Lord accepted
Job's prayer.
After Job had prayed for
his friends, the Lord restored
his fortunes and doubled his
previous possessions.

—Job 42:1–10

JUST A THOUGHT

God doesn't promise to give the
faithful twice as much as they had
before, but he does have a way of
rewarding faithfulness in terms
that can't be fully explained or
measured.

*Related Texts: Psalms 17; 37;
Matthew 5:1–6; James 5:11*

When he saw the crowds, he went up on the mountain, and after he sat down, his disciples came to him. Then he began to teach them, saying:

"Blessed are the poor in spirit,
for the kingdom of heaven
    is theirs."
—Matthew 5:1–3

The sacrifice pleasing to God is
    a broken spirit.
You will not despise a broken
    and humbled heart, God.
—Psalm 51:17

My brothers and sisters, do not show favoritism as you hold on to the faith in our glorious Lord Jesus Christ. For if someone comes into your meeting wearing a gold ring and dressed in fine clothes, and a poor person dressed in filthy clothes also comes in, if you look with favor on the one wearing the fine clothes and say, "Sit here in a good place," and yet you say to the poor person, "Stand over there," or "Sit here on the floor by my footstool," haven't you made distinctions among yourselves and become judges with evil thoughts?

Listen, my dear brothers and sisters: Didn't God choose the poor in this world to be rich in faith and heirs of the kingdom that he has promised to those who love him?
—James 2:1–5

IN OTHER WORDS

"The Beatitudes" is the title given to a special sermon from Jesus. In this sermon, Jesus introduced a radically different way of thinking. Here's what he said: Mourn and you'll be comforted. Be humble and you'll inherit the earth. Be merciful and mercy will be shown to you. Have a pure heart and you'll see God. Bring peace to others and you'll be God's child. Be treated badly for doing good and you'll be blessed.

If you can follow these teachings, you will definitely stand out as being different—there's no question about it. The promised outcomes of this life seem too good to be true.

Try it out and see what happens!

*Related Texts: Job 34:17–19;
Isaiah 57:15–19; 66:2; Luke 6:20;
Acts 10:34–35; Ephesians 6:5–9*

Blessed are those who mourn,
for they will be comforted.
−Matthew 5:4

The Spirit of the Lord GOD is
  on me,
because the LORD has anointed me
to bring good news to the poor.
He has sent me to heal
  the brokenhearted,
to proclaim liberty to the captives
and freedom to the prisoners;
to proclaim the year
  of the LORD's favor,
and the day
  of our God's vengeance;
to comfort all who mourn,
to provide for those who mourn
  in Zion;
−Isaiah 61:1−3

Then I heard a loud voice from
the throne: Look, God's dwelling
is with humanity, and he will
live with them. They will be his
peoples, and God himself will be
with them and will be their God.
He will wipe away every tear
from their eyes. Death will be no
more; grief, crying, and pain will
be no more, because the previous
things have passed away.
−Revelation 21:3−4

JUST A THOUGHT

Next time you worry about your future, remember that God has already taken care of the ultimate future, and he wants you to know it. When you know it, you'll experience a new peace and hope for living today.

Related Texts: Nehemiah 8:1−12;
Psalm 119:49−50; Ecclesiastes 3:1−8;
Luke 6:21; 2 Corinthians 10:1−5;
1 Peter 3:8−9

Blessed are the humble,
for they will inherit the earth.
—Matthew 5:5

Do not be agitated by evildoers;
do not envy those who do wrong.
For they wither quickly like grass
and wilt like tender green plants.

Trust in the LORD and do
what is good;
dwell in the land and live securely.
Take delight in the LORD,
and he will give you
your heart's desires.

Commit your way to the LORD;
trust in him, and he will act,
making your righteousness shine
like the dawn,
your justice like the noonday.

Be silent before the LORD and wait
expectantly for him;
do not be agitated by one
who prospers in his way,
by the person who carries out
evil plans.

A little while, and
the wicked person will be
no more;
though you look for him,
he will not be there.
But the humble will inherit
the land
and will enjoy
abundant prosperity.
—Psalm 37:1–7,10–11

ONE MINUTE MEMORY

"But the humble will inherit the land and will enjoy abundant prosperity" (Ps 37:11).

Related Texts: Psalms 25:12–13; 37:12–40; Matthew 11:25–30; 2 Corinthians 10:1–5; Galatians 5:19–23; 1 Peter 3:8–9

Blessed are those who hunger and thirst for righteousness, for they will be filled.

—Matthew 5:6

As a deer longs for flowing streams, so I long for you, God.
I thirst for God, the living God.
When can I come and appear
    before God?

—Psalm 42:1–2

Jesus said, "Everyone who drinks from this water will get thirsty again. But whoever drinks from the water that I will give him will never get thirsty again. In fact, the water I will give him will become a well of water springing up in him for eternal life." . . .

On the last and most important day of the festival, Jesus stood up and cried out, "If anyone is thirsty, let him come to me and drink. The one who believes in me, as the Scripture has said, will have streams of living water flow from deep within him." He said this about the Spirit. Those who believed in Jesus were going to receive the Spirit.

—John 4:13–14; 7:37–39

Both the Spirit and the bride say, "Come!" Let anyone who hears, say, "Come!" Let the one who is thirsty come. Let the one who desires take the water of life freely.

—Revelation 22:17

HERE'S THE DEAL

These are good Scriptures to recall next time you swing open the refrigerator and exclaim, "I'm starving!" Do you ever stare at all the food and say, "There's nothing to eat" and then slam the door, frustrated, hungry, and in search of some munchies? If so, you're not alone.

Though Jesus doesn't promise you'll have a lifetime supply of pizza, ice cream, and potato chips, he does guarantee that you'll never go spiritually hungry or thirsty if you believe in him. He's not referring to a growling stomach, but being completely satisfied with his love. Picture Jesus's promise as being like living next door to a grocery store that's open 24 hours every day, filled with free all-you-can-eat food. Jesus's assurance is even better than that because you never have to leave your home, and his "food" is always good for you.

How might you eat from the "bread of life" (see Jn 6:35) today?

Related Texts: Psalms 107:1–9; 146; Isaiah 55:1–2; Luke 6:21; Revelation 7:16–17

Blessed are the merciful,
for they will be shown mercy.
—Matthew 5:7

He will not leave you, destroy you,
or forget the covenant with your
ancestors that he swore to them
by oath, because the LORD your
God is a compassionate God.
—Deuteronomy 4:31

I lift my eyes to you,
the one enthroned in heaven.
Like a servant's eyes
on his master's hand,
like a servant girl's eyes
on her mistress's hand,
so our eyes are on the LORD our God
until he shows us favor.
—Psalm 123:1–2

For I desire faithful love
and not sacrifice,
the knowledge of God rather than
burnt offerings.
—Hosea 6:6

Mankind, he has told each of you
what is good
and what it is the LORD requires
of you:
to act justly,
to love faithfulness,
and to walk humbly with your God.
—Micah 6:8

Speak and act as those who are to
be judged by the law of freedom.
For judgment is without mercy to
the one who has not shown mercy.
Mercy triumphs over judgment.
—James 2:12–13

IN OTHER WORDS

Mercy is showing compassion or empathy (see Day 32). Mercy is given by God to meet the needs of his people and to care for them.

Mercy starts with God. God shows mercy to his followers because he has compassion and cares for you. But mercy doesn't stop with God to you! You can also express mercy to others in need—the way God expresses it to you.

Can you think of a person who is in need of some mercy—compassion and/or empathy? How might you show this person mercy today?

Related Texts: Psalm 6; Micah 7:18–19; Zechariah 7:9–10; Luke 6:27–38; 10:25–37; Jude 1:20–23

Blessed are the pure in heart,
for they will see God.
                    −Matthew 5:8

Who may ascend the mountain
    of the LORD?
Who may stand in his holy place?
The one who has clean hands
    and a pure heart,
who has not appealed
    to what is false,
and who has not sworn deceitfully.
He will receive blessing
    from the LORD,
and righteousness from the God
    of his salvation....

God, create a clean heart for me
and renew a steadfast spirit
    within me.
                −Psalms 24:3−5; 51:10

Flee from youthful passions, and
pursue righteousness, faith, love,
and peace, along with those who
call on the Lord from a pure heart.
                    −2 Timothy 2:22

Therefore, brothers and sisters,
since we have boldness to enter
the sanctuary through the blood
of Jesus — he has inaugurated
for us a new and living way
through the curtain (that is,
through his flesh) — and since
we have a great high priest over
the house of God, let us draw near
with a true heart in full assurance
of faith, with our hearts sprinkled
clean from an evil conscience and
our bodies washed in pure water.
                −Hebrews 10:19−22

TAKE A SHOT

In 2 Timothy 2:22, Paul provides
an action plan for remaining pure in
heart. Here it is:

1. Run from the things that give you
   evil thoughts.

2. Stay close to anything that makes
   you do right.

3. Have faith and love.

4. Enjoy the company of others who
   love God and live by this plan.

Do you currently have at least
one friend who could help you
accomplish number 4? If so, what
three qualities do you admire about
this friend? If not, how can you
become a good friend to others?

_____

_____

_____

_____

_____

_____

_____

_____

_____

_____

_____

_____

_____

Related Texts: 2 Chronicles 30:13−20;
Proverbs 20:5−11; Mark 7:1−23;
Hebrews 3; 12:14−29

B lessed are the peacemakers,
for they will be called
sons of God.

—Matthew 5:9

Come, children, listen to me;
I will teach you the fear
  of the LORD.
Who is someone who desires life,
loving a long life to enjoy
  what is good?
Keep your tongue from evil
and your lips
  from deceitful speech.
Turn away from evil and do
  what is good;
seek peace and pursue it....

—Psalm 34:11–14

"There is no peace for the wicked,"
  says the LORD.

—Isaiah 48:22

If possible, as far as it depends on
you, live at peace with everyone.

—Romans 12:18

But the wisdom from above is
first pure, then peace-loving,
gentle, compliant, full of mercy
and good fruits, unwavering,
without pretense.

—James 3:17

JUST A THOUGHT

In a world filled with violence, terrorism, war, racism, and hatred, it would be great if others could count on you as one of the world's peacemakers! How might you make peace today?

Related Texts: Isaiah 9:6–7; John 1:1–13; Romans 8:9–23; Galatians 3:26–4:7; 1 John 3:1–11

Blessed are those who
are persecuted because
of righteousness,
for the kingdom of heaven
is theirs.

"You are blessed when they
insult you and persecute you
and falsely say every kind of evil
against you because of me. Be
glad and rejoice, because your
reward is great in heaven. For
that is how they persecuted the
prophets who were before you."
—Matthew 5:10–12

But the LORD is with me
like a violent warrior.
Therefore, my persecutors
will stumble and not prevail.
Since they have not succeeded,
they will be utterly shamed,
an everlasting humiliation
that will never be forgotten.
—Jeremiah 20:11

For it brings favor if, because of a
consciousness of God, someone
endures grief from suffering
unjustly. For what credit is there
if when you do wrong and are
beaten, you endure it? But when
you do what is good and suffer,
if you endure it, this brings favor
with God.
For you were called to this,
because Christ also suffered for
you, leaving you an example, that
you should follow in his steps.
—1 Peter 2:19–21

ONE MINUTE MEMORY

"So I take pleasure in weaknesses,
insults, hardships, persecutions,
and in difficulties, for the sake of
Christ. For when I am weak, then I
am strong" (2Co 12:10).

*Related Texts: Job 36:15–17; Isaiah 53;
1 Peter 1:3–9; 4:12–19*

Who can separate us from the love of Christ? Can affliction or distress or persecution or famine or nakedness or danger or sword? . . .

For I am persuaded that neither death nor life, nor angels nor rulers, nor things present nor things to come, nor powers, nor height nor depth, nor any other created thing will be able to separate us from the love of God that is in Christ Jesus our Lord.

—Romans 8:35,38–39

And we have come to know and to believe the love that God has for us.

God is love, and the one who remains in love remains in God, and God remains in him. In this, love is made complete with us so that we may have confidence in the day of judgment, because as he is, so also are we in this world. There is no fear in love; instead, perfect love drives out fear, because fear involves punishment. So the one who fears is not complete in love . . . We love because he first loved us.

—1 John 4:16–19

HERE'S THE DEAL

Unconditional love is the way God loves you. God's love for you isn't based on your grades, your looks, your athletic performance, your friendships, your personality, your money, or your past. If God loved you for what you did, that would be called conditional love (based on your conditions). But God's love is unconditional because his love has no strings attached. There are things you do that God doesn't like, but he never stops loving you because of Jesus's death on your behalf.

Nothing you do will distance you from God's love in Christ. Believe it or not, there's no sin that's too gross, no language that's too bad, no action that's too evil, and no thought that's too wild to stop God from loving you. Wow! Doesn't that make you want to love God in response to his love for you?

Related Texts: Deuteronomy 7:7–11; 10:14–15; John 3:16–19; Romans 5:8–11; Ephesians 2:4–10

If I speak human or angelic tongues but do not have love, I am a noisy gong or a clanging cymbal. If I have the gift of prophecy and understand all mysteries and all knowledge, and if I have all faith so that I can move mountains but do not have love, I am nothing. And if I give away all my possessions, and if I give over my body in order to boast but do not have love, I gain nothing.

Love is patient, love is kind. Love does not envy, is not boastful, is not arrogant, is not rude, is not self-seeking, is not irritable, and does not keep a record of wrongs. Love finds no joy in unrighteousness but rejoices in the truth. It bears all things, believes all things, hopes all things, endures all things.

Love never ends. . . .

Now these three remain: faith, hope, and love — but the greatest of these is love.

—1 Corinthians 13:1–8,13

TAKE A SHOT

Listed below you will find several qualities of love. Give yourself a letter-grade (A–F) on how you currently live out each of these qualities. Next to your lowest grade write down a few ideas on how you might improve your "love life" with that specific quality.

- Love is patient
- Love is kind
- Love does not envy
- Love is not boastful
- Love is not conceited
- Love does not act improperly
- Love is not selfish
- Love is not provoked
- Love does not keep a record of wrongs
- Love finds no joy in unrighteousness
- Love rejoices in the truth

Now go back and cross out the word *love* and replace it with your name. How does that look?

Related Texts: Deuteronomy 6:1–15; Psalm 136; John 15:9–17; 1 John 3

These are the names of the sons of Israel who came to Egypt with Jacob; each came with his family:

>Reuben, Simeon, Levi,
>   and Judah;
>Issachar, Zebulun,
>   and Benjamin;
>Dan and Naphtali; Gad
>   and Asher.

The total number of Jacob's descendants was seventy; Joseph was already in Egypt.

Joseph and all his brothers and all that generation eventually died. But the Israelites were fruitful, increased rapidly, multiplied, and became extremely numerous so that the land was filled with them.

A new king, who did not know about Joseph, came to power in Egypt. He said to his people, "Look, the Israelite people are more numerous and powerful than we are. Come, let's deal shrewdly with them; otherwise they will multiply further, and when war breaks out, they will join our enemies, fight against us, and leave the country." So the Egyptians assigned taskmasters over the Israelites to oppress them with forced labor. They built Pithom and Rameses as supply cities for Pharaoh. But the more they oppressed them, the more they multiplied and spread so that the Egyptians came to dread the Israelites. They worked the Israelites ruthlessly . . .

Pharaoh then commanded all his people, "You must throw every son born to the Hebrews into the Nile, but let every daughter live."

—Exodus 1:1–13,22

WEIRD OR WHAT?

An Egyptian taskmaster's job description included torturing the Jewish people (the Hebrews) with slave-like jobs (slave labor).

Taskmasters tormented Hebrews from morning until night, so they wouldn't have time or strength to have children who might grow up to challenge Pharaoh's leadership.

It was not uncommon for a taskmaster to beat, even to the point of death, a Hebrew who wasn't working hard. These slaves lived with no rights under the cruel taskmasters.

Thankfully, today, if you have faith in Jesus you are a child of God and no longer a slave of someone like Pharaoh or even a slave to your sin. You are free and don't have to be a slave to anyone because of Jesus. You are free! That's good news!

Related Texts: Psalm 105:23–25; Acts 7:9–34; 1 Corinthians 7:21–23; Galatians 3:26–28

Now a man from the family of Levi married a Levite woman. The woman became pregnant and gave birth to a son; when she saw that he was beautiful, she hid him for three months. But when she could no longer hide him, she got a papyrus basket for him and coated it with asphalt and pitch. She placed the child in it and set it among the reeds by the bank of the Nile. Then his sister stood at a distance in order to see what would happen to him.

Pharaoh's daughter went down to bathe at the Nile while her servant girls walked along the riverbank. She saw the basket among the reeds, sent her slave girl, took it, opened it, and saw him, the child — and there he was, a little boy, crying. She felt sorry for him and said, "This is one of the Hebrew boys."

Then his sister said to Pharaoh's daughter, "Should I go and call a Hebrew woman who is nursing to nurse the boy for you?"

"Go," Pharaoh's daughter told her. So the girl went and called the boy's mother. Then Pharaoh's daughter said to her, "Take this child and nurse him for me, and I will pay your wages." So the woman took the boy and nursed him. When the child grew older, she brought him to Pharaoh's daughter, and he became her son. She named him Moses, "Because," she said, "I drew him out of the water."

—Exodus 2:1–10

BIBLICAL BIO

Moses is famous for many accomplishments: He delivered the Jewish people from captivity, he accessed God's power and opened the Red Sea so they could escape the Egyptians, and he was chosen to receive God's Ten Commandments. Quite the life!

It's interesting how God protected Moses as a newborn baby. After Moses's birth, the Pharaoh ordered all newborn Hebrew boys to be killed. Fearful, Moses's mother made a floatable basket and sent him down the Nile River hoping he'd remain alive. Amazingly, Pharaoh's daughter found baby Moses and adopted him into her family—now Moses was part of a famous family. It's so wild to think about!

When God wants to get something done, he doesn't mess around. God has a special purpose for your life. Today, trust in him and watch what happens.

Related Texts: Isaiah 49:13–19; Acts 7:20–22; Hebrews 11:23

Years later, after Moses had grown up, he went out to his own people and observed their forced labor. He saw an Egyptian striking a Hebrew, one of his people. Looking all around and seeing no one, he struck the Egyptian dead and hid him in the sand. The next day he went out and saw two Hebrews fighting. He asked the one in the wrong, "Why are you attacking your neighbor?"

"Who made you a commander and judge over us?" the man replied. "Are you planning to kill me as you killed the Egyptian?"

Then Moses became afraid and thought, "What I did is certainly known."

When Pharaoh heard about this, he tried to kill Moses . . .

After a long time, the king of Egypt died. The Israelites groaned because of their difficult labor, they cried out, and their cry for help because of the difficult labor ascended to God. God heard their groaning, and God remembered his covenant with Abraham, with Isaac, and with Jacob. God saw the Israelites, and God knew.

—Exodus 2:11–15,23–25

He has sent redemption
   to his people.
He has ordained
   his covenant forever.
His name is holy and awe-
   inspiring.

—Psalm 111:9

BIG TIME WORD

Moses became afraid. Fright is a natural and common reaction. Everyone has a few quirks that trigger fear: spiders, the dark, speaking to a crowd, nuclear war, terrorism, etc. Fright can cause physical and emotional reactions. It's an uncomfortable sensation that puts your entire body on the defense. To constantly live with fear would do terrible damage to your body.

Some people allow fears to control their lives and keep them from living and taking risks. Some Christians allow fears to keep them from being all God wants them to be. Do you have any fears holding you back?

If your fears are stronger than your faith, you'll probably be in trouble. Faith counteracts fear because God is bigger and stronger than the object of your fear. If you have any fears keeping you from fully following God's ways, ask him to take away those fears today.

Related Texts: Deuteronomy 7:7–11; 10:14–15; John 3:16–19; Romans 5:8–11; Ephesians 2:4–10

Meanwhile, Moses was shepherding the flock of his father-in-law Jethro, the priest of Midian. He led the flock to the far side of the wilderness and came to Horeb, the mountain of God. Then the angel of the LORD appeared to him in a flame of fire within a bush. As Moses looked, he saw that the bush was on fire but was not consumed. So Moses thought, "I must go over and look at this remarkable sight. Why isn't the bush burning up?"

When the LORD saw that he had gone over to look, God called out to him from the bush, "Moses, Moses!"

"Here I am," he answered.

"Do not come closer," he said. "Remove the sandals from your feet, for the place where you are standing is holy ground." Then he continued, "I am the God of your father, the God of Abraham, the God of Isaac, and the God of Jacob." Moses hid his face because he was afraid to look at God.

Then the LORD said, "I have observed the misery of my people in Egypt, and have heard them crying out because of their oppressors. I know about their sufferings, and I have come down to rescue them from the power of the Egyptians and to bring them from that land to a good and spacious land. . . . Therefore, go. I am sending you to Pharaoh so that you may lead my people, the Israelites, out of Egypt."

—Exodus 3:1–8,10

DIG DEEPER

Moses was in the presence of God and on holy territory. Being in God's presence was not to be taken lightly. It still isn't! This same principle of holiness and respect also applies to Jesus. Unlike many people's beliefs, Jesus is more than just a nice man and a good teacher. The Bible teaches that Jesus is God and worthy of worship.

The Bible teaches that there will be a day when the name of Jesus will cause ultimate respect. Check out Philippians 2:10–11: "so that at the name of Jesus every knee will bow—in heaven and on earth and under the earth—and every tongue will confess that Jesus Christ is Lord, to the glory of God the Father."

That's a powerful name! How do you respond when you hear it?

Related Texts: Isaiah 6; Acts 7:30–35; Revelation 15:2–4

But Moses asked God, "Who am I that I should go to Pharaoh and that I should bring the Israelites out of Egypt?"

He answered, "I will certainly be with you, and this will be the sign to you that I am the one who sent you: when you bring the people out of Egypt, you will all worship God at this mountain."

Then Moses asked God, "If I go to the Israelites and say to them, 'The God of your ancestors has sent me to you,' and they ask me, 'What is his name?' what should I tell them?"

God replied to Moses, "I AM WHO I AM. This is what you are to say to the Israelites: I AM has sent me to you." God also said to Moses, "Say this to the Israelites: The LORD, the God of your ancestors, the God of Abraham, the God of Isaac, and the God of Jacob, has sent me to you. This is my name forever; this is how I am to be remembered in every generation. . . .

Then God spoke to Moses, telling him, "I am the LORD. I appeared to Abraham, Isaac, and Jacob as God Almighty, but I was not known to them by my name 'the LORD.'"

—Exodus 3:11–15, 6:2–3

IN OTHER WORDS

Ever wondered if God has a name? God has several different names. In this passage God tells Moses his name is "I AM."

Seems like an odd name, doesn't it? I AM is the name God chose for himself. Many believe this name says it all. "Who's in charge?" I AM. "Who's the greatest?" I AM. This name—I AM—shows that God is all. There is nothing else but God.

Jesus also said this about himself in John 8:58. He did not say "I was" or "I will be," but he said "I AM."

What does all this mean to you today? It means the same thing to you as it did to Moses: God is everything you need.

Related Texts: Exodus 20:7; John 6:35; 8:12,58; 10:7,11; 11:25; 14:6; 15:1; Revelation 1:8

The Lord is a refuge
for the persecuted,
a refuge in times of trouble.
Those who know your name
trust in you
because you have not abandoned
those who seek you, Lord.
—Psalm 9:9–10

Do not misuse the name of the
Lord your God, because the Lord
will not leave anyone unpunished
who misuses his name.
—Exodus 20:7

For I will proclaim the
Lord's name.
Declare the greatness of our God!
The Rock — his work is perfect;
all his ways are just.
A faithful God, without bias,
he is righteous and true.
—Deuteronomy 32:3–4

The name of the Lord is
a strong tower;
the righteous run to it
and are protected.
—Proverbs 18:10

Lord, there is no one like you.
You are great;
your name is great in power.
—Jeremiah 10:6

BIBLICAL BIO

Lord is a title for God that clearly provides better insight into the character of God.

A traditional definition of a lord is someone who owned land and ruled with authority over people. If you have a relationship with God, God is the Lord and Master of your life. He owns you and has authority over you. This means God watches over you and takes care of you—he is your Lord. You are his creation and his property.

It's a comforting way to think of yourself—as the Lord's. You are God's personal possession. Enjoy that truth today!

*Related Texts: Exodus 15:1–3;
Isaiah 42:5–9; Colossians 3:16–17;
Hebrews 13:15*

This is why you are great, Lord GOD. There is no one like you, and there is no God besides you, as all we have heard confirms. And who is like your people Israel? God came to one nation on earth in order to redeem a people for himself, to make a name for himself, and to perform for them great and awesome acts, driving out nations and their gods before your people you redeemed for yourself from Egypt. You established your people Israel to be your own people forever, and you, LORD, have become their God.

−2 Samuel 7:22−24

Our God is a God of salvation,
and escape from death belongs
    to the LORD my Lord. . . .

For you are my hope, Lord GOD,
my confidence from my youth. . . .

Those far from you
    will certainly perish;
you destroy all who are
    unfaithful to you.
But as for me, God's presence is
    my good.
I have made the Lord GOD
    my refuge,
so I can tell about all you do.

−Psalms 68:20; 71:5; 73:27−28

DIG DEEPER

God is the one who created all, knows all, controls all, is above all, and is everywhere. There is nothing bigger or greater than God. Because of this, God is often described with the word *sovereign*. It often means "above" or "superior to all others."

Today, think about God being superior and in complete control of your life. Because God is sovereign, he's definitely capable of caring for you today.

Related Texts: Isaiah 50:4−11; Acts 4:23−35; Ephesians 5:19−20

L ift up your heads, you gates!
Rise up, ancient doors!
Then the King of glory
will come in.
Who is this King of glory?
The LORD, strong and mighty,
the LORD, mighty in battle.
Lift up your heads, you gates!
Rise up, ancient doors!
Then the King of glory
will come in.
Who is he, this King of glory?
The LORD of Armies,
he is the King of glory.

–Psalm 24:7–10

I also saw something like a sea of glass mixed with fire, and those who had won the victory over the beast, its image, and the number of its name, were standing on the sea of glass with harps from God. They sang the song of God's servant Moses and the song of the Lamb:

Great and awe-inspiring are
your works,
Lord God, the Almighty;
just and true are your ways,
King of the nations.
Lord, who will not fear
and glorify your name?
For you alone are holy.
All the nations will come
and worship before you
because your righteous acts
have been revealed.

–Revelation 15:2–4

TAKE A SHOT

What are a few qualities that you know a king to be traditionally known for? Do these same words also describe your understanding of God? Why is "King" a good title for God? Or is it?

Related Texts: 1 Samuel 17:39–51; Isaiah 54:5; Revelation 4:1–8

Therefore listen to me,
    you men of understanding.
It is impossible for God
    to do wrong,
and for the Almighty
    to act unjustly.
For he repays a person
    according to his deeds,
and he gives him what his conduct
    deserves.
Indeed, it is true that God does not
    act wickedly
and the Almighty does not
    pervert justice....

The Almighty — we cannot
    reach him —
he is exalted in power!
He will not violate justice and
    abundant righteousness,
therefore, men fear him.
He does not look favorably on any
    who are wise in heart.
                    —*Job 34:10–12; 37:23–24*

The one who lives
    under the protection
    of the Most High
dwells in the shadow
    of the Almighty.

I will say concerning the LORD,
    who is my refuge
    and my fortress,
my God in whom I trust.
                    —*Psalm 91:1–2*

"I am the Alpha and the Omega,"
says the Lord God, "the one who
is, who was, and who is to come,
the Almighty."
                    —*Revelation 1:8*

IN OTHER WORDS

God uses the alphabet to better describe another of his many qualities. In the Greek language in which the New Testament was originally written, alpha and omega were the first and last letters of the alphabet. So in Revelation 1:8, he is saying, "I am the A and the Z." He is reminding everyone that he is the beginning (A) and the end (Z).

God was around before the earth, before the stars, before your grandparents, before the invention of TV, and way before you (that's the A). God is also the end of everything (that's the Z), which means you are somewhere in the middle of his big plan—maybe around the letter K—nobody knows.

The only thing known is his promise to return. When that happens, you'll need to know more than just the alphabet. You'll need to know Jesus as your Savior. Are you ready for his return?

Related texts: Genesis 17:1; 28:3; 35:11; 43:14; 48:3; 49:25; Exodus 6:2–4; Revelation 21:22–27

For the LORD your God is the God of gods and Lord of lords, the great, mighty, and awe-inspiring God, showing no partiality and taking no bribe. He executes justice for the fatherless and the widow, and loves the resident alien, giving him food and clothing.
—Deuteronomy 10:17–18

LORD, our Lord,
how magnificent is your name
　throughout the earth! . . .

Lord, you have been our refuge
in every generation.
Before the mountains were born,
before you gave birth to the earth
　and the world,
from eternity to eternity,
　you are God.
—Psalms 8:9; 90:1–2

If you confess with your mouth, "Jesus is Lord," and believe in your heart that God raised him from the dead, you will be saved. One believes with the heart, resulting in righteousness, and one confesses with the mouth, resulting in salvation.
—Romans 10:9–10

So then, just as you have received Christ Jesus as Lord, continue to walk in him, being rooted and built up in him and established in the faith, just as you were taught, and overflowing with gratitude.
—Colossians 2:6–7

ONE MINUTE MEMORY

"So then, just as you have received Christ Jesus as Lord, continue to walk in him, being rooted and built up in him and established in the faith, just as you were taught, and overflowing with gratitude" (Col 2:6–7).

Related Texts: Job 28; Psalms 8; 86; 110; Daniel 9:1–19; Philippians 2:5–11

My shield is with God,
   who saves the upright
in heart....

God is our refuge and strength,
a helper who is always found
in times of trouble.
Therefore we will not be afraid,
though the earth trembles
and the mountains topple
into the depths of the seas,
though its water roars and foams
and the mountains quake
   with its turmoil.

There is a river —
its streams delight the city of God,
the holy dwelling place
   of the Most High.
God is within her;
   she will not be toppled.
God will help her
   when the morning dawns.
Nations rage, kingdoms topple;
the earth melts when he lifts
   his voice.
The Lord of Armies is with us;
the God of Jacob is our stronghold.

It is good to give thanks
   to the Lord,
to sing praise to your name,
   Most High,
to declare your faithful love
   in the morning
and your faithfulness at night,
with a ten-stringed harp
and the music of a lyre.
   —Psalms 7:10; 46:1–7; 92:1–3

JUST A THOUGHT

If God is known to help and protect the faithful and he's done it many times, don't you think it's worth putting him in total control of your life?

Related Texts: Genesis 14:18–24; Psalms 7; 9:1–2; Luke 1:26–38

So remember your Creator in
the days of your youth:
Before the days of adversity come,
and the years approach
    when you will say,
"I have no delight in them";
before the sun and the light
    are darkened,
and the moon and the stars,
and the clouds return
    after the rain;
on the day when the guardians
    of the house tremble,
and the strong men stoop,
the women who grind grain cease
    because they are few,
and the ones who watch
    through the windows see dimly,
the doors at the street are shut
while the sound of the mill fades;
when one rises at the sound
    of a bird,
and all the daughters of song
    grow faint.
Also, they are afraid of heights
    and dangers on the road;
the almond tree blossoms,
the grasshopper loses its spring,
and the caper berry has no effect;
for the mere mortal is headed
    to his eternal home,
and mourners will walk around
    in the street;
before the silver cord is snapped,
and the gold bowl is broken,
and the jar is shattered
    at the spring,
and the wheel is broken
    into the well;
and the dust returns to the earth
    as it once was,
and the spirit returns to God
    who gave it.
                —Ecclesiastes 12:1–7

DIG DEEPER

You've probably heard it said, "Time
flies when you're having fun!"
Well, time flies even if you aren't
having fun. Time and life move very
quickly. It's easy to waste time and
move through life being bored when
you don't fully understand the big
picture of why you're on earth. The
Bible teaches that you're here to
love God, celebrate life, love others,
and do good things that will make a
difference in the world.

Check out the advice from the
psalmist regarding time: "Teach
us to number our days carefully so
that we may develop wisdom in our
hearts" (Ps 90:12).

Spend a minute today asking God
for his direction on how you spend
today's time. If God is a part of the
day, it's never wasted.

*Related Texts: Genesis 1; 14:18–24;
Ecclesiastes 12:9–14; Isaiah 40:27–31;
Revelation 4:11*

Jacob, why do you say,
   and Israel, why do you assert,
"My way is hidden from the LORD,
and my claim is ignored
   by my God"?
Do you not know?
Have you not heard?
The LORD is the everlasting God,
the Creator of the whole earth.
He never becomes faint or weary;
there is no limit
   to his understanding.
He gives strength to the faint
and strengthens the powerless.
Youths may become faint
   and weary,
and young men stumble and fall,
but those who trust in the LORD
will renew their strength;
they will soar on wings like eagles;
they will run and not
   become weary,
they will walk and not faint.
                    —Isaiah 40:27–31

This saying is trustworthy and
deserving of full acceptance:
"Christ Jesus came into the
world to save sinners" — and
I am the worst of them. But I
received mercy for this reason,
so that in me, the worst of them,
Christ Jesus might demonstrate
his extraordinary patience
as an example to those who
would believe in him for eternal
life. Now to the King eternal,
immortal, invisible, the only God,
be honor and glory forever and
ever. Amen.
                    —1 Timothy 1:15–17

TAKE A SHOT

In the space provided, record your feelings immediately after reading the following verse: "Those who trust in the LORD will renew their strength; they will soar on wings like eagles; they will run and not become weary; they will walk and not faint" (Is 40:31)

Related Texts: Deuteronomy 33:27; Psalm 90:1–2; Romans 16:25–27; Hebrews 9:14

But you are holy,
enthroned on the praises
of Israel.
Our ancestors trusted in you;
they trusted,
and you rescued them.
They cried to you and were
set free;
they trusted in you
and were not disgraced.
—Psalm 22:3–5

The fear of the LORD is
the beginning of wisdom,
and the knowledge of the Holy One
is understanding.
—Proverbs 9:10

The Holy One of Israel is
our Redeemer;
The LORD of Armies is his name.
—Isaiah 47:4

In the synagogue there was a
man with an unclean demonic
spirit who cried out with a loud
voice, "Leave us alone! What do
you have to do with us, Jesus
of Nazareth? Have you come to
destroy us? I know who you are
— the Holy One of God!"
But Jesus rebuked him and said,
"Be silent and come out of him!"
And throwing him down before
them, the demon came out of him
without hurting him at all.
Amazement came over them
all, and they were saying to one
another, "What is this message?
For he commands the unclean
spirits with authority and power,
and they come out!"
– Luke 4:33–36

BIG TIME WORD

Holy is a biblical term given
to things associated with God.
Something that is holy is set apart
from sin. Holiness is very rare.

Holiness starts with God because
God is holy. God then calls you and
encourages you to be holy—to be
set apart from sin.

Since God has given you his Son
to make you right with him, holiness
is a goal for those wanting to mature
and grow in their faith. Make it
a goal—aim for holiness. It has
been said, "If you aim at nothing,
you'll hit it every time." "Nothing"
is a lousy target. Take aim at
holiness today.

*Related Texts: Psalm 16; Isaiah 40:25–
31; 54:5; Acts 2:22–39*

But the LORD sits enthroned
forever;
he has established his throne
for judgment.
And he judges the world
with righteousness;
he executes judgment
on the nations with fairness.

LORD, God of vengeance —
God of vengeance, shine!
Rise up, Judge of the earth;
repay the proud
what they deserve.
—Psalm 9:7–8; 94:1–2

Then a shoot will grow
from the stump of Jesse,
and a branch from his roots
will bear fruit.
The Spirit of the LORD will rest
on him —
a Spirit of wisdom
and understanding,
a Spirit of counsel and strength,
a Spirit of knowledge
and of the fear of the LORD.
His delight will be in the fear
of the LORD.
He will not judge
by what he sees with his eyes,
he will not execute justice
by what he hears with his ears,
but he will judge
the poor righteously
and execute justice
for the oppressed of the land.

For the LORD is our Judge,
the LORD is our Lawgiver,
the LORD is our King.
He will save us.
—Isaiah 11:1–4; 33:22

DIG DEEPER

In the Old Testament, God is often seen as the judge. While in the New Testament, Jesus is given the responsibility of judgment. But since God and Jesus are one, they will work together and decide the details connected with the judgment on your life. Judgment Day is a mystery day; no one knows when . . . except God.

Check out how this verse teaches that you can be prepared for that day: "All the prophets testify about him [Jesus] that through his name everyone who believes in him receives forgiveness of sins" (Ac 10:43).

It's not always an easy decision to completely trust Jesus with every part of your life, but it's sure an easy choice between spending eternal life with God or without God. What's your choice?

Related Texts: Judges 11:27; Psalms 7; 82; 96; John 5:25–30; Acts 10:34–43; James 4:11–12; Revelation 19:11–16

The Lord sits enthroned
over the flood;
The Lord sits enthroned,
King forever.
The Lord gives
his people strength.
—Psalm 29:10–11

I am the Lord, your Holy One,
the Creator of Israel, your King.
—Isaiah 43:15

Then I saw heaven opened, and
there was a white horse. Its rider
is called Faithful and True, and
with justice he judges and makes
war. His eyes were like a fiery
flame, and many crowns were on
his head. He had a name written
that no one knows except himself.
He wore a robe dipped in blood,
and his name is called the Word
of God. The armies that were in
heaven followed him on white
horses, wearing pure white linen.
A sharp sword came from his
mouth, so that he might strike
the nations with it. He will rule
them with an iron rod. He will
also trample the winepress of the
fierce anger of God, the Almighty.
And he has a name written on
his robe and on his thigh: King of
Kings and Lord of Lords.
—Revelation 19:11–16

JUST A THOUGHT

God showed his awesome power
in creating this world, and he has
displayed his great love for people
long before you were alive. The good
news for today is that his power and
love are available for you!

*Related Texts: Psalms 47; 95:1–7;
Isaiah 44:6–8; Jeremiah 10:6–10;
Matthew 21:1–5; 1 Timothy 1:17; 6:15*

Instead of your being deserted
and hated,
with no one passing through,
I will make you an object
    of eternal pride,
a joy from age to age.
You will nurse on the milk
    of nations,
and nurse at the breast of kings;
you will know that I, the LORD,
    am your Savior
and Redeemer, the Mighty One
    of Jacob.

—Isaiah 60:15–16

And Mary said:
    My soul magnifies the Lord,
    and my spirit rejoices in God
        my Savior,
    because he has looked
        with favor
    on the humble condition
        of his servant.
    Surely, from now on
        all generations
    will call me blessed,
    because the Mighty One
    has done great things for me,
    and his name is holy.
    His mercy is from generation
        to generation
    on those who fear him.
    He has done a mighty deed
        with his arm;
    he has scattered the proud
    because of the thoughts
        of their hearts;
    he has toppled the mighty
        from their thrones
    and exalted the lowly.

—Luke 1:46–52

TAKE A SHOT

In a moment of joy, Mary said,
"(God) has done great things for
me." What are four great things God
has done for you?

1.

2.

3.

4.

Take a minute to thank God and give
him praise for the great things he
has done in your life . . . and will
continue to do.

*Related Texts: Joshua 22:22; Psalms 50;
132; Isaiah 49:24–26; Mark 14:60–62*

But I know that my Redeemer lives,
and at the end he will stand
    on the dust.
Even after my skin
    has been destroyed,
yet I will see God in my flesh.
I will see him myself;
my eyes will look at him, and not
    as a stranger.
My heart longs within me.
*   —Job 19:25–27*

Who perceives
    his unintentional sins?
Cleanse me from my hidden faults.
Moreover, keep your servant
    from willful sins;
do not let them rule me.
Then I will be blameless
and cleansed
    from blatant rebellion.
May the words of my mouth
and the meditation of my heart
be acceptable to you,
LORD, my rock and my Redeemer.
*   —Psalm 19:12–14*

This is what the LORD, the King of
Israel and its Redeemer, the LORD
of Armies, says:
    I am the first and I am the last.
    There is no God but me.
    Who, like me, can announce
        the future?
    Let him say so and make a case
        before me,
    since I have established
        an ancient people.
    Let these gods declare
        the coming things,
    and what will take place.
*   —Isaiah 44:6–7*

IN OTHER WORDS

God is called a Redeemer because
he saves people from being
prisoners to the power of sin. Since
God cannot tolerate sin, you (as a
sinner) must be saved or redeemed
from sin's captivity. God did this
(redeemed humanity) through
Jesus's death on the cross.

Jesus's death on the cross paid
for your sins! He bought you back
through death on the cross and
rescued you (those who believe)
from the penalty of sin—which is
death and separation from God.
When you believe in what Jesus did
on the cross, you are saved from
being a prisoner to sin, and you
experience salvation.

Be sure to ask questions if you
need help understanding this
term—it's very important and
powerful!

Related Texts: Isaiah 44:24–28; 54;
Luke 24:13–36; Galatians 4:4–5;
Titus 2:11–14

The LORD is a refuge
for the persecuted,
a refuge in times of trouble.
Those who know your name
trust in you
because you have not abandoned
those who seek you, LORD. . . .

God, hear my cry;
pay attention to my prayer.
I call to you from the ends
of the earth
when my heart is
without strength.
Lead me to a rock that is
high above me,
for you have been a refuge for me,
a strong tower in the face
of the enemy.
I will dwell in your tent forever
and take refuge under the shelter
of your wings.

You are my shelter and my shield;
I put my hope in your word.
– Psalms 9:9–10; 61:1–4; 119:114

LORD, my strength
and my stronghold,
my refuge in a time of distress,
the nations will come to you
from the ends of the earth,
and they will say,
"Our ancestors inherited only lies,
worthless idols of no benefit
at all."
Can one make gods for himself?
But they are not gods.
"Therefore, I am about
to inform them,
and this time I will
make them know
my power and my might;
then they will know that my name
is the LORD."
– Jeremiah 16:19–21

HERE'S THE DEAL

These verses are great to return to when you feel lonely, hurt, or scared (which can be often). It's exciting to know that God promises to comfort you during times of trouble.

A typical move during tough times is to run to friends. This can be both good and bad. Friends can provide comfort and direction. But friends can also turn their backs on you or even make things worse (remember Job's friends?).

God is different from a friend. He's more consistent, for one thing. But he's also stronger, wiser, more powerful, and able to provide you with hope and strength for your specific hurt.

Allow these verses to remind you not to overlook God as the source of comfort. If you don't think he's strong enough, just wait until tomorrow's reading—you'll see.

Related Texts: 2 Samuel 22:3; 31; Psalms 46; 59:16–17; 71; 91; Isaiah 25:1–5

P ay attention, heavens, and I
will speak;
listen, earth, to the words
    from my mouth.
Let my teaching fall like rain
and my word settle like dew,
like gentle rain on new grass
and showers on tender plants.
For I will proclaim the
    LORD's name.
Declare the greatness of our God!
The Rock — his work is perfect;
all his ways are just.
A faithful God, without bias,
he is righteous and true.
*   —Deuteronomy 32:1–4*

Hannah prayed:
    My heart rejoices in the LORD;
    my horn is lifted up by the LORD.
    My mouth boasts
        over my enemies,
    because I rejoice
        in your salvation.
    There is no one holy
        like the LORD.
    There is no one besides you!
    And there is no rock
        like our God.
*   —1 Samuel 2:1–2*

The LORD is my rock,
my fortress, and my deliverer,
my God, my rock
    where I seek refuge,
my shield and the horn
    of my salvation,
my stronghold.
I called to the LORD, who is
    worthy of praise,
and I was saved from my enemies.
*   —Psalm 18:2–3*

DIG DEEPER

In the New Testament Jesus is referred to as a stone. Check out 1 Peter 2:4–6 where, in addition to Jesus's being called a stone, you also receive two identities—"living stones" and "holy priesthood." Read the following passage and underline your given identity.

"As you come to him, a living stone—rejected by people but chosen and honored by God—you yourselves, as living stones, a spiritual house, are being built to be a holy priesthood to offer spiritual sacrifices acceptable to God through Jesus Christ" (2:4–5).

Give it a try—put on your new identity today!

Related Texts: Deuteronomy 32; 2 Samuel 22; Psalm 62; Romans 9:30– 33; 1 Corinthians 10:1–4; 1 Peter 2:1–8

W hy, my soul, are you
so dejected?
Why are you in such turmoil?
Put your hope in God, for I will
   still praise him,
my Savior and my God.
—Psalm 42:11

"You are my witnesses" —
   this is the LORD's declaration —
"and my servant
   whom I have chosen,
so that you may know
   and believe me
and understand that I am he.
No god was formed before me,
and there will be none after me.
I — I am the LORD.
Besides me, there is no Savior.
I alone declared, saved,
   and proclaimed —
and not some foreign god
   among you.
So you are my witnesses" —
   this is the LORD's declaration —
"and I am God.
Also, from today on I am he alone,
and none can rescue
   from my power.
I act, and who can reverse it?"
—Isaiah 43:10–13

For the grace of God has
appeared, bringing salvation for
all people, instructing us to deny
godlessness and worldly lusts and
to live in a sensible, righteous,
and godly way in the present age,
while we wait for the blessed
hope, the appearing of the glory
of our great God and Savior, Jesus
Christ. He gave himself for us to
redeem us from all lawlessness
and to cleanse for himself a
people for his own possession,
eager to do good works.
—Titus 2:11–14

IN OTHER WORDS

Th word *salvation* represents one
of the main messages throughout
the Bible. When someone says,
"I've been saved," he is saying he
has been saved from sin's grip and
returned to God.

The only way to experience
salvation is by trusting in Jesus's
death as the payment for your
sins. The Bible reveals that there's
no other way to be saved or no
other plan or method to get to
God. "There is salvation in no one
else [but Jesus], for there is no
other name under heaven given to
people by which we must be saved"
(Ac 4:12).

*Related Texts: Psalm 68:19–20; Micah
7:1–7; Habakkuk 3:16–19; Luke 1:47–
55; 2:8–20; John 4:40–42; Acts 5:29–32*

The LORD is my shepherd;
I have what I need.
—Psalm 23:1

He protects his flock
like a shepherd;
he gathers the lambs in his arms
and carries them in the fold
of his garment.
He gently leads those
that are nursing.
—Isaiah 40:11

Now may the God of peace, who
brought up from the dead our
Lord Jesus — the great Shepherd
of the sheep — through the blood
of the everlasting covenant, equip
you with everything good to do
his will, working in us what is
pleasing in his sight, through
Jesus Christ, to whom be glory
forever and ever. Amen.
—Hebrews 13:20–21

For this reason they are
before the throne of God,
and they serve him day and night
in his temple.
The one seated on the throne
will shelter them:
They will no longer hunger;
they will no longer thirst;
the sun will no longer strike them,
nor will any scorching heat.
For the Lamb who is at the center
of the throne
will shepherd them;
he will guide them to springs
of the waters of life,
and God will wipe away every tear
from their eyes.
—Revelation 7:15–17

TAKE A SHOT

A shepherd's primary responsibility
is to care for sheep. Listed below
are three qualities of a shepherd.
Next to those qualities, write down
how God might be like a shepherd
in your life.

A shepherd [God]:

1. Knows his sheep.

2. Keeps the sheep from danger.

3. Feeds the sheep.

Related Texts: Psalms 23; 80:1–7;
Ezekiel 34; Micah 5:2–5; John 10:11–15;
1 Peter 2:21–25; 5:1–4

Now the works of the flesh are obvious: sexual immorality, moral impurity, promiscuity, idolatry, sorcery, hatreds, strife, jealousy, outbursts of anger, selfish ambitions, dissensions, factions, envy, drunkenness, carousing, and anything similar. I am warning you about these things — as I warned you before — that those who practice such things will not inherit the kingdom of God.

But the fruit of the Spirit is love, joy, peace, patience, kindness, goodness, faithfulness, gentleness, and self-control. The law is not against such things.
–Galatians 5:19–23

For you were once darkness, but now you are light in the Lord. Walk as children of light — for the fruit of the light consists of all goodness, righteousness, and truth — testing what is pleasing to the Lord. Don't participate in the fruitless works of darkness, but instead expose them.
–Ephesians 5:8–11

A good person produces good out of the good stored up in his heart. An evil person produces evil out of the evil stored up in his heart, for his mouth speaks from the overflow of the heart.
–Luke 6:45

IN OTHER WORDS

The fruits of the Spirit (Gl 5:22–23) are:

- love
- joy
- peace
- patience
- kindness
- goodness
- faithfulness
- gentleness
- self-control

The challenge in these verses is for these fruits to reside in your life. To help you better understand this concept, replace the word *fruit* with the word *actions*. Think of them as "actions as a result of God's Spirit being in you."

In today's passage, there is a list of bad fruit—it's pretty ugly. The challenge is to not "practice such things" (5:21). Good advice. Even better would be to set the course of your life to practice the fruits of the Spirit. When you live your life in faithfulness and obedience to God, his Spirit will energize you to produce these actions in how you think, feel, and act.

Read the list again and ask God to help you become a person who reveals good fruit.

Related Texts: Psalms 1; 112; Isaiah 27:2–3; John 15:1–16; Romans 7:1–6

J esus answered, "The most important is **Listen, Israel! The Lord our God, the Lord is one. Love the Lord your God with all your heart, with all your soul, with all your mind, and with all your strength.** The second is, **Love your neighbor as yourself.** There is no other command greater than these."
—Mark 12:29–31

"I give you a new command: Love one another. Just as I have loved you, you are also to love one another. By this everyone will know that you are my disciples, if you love one another."
—John 13:34–35

"You have heard that it was said, **Love your neighbor** and hate your enemy. But I tell you, love your enemies and pray for those who persecute you, so that you may be children of your Father in heaven. For he causes his sun to rise on the evil and the good, and sends rain on the righteous and the unrighteous. For if you love those who love you, what reward will you have? Don't even the tax collectors do the same?"
—Matthew 5:43–46

Above all, put on love, which is the perfect bond of unity …
—Colossians 3:14

JUST A THOUGHT

The secret to trying to change enemies, friends, parents, teachers, or even little brothers or sisters is to make attempts to love them just like Jesus loves you. People can't stay the same when they're drenched with the type of love Jesus displays—love will change them.

Related Texts: Deuteronomy 6:4–6; John 14–15; 21:15–17; 1 Corinthians 13; 1 Peter 4:7–8; 1 John 4:17–21

The LORD came down in a cloud, stood with him there, and proclaimed his name, "the LORD." The LORD passed in front of him and proclaimed:

The LORD — the LORD is a compassionate and gracious God, slow to anger and abounding in faithful love and truth, maintaining faithful love to a thousand generations, forgiving iniquity, rebellion, and sin. But he will not leave the guilty unpunished, bringing the consequences of the fathers' iniquity on the children and grandchildren to the third and fourth generation.

−Exodus 34:5−7

He loves righteousness and justice; the earth is full of the LORD's unfailing love.

−Psalm 33:5

For God loved the world in this way: He gave his one and only Son, so that everyone who believes in him will not perish but have eternal life.

−John 3:16

But God proves his own love for us in that while we were still sinners, Christ died for us. . . .

For I am persuaded that neither death nor life, nor angels nor rulers, nor things present nor things to come, nor powers, nor height nor depth, nor any other created thing will be able to separate us from the love of God that is in Christ Jesus our Lord.

−Romans 5:8; 8:38−39

ONE MINUTE MEMORY

"For God loved the world in this way: He gave his one and only Son, so that everyone who believes in him will not perish but have eternal life" (Jn 3:16).

If you already have this verse memorized, try this one: "But God proves his own love for us in that while we were still sinners, Christ died for us" (Rm 5:8).

Related Texts: Psalms 1; 112; Isaiah 27:2−3; John 15:1−16; Romans 7:1−6

R ejoice in the LORD,
you righteous ones;
praise from the upright
is beautiful.
Praise the LORD with the lyre;
make music to him with a ten-
stringed harp.
Sing a new song to him;
play skillfully on the strings,
with a joyful shout.

For the word of the LORD is right,
and all his work is trustworthy.
—Psalm 33:1–4

Though the fig tree does not bud
and there is no fruit on the vines,
though the olive crop fails
and the fields produce no food,
though the flocks disappear
from the pen
and there are no herds
in the stalls,
yet I will celebrate in the LORD;
I will rejoice in the God
of my salvation!
—Habakkuk 3:17–18

Now may the God of hope fill
you with all joy and peace as you
believe so that you may overflow
with hope by the power of the
Holy Spirit.
—Romans 15:13

Rejoice in the Lord always. I will
say it again: Rejoice!
—Philippians 4:4

JUST A THOUGHT

When you wake up tomorrow morning, try out this joyful phrase, "Good morning, God!" Try it out and watch it jumpstart your day with a joyful attitude.

Related Texts: Nehemiah 8:1–12; Psalms 28:6–9; 30:4–5; Isaiah 61

May the glory of the LORD
endure forever;
may the LORD rejoice in his works.
He looks at the earth,
    and it trembles;
he touches the mountains,
and they pour out smoke.
I will sing to the LORD all my life;
I will sing praise to my God
    while I live.
May my meditation be pleasing
    to him;
I will rejoice in the LORD.
                —*Psalm 104:31–34*

On that day it will be said
    to Jerusalem:
"Do not fear;
Zion, do not let your hands
    grow weak.
The LORD your God is among you,
a warrior who saves.
He will rejoice over you
    with gladness.
He will be quiet in his love.
He will delight in you
    with singing."
                —*Zephaniah 3:16–17*

Keeping our eyes on Jesus, the
pioneer and perfecter of our faith.
For the joy that lay before him, he
endured the cross, despising the
shame, and sat down at the right
hand of the throne of God.
    For consider him who endured
such hostility from sinners
against himself, so that you won't
grow weary and give up.
                —*Hebrews 12:2–3*

BIG TIME WORD

Did you know that the word *joy* is different from the word *happiness*? Happiness is usually based on some circumstantial happening.

True joy is different because it isn't dependent on circumstances. Joy is an attitude that lives within you. Someone who possesses joy doesn't change when situations change.

Even though it may seem impossible, joy can exist in the midst of difficulty. In the Bible, followers of Jesus are encouraged to be joyful when they encounter problems and have joy during difficult times because Jesus has overcome the world.

Pain is unavoidable, and being happy is conditional, but joy is a fruit of the Spirit that becomes available when you depend on God.

Related Texts: 1 Chronicles 16:23–33; Nehemiah 8:1–12; Psalm 21:1–7; Isaiah 62:4–7

M ay the LORD bless you
and protect you;
may the LORD make his face shine
on you
and be gracious to you;
may the LORD look with favor
on you
and give you peace.
—Numbers 6:24–26

Abundant peace belongs to those
who love your instruction;
nothing makes them stumble.
—Psalm 119:165

You will keep the mind that is
dependent on you
in perfect peace,
for it is trusting in you.
Trust in the LORD forever,
because in the LORD,
the LORD himself, is
an everlasting rock!
—Isaiah 26:3–4

"Peace I leave with you. My peace
I give to you. I do not give to you
as the world gives. Don't let your
heart be troubled or fearful."
—John 14:27

Don't worry about anything, but
in everything, through prayer
and petition with thanksgiving,
present your requests to God.
And the peace of God, which
surpasses all understanding, will
guard your hearts and minds in
Christ Jesus.
—Philippians 4:6–7

And let the peace of Christ, to
which you were also called in one
body, rule your hearts. And be
thankful.
—Colossians 3:15

ONE MINUTE MEMORY

"Don't worry about anything, but
in everything, through prayer and
petition with thanksgiving, present
your requests to God" (Php 4:6).

*Related Texts: Proverbs 12:20;
Isaiah 32:17; 57:21; Micah 4:1–5;
Luke 2:13–14; Romans 8:1–6*

The LORD gives
his people strength;
the LORD blesses his people
with peace.

—Psalm 29:11

For a child will be born for us,
a son will be given to us,
and the government will be
on his shoulders.
He will be named
Wonderful Counselor, Mighty God,
Eternal Father, Prince of Peace.
The dominion will be vast,
and its prosperity will never end.
He will reign on the throne
of David
and over his kingdom,
to establish and sustain it
with justice and righteousness
from now on and forever.
The zeal of the LORD of Armies
will accomplish this.

—Isaiah 9:6–7

Now may the God of peace
himself sanctify you completely.
And may your whole spirit, soul,
and body be kept sound and
blameless at the coming of our
Lord Jesus Christ.

—1 Thessalonians 5:23

May the Lord of peace himself
give you peace always in every
way. The Lord be with all of you.

—2 Thessalonians 3:16

WEIRD OR WHAT?

In the Old Testament, the Hebrew word for "peace" is *shalom*. This is the same word you might hear as a greeting or closing remark in many present-day Jewish temples. Shalom is used to communicate a blessing to another person.

The meaning of this blessing has its source in God. To withhold shalom is to withhold the blessing and might be interpreted in a similar manner as cursing at someone.

Related Texts: Ecclesiastes 3:1–8; Romans 15:33; 16:20; 2 Corinthians 13:11; Philippians 4:6–9

Be silent before the LORD
and wait expectantly for him;
do not be agitated by one
who prospers in his way,
by the person who carries out
evil plans.

Refrain from anger and give up
your rage;
do not be agitated — it can only
bring harm.
For evildoers will be destroyed,
but those who put their hope
in the LORD
will inherit the land.

I waited patiently for the LORD,
and he turned to me and heard
my cry for help.
He brought me up
from a desolate pit,
out of the muddy clay,
and set my feet on a rock,
making my steps secure.
He put a new song in my mouth,
a hymn of praise to our God.
Many will see and fear,
and they will trust in the LORD.
              —Psalms 37:7–9; 40:1–3

A patient person shows great
understanding,
but a quick-tempered one
promotes foolishness.
                    —Proverbs 14:29

Love is patient, love is kind. Love
does not envy, is not boastful, is
not arrogant, is not rude.
              —1 Corinthians 13:4–5

Therefore, brothers and sisters,
be patient until the Lord's coming.
                    —James 5:7

HERE'S THE DEAL

Showing patience in today's world is tough! In a time-crazed society, "quick serve," getting "in and out," fast food, instant messaging, and no lines are important values for survival. Patience is minimized when time is so important.

Is it difficult to show patience when you desperately want something to happen? What's even more difficult is being a follower of Jesus and learning to be patient with God's timing. Most people want God to answer their prayers now. But whether or not they like it, God answers them when he wants to, and his timing is always better than theirs. Why? Because he's God.

Try out a little patience today. See what happens; you won't explode. Next time you ask God for something, accept his timing. Be confident that he hears your prayers.

Related Texts: Proverbs 15:18;
16:32; 19:11; 25:15; Ecclesiastes 7:8;
Romans 12:9–12

This saying is trustworthy and deserving of full acceptance: "Christ Jesus came into the world to save sinners" — and I am the worst of them. But I received mercy for this reason, so that in me, the worst of them, Christ Jesus might demonstrate his extraordinary patience as an example to those who would believe in him for eternal life.

−1 Timothy 1:15−16

The Lord does not delay his promise, as some understand delay, but is patient with you, not wanting any to perish but all to come to repentance.

But the day of the Lord will come like a thief; on that day the heavens will pass away with a loud noise, the elements will burn and be dissolved, and the earth and the works on it will be disclosed....

Also, regard the patience of our Lord as salvation, just as our dear brother Paul has written to you according to the wisdom given to him.

−2 Peter 3:9−10,15

JUST A THOUGHT

The greatest news any of your friends could ever hear is that God loves them more than they love themselves, and he wants them to have everlasting life.

Can you do anything to let them know this good news today?

Related Texts: Isaiah 7:13; 65:17−25; Romans 2:1−4; 3:21−28; 1 Peter 3:18−20; Revelation 21:1−8

A gracious woman gains honor,
but violent people gain
only riches.

A kind man benefits himself,
but a cruel person brings ruin
on himself. . . .

The one who oppresses the poor
person insults his Maker,
but one who is kind to the needy
honors him. . . .

Kindness to the poor is a loan
to the LORD,
and he will give a reward
to the lender.
—*Proverbs 11:16–17; 14:31; 19:17*

And be kind and compassionate
to one another, forgiving one
another, just as God also forgave
you in Christ.
—*Ephesians 4:32*

Therefore, as God's chosen ones,
holy and dearly loved, put on
compassion, kindness, humility,
gentleness, and patience, bearing
with one another and forgiving
one another if anyone has a
grievance against another. Just as
the Lord has forgiven you, so you
are also to forgive. Above all, put
on love, which is the perfect bond
of unity.
—*Colossians 3:12–14*

TAKE A SHOT

When you help the poor, you are
lending to the Lord. The good
news connected to this action is
that God will reward the lender
(see Pr 19:17). This doesn't mean
God will shower you with riches.
His spiritual rewards are far better
than that.

Try to list five specific ways
you can help the poor (in your
community and around the world).

1.

2.

3.

4.

5.

Circle your best idea and get started
in God's program to care for those in
need today. Not only will the poor be
blessed by your generosity, but you
will be too.

Related Texts: Ruth 1:1–3:10;
Proverbs 14:21; 1 Thessalonians 5:15

I will make known
the LORD's faithful love
and the LORD's praiseworthy acts,
because of all the LORD has done
for us —
even the many good things
he has done for the house of Israel,
which he did for them based on
his compassion
and the abundance of
his faithful love.

—Isaiah 63:7

This is what the LORD says:
The wise person should not boast
in his wisdom;
the strong should not boast
in his strength;
the wealthy should not boast
in his wealth.
But the one who boasts
should boast in this:
that he understands
and knows me —
that I am the LORD,
showing faithful love,
justice, and righteousness
on the earth,
for I delight in these things.
This is the LORD's declaration.

—Jeremiah 9:23–24

For we too were once foolish,
disobedient, deceived, enslaved
by various passions and
pleasures, living in malice and
envy, hateful, detesting one
another.
But when the kindness of
God our Savior and his love
for mankind appeared, he
saved us — not by works of
righteousness that we had done,
but according to his mercy.

—Titus 3:3–5

DIG DEEPER

Prophets were people who foretold God's ultimate act of kindness prior to the birth of Jesus. Check out what was written in Isaiah 53:4–6 about God's plan for Jesus and you thousands of years ago:

Yet he himself bore our sicknesses, and he carried our pains; but we in turn regarded him stricken, struck down by God, and afflicted. But he was pierced because of our rebellion, crushed because of our iniquities; punishment for our peace was on him, and we are healed by his wounds. We all went astray like sheep; we all have turned to our own way; and the LORD has punished him for the iniquity of us all.

Go back through the passage and circle the words "our" and "we" and then thank God that his ultimate plan included you.

Related Texts: Isaiah 53:1–8; Romans 2:1–8; 11:11–24

One who is good obtains favor
from the LORD,
but he condemns a person
who schemes.

—Proverbs 12:2

I know that there is nothing
better for them than to rejoice
and enjoy the good life. It is also
the gift of God whenever anyone
eats, drinks, and enjoys all his
efforts.

—Ecclesiastes 3:12–13

Let us not get tired of doing good,
for we will reap at the proper time
if we don't give up. Therefore, as
we have opportunity, let us work
for the good of all, especially
for those who belong to the
household of faith.

—Galatians 6:9–10

For we are his workmanship,
created in Christ Jesus for good
works, which God prepared
ahead of time for us to do.

—Ephesians 2:10

Dear friend, do not imitate what
is evil, but what is good. The one
who does good is of God; the one
who does evil has not seen God.

—3 John 11

ONE MINUTE MEMORY

"For we are his workmanship, created in Christ Jesus for good works, which God prepared ahead of time for us to do" (Eph 2:10).

Related Texts: Psalm 34:8–14; Proverbs 3:27; 11:27; 1 Peter 2:12–15

Taste and see that the LORD
  is good.
How happy is the person who
    takes refuge in him! ...

I will praise you forever for what
    you have done.
In the presence
    of your faithful people,
I will put my hope in your name,
    for it is good. ...

God is indeed good to Israel,
to the pure in heart. ...

For the LORD is good, and his
    faithful love endures forever;
his faithfulness,
    through all generations. ...

Give thanks to the LORD,
    for he is good;
his faithful love
    endures forever. ...

You are good, and you do
    what is good;
teach me your statutes. ...

Praise the LORD, for the LORD
    is good;
sing praise to his name,
    for it is delightful. ...

The LORD is good to everyone;
his compassion rests
    on all he has made.
    —*Psalms 34:8; 52:9; 73:1; 100:5;*
      118:29; 119:68; 135:3; 145:9

HERE'S THE DEAL

God is good! You can see his goodness; you can hear it; you can touch his goodness and even smell it every single day. See for yourself! Experience his goodness with any one of these ideas:

- Watch a sunset
- Smell a flower
- Examine the legs of a centipede
- Listen to the waves break on the beach
- Ask a follower of Jesus to tell you their spiritual story of knowing God
- Listen to the sounds of nature in a quiet location
- Watch a caterpillar turn into a butterfly
- Look at the stars on a clear night
- Kiss a newborn baby
- Look out a window at God's incredible playground—earth.

Related Texts: 2 Chronicles 6:41;
Psalm 84:9–12; Mark 10:17–18;
Romans 8:18–28; 3 John 11

A bove all, fear the LORD and worship him faithfully with all your heart; consider the great things he has done for you.

−1 Samuel 12:24

With the faithful
you prove yourself faithful,
with the blameless
you prove yourself blameless,
with the pure
you prove yourself pure,
but with the crooked
you prove yourself shrewd.
You rescue an oppressed people,
but your eyes are set
   against the proud —
you humble them.

−2 Samuel 22:26−28

This saying is trustworthy:
   For if we died with him,
   we will also live with him;
   if we endure, we will also reign
     with him;
   if we deny him, he will also
     deny us;
   if we are faithless,
   he remains faithful,
   for he cannot deny himself.

−2 Timothy 2:11−13

BIG TIME WORD

Faith is believing that an unseen God is big enough to know everything about you, to intimately care for you, and to provide for all your needs. Being faithful is living your life like you believe that definition of faith.

It's easy to be faithful when everything is going well. It's a lot more difficult to be faithful when you experience pain and tragedy. Trusting that God is going to be God and that you're going to be okay is a process you'll be working on for years.

Practice being faithful today and don't worry about tomorrow until it gets here.

Related Texts: Psalm 101; Proverbs 3:1−4; Matthew 24:45−51; 25:14−30

Know that the LORD your God is God, the faithful God who keeps his gracious covenant loyalty for a thousand generations with those who love him and keep his commands. But he directly pays back and destroys those who hate him. He will not hesitate to pay back directly the one who hates him.
—*Deuteronomy 7:9–10*

Yet I call this to mind, and therefore I have hope:

Because of the LORD's faithful love we do not perish, for his mercies never end. They are new every morning; great is your faithfulness!
—*Lamentations 3:21–23*

So, whoever thinks he stands must be careful not to fall. No temptation has come upon you except what is common to humanity. But God is faithful; he will not allow you to be tempted beyond what you are able, but with the temptation he will also provide the way out so that you may be able to bear it.
—*1 Corinthians 10:12–13*

If we confess our sins, he is faithful and righteous to forgive us our sins and to cleanse us from all unrighteousness.
—*1 John 1:9*

ONE MINUTE MEMORY

"If we confess our sins, he is faithful and righteous to forgive us our sins and to cleanse us from all unrighteousness" (1Jn 1:9).

Related Texts: Deuteronomy 31:30–32:4; 2 Thessalonians 3:3; 2 Timothy 2:11–13; Revelation 19:11–16

A gentle answer
turns away anger,
but a harsh word stirs up wrath. . . .

A ruler can be persuaded
    through patience,
and a gentle tongue can break
    a bone.
—Proverbs 15:1; 25:15

With all humility and gentleness,
with patience, bearing with one
another in love, making every
effort to keep the unity of the
Spirit through the bond of peace.
—Ephesians 4:2–3

Who then will harm you if you
are devoted to what is good?
But even if you should suffer
for righteousness, you are
blessed. **Do not fear them or
be intimidated,** but in your
hearts regard Christ the Lord as
holy, ready at any time to give a
defense to anyone who asks you
for a reason for the hope that is in
you. Yet do this with gentleness
and reverence, keeping a clear
conscience, so that when you are
accused, those who disparage
your good conduct in Christ will
be put to shame.
— 1 Peter 3:13–16

BIG TIME WORD

Being gentle in today's world is a
rare quality. Unfortunately, gentle
people are often overlooked and
those who are loud, wild, and
obnoxious tend to get most of
the attention. But the truth is,
gentleness is a very important
quality.

Being gentle is often associated
with weakness. But it's actually
just the opposite. Gentleness is
a character quality associated
with strength. People who display
gentleness have a quiet, controlled
confidence about themselves and a
strong faith in God.

Pray for more gentleness today
and think about being confident
in the person God planned for you
to become.

*Related Texts: Isaiah 8:12–15;
1 Timothy 6:3–11; 2 Timothy 2:24–25;
1 Peter 3:1–6*

See, the Lord GOD comes
with strength,
and his power establishes his rule.
His wages are with him,
and his reward accompanies him.
He protects his flock
   like a shepherd;
he gathers the lambs in his arms
and carries them in the fold
   of his garment.
He gently leads those
   that are nursing.
—Isaiah 40:10–11

Rejoice greatly, Daughter Zion!
Shout in triumph,
   Daughter Jerusalem!
Look, your King is coming to you;
he is righteous and victorious,
humble and riding on a donkey,
on a colt, the foal of a donkey.
—Zechariah 9:9

"Come to me, all of you who are
weary and burdened, and I will
give you rest. Take up my yoke
and learn from me, because I
am lowly and humble in heart,
and you will find rest for your
souls. For my yoke is easy and my
burden is light."
—Matthew 11:28–30

TAKE A SHOT

A burden is something that troubles you or creates difficult times in your life.

What burdens or problems are currently heavy in your life and need to be lightened today?

1.

2.

3.

Ask God for his gentleness to comfort these burdens. He wants to make your burdens light.

*Related Texts: 1 Kings 19:9–12;
Matthew 21:1–12; 2 Corinthians 10:1;*

A person who does not control
his temper
is like a city whose wall
  is broken down.
                    —Proverbs 25:28

But you are to proclaim things
consistent with sound teaching.
Older men are to be self-
controlled, worthy of respect,
sensible, and sound in faith, love,
and endurance. In the same way,
older women are to be reverent
in behavior, not slanderers, not
slaves to excessive drinking. They
are to teach what is good, so that
they may encourage the young
women to love their husbands
and to love their children, to be
self-controlled, pure, workers at
home, kind, and in submission
to their husbands, so that God's
word will not be slandered.
    In the same way, encourage the
young men to be self-controlled.
                    —Titus 2:1–6

For this very reason, make
every effort to supplement your
faith with goodness, goodness
with knowledge, knowledge
with self-control, self-control
with endurance, endurance
with godliness, godliness
with brotherly affection, and
brotherly affection with love. For
if you possess these qualities in
increasing measure, they will
keep you from being useless or
unfruitful in the knowledge of
our Lord Jesus Christ.
                    —2 Peter 1:5–8

BIG TIME WORD

The term self-control has to do with
having power over yourself. Self-
control expresses the power not
to do something that might seem
natural or something you really want
to do. For instance, keeping your
mouth closed when you want to
yell at a younger sibling for putting
hair ointment on your toothbrush.
Or, controlling your sexual urges
when you feel like disobeying God's
standards.

    Having self-control doesn't mean
you will express complete control
in all situations. Self-control comes
with maturity, practice, and prayer.
It's learned on a daily basis through
trial and error. It's worth having. If
you don't have it, ask God for it and
begin trusting in his power today for
self-control.

*Related Texts: Proverbs 1:1–17; 23:23;
1 Thessalonians 5:5–10; 2 Timothy 1:7;
Titus 2:11–14; 1 Peter 4:7*

The Lord is compassionate
and gracious,
slow to anger and abounding
in faithful love.
He will not always accuse us
or be angry forever.
He has not dealt with us as
our sins deserve
or repaid us according to
our iniquities.

For as high as the heavens
are above the earth,
so great is his faithful love
toward those who fear him.
As far as the east is from the west,
so far has he removed
our transgressions from us....

The Lord is gracious
and compassionate,
slow to anger and great
in faithful love.
The Lord is good to everyone;
his compassion rests
on all he has made.
—Psalms 103:8–12; 145:8–9

The Lord is a jealous
and avenging God;
the Lord takes vengeance
and is fierce in wrath.
The Lord takes vengeance
against his foes;
he is furious with his enemies.
The Lord is slow to anger but great
in power;
the Lord will never leave
the guilty unpunished.
His path is in the whirlwind
and storm,
and clouds are the dust
beneath his feet.
—Nahum 1:2–3

DIG DEEPER

God may be slow to anger, but he does give indication that he will return, in his own time, and express his anger and judgment on those who don't know Jesus. Check out what is written in 2 Peter 3:8–10:

Dear friends, don't overlook this one fact: With the Lord one day is like a thousand years, and a thousand years like one day. The Lord does not delay his promise, as some understand delay, but is patient with you, not wanting any to perish but all to come to repentance.

But the day of the Lord will come like a thief; on that day the heavens will pass away with a loud noise, the elements will burn and be dissolved, and the earth and the works on it will be disclosed.

Are you ready for God to return and show his anger?

_____
_____
_____
_____
_____
_____
_____
_____
_____
_____
_____
_____

Related Texts: Exodus 34:5–7;
Psalm 86:15–17; Joel 2:12–14;
Jonah 3–4; 2 Peter 3:8–15

God also said to Moses, "Say this to the Israelites: The LORD, the God of your ancestors, the God of Abraham, the God of Isaac, and the God of Jacob, has sent me to you. This is my name forever; this is how I am to be remembered in every generation.

"Go and assemble the elders of Israel and say to them: The LORD, the God of your ancestors, the God of Abraham, Isaac, and Jacob, has appeared to me and said: I have paid close attention to you and to what has been done to you in Egypt. And I have promised you that I will bring you up from the misery of Egypt to the land of the Canaanites, Hethites, Amorites, Perizzites, Hivites, and Jebusites — a land flowing with milk and honey. They will listen to what you say. Then you, along with the elders of Israel, must go to the king of Egypt and say to him: The LORD, the God of the Hebrews, has met with us. Now please let us go on a three-day trip into the wilderness so that we may sacrifice to the LORD our God.

"However, I know that the king of Egypt will not allow you to go, even under force from a strong hand. But when I stretch out my hand and strike Egypt with all my miracles that I will perform in it, after that, he will let you go. And I will give these people such favor with the Egyptians that when you go, you will not go empty-handed. Each woman will ask her neighbor and any woman staying in her house for silver and gold jewelry, and clothing, and you will put them on your sons and daughters. So you will plunder the Egyptians."
–*Exodus 3:15–22*

IN OTHER WORDS

During the days of Jacob, the Israelites immigrated to Egypt where they eventually became slaves to the Egyptian people. For four-hundred years they suffered hardship and torture and were robbed of their freedom.

God chose Moses to return to Egypt and free the Israelites from their suffering. God wanted to deliver them and move them into the promised land. This promised land was a place for the Israelites to raise their families, prosper, and enjoy their relationship with God. It's a long story, but they eventually got there. Keep reading and you'll see several illustrations of God's amazing power — it's quite the journey!

Related Texts: Genesis 13:12–17; 15:12–16; Haggai 2:4–8; Acts 7:30–36

The Lord instructed Moses, "When you go back to Egypt, make sure you do before Pharaoh all the wonders that I have put within your power. But I will harden his heart so that he won't let the people go. And you will say to Pharaoh: This is what the Lord says: Israel is my firstborn son. I told you: Let my son go so that he may worship me, but you refused to let him go. Look, I am about to kill your firstborn son!"...

Now the Lord had said to Aaron, "Go and meet Moses in the wilderness." So he went and met him at the mountain of God and kissed him. Moses told Aaron everything the Lord had sent him to say, and about all the signs he had commanded him to do. Then Moses and Aaron went and assembled all the elders of the Israelites. Aaron repeated everything the Lord had said to Moses and performed the signs before the people. The people believed, and when they heard that the Lord had paid attention to them and that he had seen their misery, they knelt low and worshiped.

Later, Moses and Aaron went in and said to Pharaoh, "This is what the Lord, the God of Israel, says: Let my people go, so that they may hold a festival for me in the wilderness."

But Pharaoh responded, "Who is the Lord that I should obey him by letting Israel go? I don't know the Lord, and besides, I will not let Israel go."

—Exodus 4:21–23,27–31; 5:1–2

BIBLICAL BIO

Aaron was Moses's oldest brother and also his spokesperson. God mainly communicated to Moses, but Aaron passed that information on to the others.

As the people of Israel left Egypt and wandered through the wilderness, Moses became the headmaster and Aaron became the "priest." This was the first "priesthood" of Israel. In this position Aaron represented the people of Israel and brought their voice to Moses and God.

Aaron is another example of a faithful and normal person whom God used to do great things. Are you ready to be used by God and do great things? God has a habit of using ordinary people to do extraordinary things.

You never know what he has planned for you today!

Related Texts: Exodus 1:8–13; 9:13–16; Proverbs 29:1–2; John 10:33–38

The LORD answered Moses, "See, I have made you like God to Pharaoh, and Aaron your brother will be your prophet. You must say whatever I command you; then Aaron your brother must declare it to Pharaoh so that he will let the Israelites go from his land. But I will harden Pharaoh's heart and multiply my signs and wonders in the land of Egypt. Pharaoh will not listen to you, but I will put my hand into Egypt and bring the military divisions of my people the Israelites out of the land of Egypt by great acts of judgment. The Egyptians will know that I am the LORD when I stretch out my hand against Egypt and bring out the Israelites from among them." . . .

The LORD said to Moses and Aaron, "When Pharaoh tells you, 'Perform a miracle,' tell Aaron, 'Take your staff and throw it down before Pharaoh. It will become a serpent.'" So Moses and Aaron went in to Pharaoh and did just as the LORD had commanded. Aaron threw down his staff before Pharaoh and his officials, and it became a serpent. But then Pharaoh called the wise men and sorcerers — the magicians of Egypt, and they also did the same thing by their occult practices. Each one threw down his staff, and it became a serpent. But Aaron's staff swallowed their staffs. However, Pharaoh's heart was hard, and he did not listen to them, as the LORD had said.

—Exodus 7:1–5,8–13

WEIRD OR WHAT?

Pharaoh's magicians were most likely from a group of Egyptian priests or wise men called snake charmers. The actual illusion of the sticks turning into snakes appears to be quite amazing. The wise men were trained in magic and the snake charmers knew how to put the serpents into a rigid or stiff position, which gave the illusion of snakes being transformed into sticks.

The fact that Moses's staff ate the other two snakes demonstrated God's supernatural power over the natural or man-made illusion of Pharaoh's snake charmers.

Today, be on the lookout for God's supernatural power displayed in some event or person's life.

Related Texts: Exodus 8:7,18–19; Romans 9:14–21; 2 Timothy 3:8–9

My people,
　　hear my instruction;
listen to the words
　　from my mouth.
I will declare wise sayings;
I will speak mysteries
　　from the past —
things we have heard and known
and that our ancestors
　　have passed down to us.
We will not hide them
　　from their children,
but will tell a future generation
the praiseworthy acts of the LORD,
his might,
　　and the wondrous works
he has performed. . . .

He turned their rivers into blood,
and they could not drink
　　from their streams.
He sent among them swarms
　　of flies,
which fed on them,
and frogs, which devastated them.
He gave their crops
　　to the caterpillar
and the fruit of their labor
　　to the locust.
He killed their vines with hail
and their sycamore fig trees
　　with a flood.
He handed over their livestock
　　to hail
and their cattle to lightning bolts.
He sent his burning anger
　　against them:
fury, indignation, and calamity —
a band of deadly messengers.
He cleared a path for his anger.
He did not spare them from death
but delivered their lives
　　to the plague.
He struck all the firstborn in Egypt,
the first progeny of the tents
　　of Ham.

—Psalm 78:1–4,44–51

IN OTHER WORDS

Most of the Egyptian people lived with a sense of security because they believed in the power of their gods. The Egyptian leaders believed their magicians or wise men were a powerful advantage because their gods could perform miracles, or the appearance of miracles.

This is why every time Moses performed a miracle, the Pharaoh would summon his magicians to do the same. Because the Pharaoh's magicians performed similar miracles to Moses, Pharaoh questioned the power of God and this resulted in a hardened heart.

As you'll read in two days, God's plague of death upon the firstborn was something Pharaoh's magicians could not duplicate nor could they stop. Once again God showed himself to be the one true God. This truth is the same today as it was in the days of Moses.

Related Texts: Exodus 7:15–10:29; Deuteronomy 4:32–38; 1 Samuel 4:2-8; Acts 7:30-36

The LORD said to Moses, "I will bring one more plague on Pharaoh and on Egypt. After that, he will let you go from here. When he lets you go, he will drive you out of here . . .

So Moses said, "This is what the LORD says: About midnight I will go throughout Egypt, and every firstborn male in the land of Egypt will die, from the firstborn of Pharaoh who sits on his throne to the firstborn of the servant girl who is at the grindstones, as well as every firstborn of the livestock. Then there will be a great cry of anguish through all the land of Egypt such as never was before or ever will be again. But against all the Israelites, whether people or animals, not even a dog will snarl, so that you may know that the LORD makes a distinction between Egypt and Israel. All these officials of yours will come down to me and bow before me, saying: Get out, you and all the people who follow you. After that, I will get out." And he went out from Pharaoh's presence fiercely angry.

The LORD said to Moses, "Pharaoh will not listen to you, so that my wonders may be multiplied in the land of Egypt." Moses and Aaron did all these wonders before Pharaoh, but the LORD hardened Pharaoh's heart, and he would not let the Israelites go out of his land.

—Exodus 11:1,4–10

BIBLICAL BIO

Pharaoh is more of a title than a person. A pharaoh is equivalent to a king in many countries or similar to the role of President in the United States.

One difference would be that a pharaoh was considered a god. He was thought to be a son of the great sun god. Many believed that once a pharaoh died he would become the sun-god Osiris. They believed that after the Pharaoh died, he became part of the divine gods of the afterworld.

Related Texts: Exodus 4:22–23; Psalms 105:23–38; 135:8–9; 136:10–12; Romans 9:14–21; Hebrews 11:28

Then Moses summoned all the elders of Israel and said to them, "Go, select an animal from the flock according to your families, and slaughter the Passover animal. Take a cluster of hyssop, dip it in the blood that is in the basin, and brush the lintel and the two doorposts with some of the blood in the basin. None of you may go out the door of his house until morning. When the LORD passes through to strike Egypt and sees the blood on the lintel and the two doorposts, he will pass over the door and not let the destroyer enter your houses to strike you.

"Keep this command permanently as a statute for you and your descendants. When you enter the land that the LORD will give you as he promised, you are to observe this ceremony. When your children ask you, 'What does this ceremony mean to you?' you are to reply, 'It is the Passover sacrifice to the LORD, for he passed over the houses of the Israelites in Egypt when he struck the Egyptians, and he spared our homes.'" So the people knelt low and worshiped.

–Exodus 12:21–27

IN OTHER WORDS

The history of Passover starts with the tenth plague God sent to the people of Egypt—which was death to the firstborn. The Israelites were warned with special instructions on how to save their firstborn: by smearing blood from a lamb over their front door. The blood would serve as a sign to the "destroyer," or the "Angel of Death," to pass over those homes (and not harm the children). Those who didn't have blood over their doors, mostly Egyptians, experienced a massive death throughout the Passover night.

That night was a tragedy, but at the same time was a beautiful example of God's saving power and his commitment to save the Israelite people from Egyptian captivity.

God has a long history of keeping his promises!

Related Texts: Numbers 9:1–14; Deuteronomy 16:1–8; 2 Chronicles 30; 1 Corinthians 5:6–8

H e was despised and rejected
   by men,
a man of suffering who knew
   what sickness was.
He was like someone
   people turned away from;
he was despised, and we didn't
   value him.

Yet he himself bore our sicknesses,
and he carried our pains;
but we in turn
   regarded him stricken,
struck down by God, and afflicted.
But he was pierced because of
   our rebellion,
crushed because of our iniquities;
punishment for our peace was
   on him,
and we are healed by his wounds.
We all went astray like sheep;
we all have turned to our own way;
and the LORD has punished him
for the iniquity of us all.

He was oppressed and afflicted,
yet he did not open his mouth.
Like a lamb led to the slaughter
and like a sheep silent
   before her shearers,
he did not open his mouth....

Yet the LORD was pleased
   to crush him severely.
When you make him
   a guilt offering,
he will see his seed,
   he will prolong his days,
and by his hand, the LORD's pleasure
   will be accomplished.
      —Isaiah 53:3–7,10

ONE MINUTE MEMORY

"We all went astray like sheep; we all have turned to our own way; and the LORD has punished him for the iniquity of us all" (Is 53:6)

Related Texts: Psalm 22; Mark 10:45; Acts 8:26–39; 1 Peter 2:21–25

The next day John saw Jesus coming toward him and said, "Look, the Lamb of God, who takes away the sin of the world! This is the one I told you about: 'After me comes a man who ranks ahead of me, because he existed before me.' I didn't know him, but I came baptizing with water so that he might be revealed to Israel." And John testified, "I saw the Spirit descending from heaven like a dove, and he rested on him. I didn't know him, but he who sent me to baptize with water told me, 'The one you see the Spirit descending and resting on — he is the one who baptizes with the Holy Spirit.' I have seen and testified that this is the Son of God."

—John 1:29–34

Then I looked and heard the voice of many angels around the throne, and also of the living creatures and of the elders. Their number was countless thousands, plus thousands of thousands. They said with a loud voice,
Worthy is the Lamb who was slaughtered
to receive power and riches and wisdom and strength and honor and glory and blessing!
—Revelation 5:11–12

BIBLICAL BIO

John the Baptist didn't have anything to do with the Baptist church you may know of today. He was a wild preacher who spoke of forgiveness and salvation. While preaching one day, John spotted Jesus and boldly said, "This was the one of whom I said, 'The one coming after me ranks ahead of me, because he existed before me'" (Jn 1:15). God used John the Baptist to "roll out the red carpet" for Jesus as he was beginning his public ministry.

You might have something in common with John the Baptist—you can prepare people for the coming of Jesus. How might you do that today?

Related Texts: Genesis 22:1–19; Hebrews 9:11–28; 1 Peter 1:18–20; Revelation 5–7; 21:9–22:4

Jesus called them over and said to them, "You know that those who are regarded as rulers of the Gentiles lord it over them, and those in high positions act as tyrants over them. But it is not so among you. On the contrary, whoever wants to become great among you will be your servant, and whoever wants to be first among you will be a slave to all. For even the Son of Man did not come to be served, but to serve, and to give his life as a ransom for many."

—Mark 10:42–45

While he was praying in private and his disciples were with him, he asked them, "Who do the crowds say that I am?"

They answered, "John the Baptist; others, Elijah; still others, that one of the ancient prophets has come back."

"But you," he asked them, "who do you say that I am?"

Peter answered, "God's Messiah."

But he strictly warned and instructed them to tell this to no one, saying, "It is necessary that the Son of Man suffer many things and be rejected by the elders, chief priests, and scribes, be killed, and be raised the third day."

—Luke 9:18–22

JUST A THOUGHT

The greatest person ever to live (Jesus) flipped the world upside down when he claimed that the route to greatness can only be reached by following the road of servanthood.

Related Texts: Psalm 16;
Matthew 12:38–41; Mark 10:32–34;
Luke 24:13–32; Acts 2:14–40

When they approached Jerusalem and came to Bethphage at the Mount of Olives, Jesus then sent two disciples, telling them, "Go into the village ahead of you. At once you will find a donkey tied there with her colt. Untie them and bring them to me. If anyone says anything to you, say that the Lord needs them, and he will send them at once."

This took place so that what was spoken through the prophet might be fulfilled:
Tell Daughter Zion,
"See, your King is coming
to you,
gentle, and mounted
on a donkey,
and on a colt,
the foal of a donkey."

The disciples went and did just as Jesus directed them. They brought the donkey and the colt; then they laid their clothes on them, and he sat on them. A very large crowd spread their clothes on the road; others were cutting branches from the trees and spreading them on the road. Then the crowds who went ahead of him and those who followed shouted:
Hosanna to the Son of David!
Blessed is he who comes
in the name
of the Lord!
Hosanna in the highest heaven!
When he entered Jerusalem, the whole city was in an uproar, saying, "Who is this?" The crowds were saying, "This is the prophet Jesus from Nazareth in Galilee."
—Matthew 21:1–11

HERE'S THE DEAL

When you learn about the person of Jesus, you'll see how different he was from the rest in the world. For one thing, he wasn't selfish; he was a servant. His entire life modeled this truth. He was born in a barn instead of a palace. He entered Jerusalem on a donkey instead of a powerful and prestigious horse, and he washed his followers' feet, saying, "For I have given you an example, that you also should do just as I have done for you" (Jn 13:15). Jesus provided a model to follow.

The model is to serve others (also called servanthood). It's not about being first, the biggest, or the best. Servanthood is about putting the needs of others before your own. Jesus said, "Whoever wants to be great among you must be your servant"(Mt 20:26). It's as easy or as tough as this: if you want to be great in God's eyes, you must serve.

Consider how you might serve today. Give it a try and see if you find God's reward of greatness.

Related Texts: Psalm 118;
Zechariah 9:9; Mark 11:1–11;
Luke 19:28–40; John 12:12–16

As he approached and saw the city, he wept for it, saying, "If you knew this day what would bring peace — but now it is hidden from your eyes. For the days will come on you when your enemies will build a barricade around you, surround you, and hem you in on every side. They will crush you and your children among you to the ground, and they will not leave one stone on another in your midst, because you did not recognize the time when God visited you."

–Luke 19:41–44

Jesus went into the temple and threw out all those buying and selling. He overturned the tables of the money changers and the chairs of those selling doves. He said to them, "It is written, **my house will be called a house of prayer**, but you are making it **a den of thieves!**"

The blind and the lame came to him in the temple, and he healed them. When the chief priests and the scribes saw the wonders that he did and the children shouting in the temple, "*Hosanna to the Son of David!*" they were indignant and said to him, "Do you hear what these children are saying?"

Jesus replied, "Yes, have you never read:

You have prepared praise from the mouths of infants and nursing babies?"

–Matthew 21:12–16

IN OTHER WORDS

You can get a feel for the anger of Jesus by reading this event.

Jesus was mad! His anger was directed at the people who had turned the temple into a place to make a profit. The anger was directed at those who were more concerned about selling their overpriced doves and sacrificial animals than they were for the house of God.

Jesus is concerned about your inner world—your motives and the condition of your heart. On this occasion, the merchants and moneychangers didn't have the motive to please God with their business. They intended to make a quick dollar by cheating the worshipers into buying unfit animals at high prices.

What would Jesus clean out of your life if you gave him the chance? Keep an eye on your inner motives!

Related Texts: Psalm 8; Isaiah 56; Jeremiah 7:9–11; Mark 11:15–18; John 2:13–17

While the Pharisees were together, Jesus questioned them, "What do you think about the Messiah? Whose son is he?"

They replied, "David's."

He asked them, "How is it then that David, inspired by the Spirit, calls him 'Lord':

The Lord declared to my Lord,
'Sit at my right hand
until I put your enemies
under your feet'?

"If David calls him 'Lord,' how, then, can he be his son?" No one was able to answer him at all, and from that day no one dared to question him anymore.

—Matthew 22:41–46

After six days Jesus took Peter, James, and John and led them up a high mountain by themselves to be alone. He was transfigured in front of them, and his clothes became dazzling — extremely white as no launderer on earth could whiten them....

A cloud appeared, overshadowing them, and a voice came from the cloud: "This is my beloved Son; listen to him!"

—Mark 9:2–3,7

IN OTHER WORDS

Transfiguration is a big word to describe the bodily change that happened to Jesus on the day you just read. On the top of the mountain, Jesus's appearance was transformed or changed into a likeness of God's presence. When Jesus was transfigured it was evident to Peter, James, and John. His presence became like a radiant light. For a brief moment Jesus's radiance was allowed to shine through in the presence of his Father.

Unlike Jesus, you can't be transfigured. But with his power you can change your ways to become more like the person God wants you to become—more like Jesus.

Related Texts: Psalm 110; Matthew 27:45–54; Mark 1:9–11; Luke 9:28–36; Acts 2

Then the Day of Unleavened Bread came when the Passover lamb had to be sacrificed. Jesus sent Peter and John, saying, "Go and make preparations for us to eat the Passover." . . .

When the hour came, he reclined at the table, and the apostles with him. Then he said to them, "I have fervently desired to eat this Passover with you before I suffer. For I tell you, I will not eat it again until it is fulfilled in the kingdom of God." Then he took a cup, and after giving thanks, he said, "Take this and share it among yourselves. For I tell you, from now on I will not drink of the fruit of the vine until the kingdom of God comes."

And he took bread, gave thanks, broke it, gave it to them, and said, "This is my body, which is given for you. Do this in remembrance of me."

In the same way he also took the cup after supper and said, "This cup is the new covenant in my blood, which is poured out for you. But look, the hand of the one betraying me is at the table with me. For the Son of Man will go away as it has been determined, but woe to that man by whom he is betrayed!"

−Luke 22:7−8,14−22

IN OTHER WORDS

Since the death of Jesus, Christians have followed the model of Jesus's last meal with his friends: the Lord's Supper (or, Communion). It's intended to remind us of Jesus's death on the cross. The wafer or bread used during Communion is symbolic and represents the body of Jesus that was broken on the cross. The wine or grape juice represents the blood that Jesus shed on the cross for all of humanity.

Celebrating Communion helps you remember what Jesus did on the cross two thousand years ago. He died for everyone's sins. More specifically, his death was for you! Take a minute to pause and remember Jesus's death and celebrate your new life today!

Related Texts: Jeremiah 31:31−36; Matthew 26:17−30; Mark 14:12−26; Revelation 19:4−9

After Jesus had said these things, he went out with his disciples across the Kidron Valley, where there was a garden, and he and his disciples went into it. Judas, who betrayed him, also knew the place, because Jesus often met there with his disciples. So Judas took a company of soldiers and some officials from the chief priests and the Pharisees and came there with lanterns, torches, and weapons.

Then Jesus, knowing everything that was about to happen to him, went out and said to them, "Who is it that you're — seeking?"

"Jesus of Nazareth," they answered.

"I am he," Jesus told them.

Judas, who betrayed him, was also standing with them. When Jesus told them, "I am he," they stepped back and fell to the ground.

Then he asked them again, "Who is it that you're seeking?"

"Jesus of Nazareth," they said.

"I told you I am he," Jesus replied. "So if you're looking for me, let these men go." This was to fulfill the words he had said: "I have not lost one of those you have given me."

—John 18:1–9

BIBLICAL BIO

Judas Iscariot was one of the twelve disciples of Jesus. His primary job was to oversee money, but he's best known for his deception and betrayal of Jesus.

He was a greedy man who deserted his commitment to Jesus. Judas led a crowd of officers to arrest Jesus for money—thirty pieces of silver. After Jesus was crucified, Judas felt guilty and gave back the money . . . but, he also hung himself.

Unfortunately, even those closest to Jesus didn't completely follow him and totally change their ways. It's a reminder to watch yourself so you don't get bribed or conned into betraying Jesus in your life.

Related Texts: Genesis 37;
Matthew 26:47–56; Mark 14:43–50;
Luke 22:47–54; John 6:35–40; 17:1–12

The chief priests and the whole Sanhedrin were looking for false testimony against Jesus so that they could put him to death, but they could not find any, even though many false witnesses came forward. Finally, two who came forward stated, "This man said, 'I can destroy the temple of God and rebuild it in three days.'"

The high priest stood up and said to him, "Don't you have an answer to what these men are testifying against you?" But Jesus kept silent. The high priest said to him, "I charge you under oath by the living God: Tell us if you are the Messiah, the Son of God."

"You have said it," Jesus told him. "But I tell you, in the future you will see **the Son of Man seated at the right hand** of Power and **coming on the clouds of** heaven."

Then the high priest tore his robes and said, "He has blasphemed! Why do we still need witnesses? See, now you've heard the blasphemy. What is your decision?"

They answered, "He deserves death!" Then they spat in his face and beat him; others slapped him and said, "Prophesy to us, Messiah! Who was it that hit you?"

–Matthew 26:59–68

IN OTHER WORDS

Blasphemy is a word used to describe an abusive comment or action directed at something sacred or holy. Blasphemy is more than uttering profanity with God's name, it's a total disrespect for God or godliness in general.

The high priest shouted, "He has blasphemed!" because Jesus claimed he was God's Son. They were angered because they didn't believe Jesus was who he said he was.

The priests said Jesus's claim to be God's Son was blasphemous, so they charged him with a religious crime.

After the resurrection, it was obvious that Jesus proved who he claimed to be and his claim wasn't blasphemous.

Take a minute to thank God for this truth.

Related Texts: Leviticus 24:13–16; Daniel 7:13–14; Mark 14:55–65; Luke 23:63–71

Now it was nine in the morning when they crucified him. The inscription of the charge written against him was: THE KING OF THE JEWS. They crucified two criminals with him, one on his right and one on his left.

Those who passed by were yelling insults at him, shaking their heads, and saying, "Ha! The one who would destroy the temple and rebuild it in three days, save yourself by coming down from the cross!" In the same way, the chief priests with the scribes were mocking him among themselves and saying, "He saved others, but he cannot save himself! Let the Messiah, the King of Israel, come down now from the cross, so that we may see and believe." Even those who were crucified with him taunted him. . . .

Jesus let out a loud cry and breathed his last. Then the curtain of the temple was torn in two from top to bottom. When the centurion, who was standing opposite him, saw the way he breathed his last, he said, "Truly this man was the Son of God!"

—Mark 15:25–32,37–39

WEIRD OR WHAT?

Crucifying someone on a cross was one of the most abusive punishments ever devised because of its slow, torturous death of suffocation.

The inscription that was put over Jesus's head was not unusual. Inscriptions informed visitors of the crimes worthy of this type of brutal death. Typically, criminals were crucified publicly so everyone could see the consequences of their crime. Jesus was crucified for being "king of the Jews." Jesus died a real and painful death. He died so that you might have new life today.

Related Texts: Psalm 22; Isaiah 53; Matthew 27:33–56; Luke 23:26–48; John 3:13–16; 19:16–37

After the Sabbath, as the first day of the week was dawning, Mary Magdalene and the other Mary went to view the tomb. There was a violent earthquake, because an angel of the Lord descended from heaven and approached the tomb. He rolled back the stone and was sitting on it. His appearance was like lightning, and his clothing was as white as snow. The guards were so shaken by fear of him that they became like dead men.

The angel told the women, "Don't be afraid, because I know you are looking for Jesus who was crucified. He is not here. For he has risen, just as he said. Come and see the place where he lay. Then go quickly and tell his disciples, 'He has risen from the dead and indeed he is going ahead of you to Galilee; you will see him there.' Listen, I have told you."

So, departing quickly from the tomb with fear and great joy, they ran to tell his disciples the news. Just then Jesus met them and said, "Greetings!" They came up, took hold of his feet, and worshiped him. Then Jesus told them, "Do not be afraid. Go and tell my brothers to leave for Galilee, and they will see me there."

—Matthew 28:1–10

JUST A THOUGHT

He's alive! He has risen from the dead! He's alive! Shout it out: "He's alive!"

Celebrate this Easter with the presence of Jesus alive in your life. Tell a friend: He's alive!

Related Texts: Psalm 16:8–11;
Mark 16:1–8; Luke 24:1–10;
John 20:1–18; 1 Corinthians 15

Now if Christ is proclaimed as raised from the dead, how can some of you say, "There is no resurrection of the dead"? If there is no resurrection of the dead, then not even Christ has been raised; and if Christ has not been raised, then our proclamation is in vain, and so is your faith. Moreover, we are found to be false witnesses about God, because we have testified wrongly about God that he raised up Christ — whom he did not raise up, if in fact the dead are not raised. For if the dead are not raised, not even Christ has been raised. And if Christ has not been raised, your faith is worthless; you are still in your sins. Those, then, who have fallen asleep in Christ have also perished. If we have put our hope in Christ for this life only, we should be pitied more than anyone.

But as it is, Christ has been raised from the dead, the firstfruits of those who have fallen asleep. For since death came through a man, the resurrection of the dead also comes through a man. For just as in Adam all die, so also in Christ all will be made alive.

–1 Corinthians 15:12–22

JUST A THOUGHT

Belief in the resurrection of Jesus is the backbone of the Christian faith. If Jesus didn't rise from the dead, then he's a liar and just another person in a grave. Who would worship a dead guy?

Related Texts: Job 19:23–27; Romans 6:1–11; Acts 2:22–36; 1 Corinthians 15:23–58;

Your boasting is not good. Don't you know that a little leaven leavens the whole batch of dough? Clean out the old leaven so that you may be a new unleavened batch, as indeed you are. For Christ our Passover lamb has been sacrificed. Therefore, let us observe the feast, not with old leaven or with the leaven of malice and evil, but with the unleavened bread of sincerity and truth.

–1 Corinthians 5:6–8

If you appeal to the Father who judges impartially according to each one's work, you are to conduct yourselves in reverence during your time living as strangers. For you know that you were redeemed from your empty way of life inherited from your ancestors, not with perishable things like silver or gold, but with the precious blood of Christ, like that of an unblemished and spotless lamb. He was foreknown before the foundation of the world but was revealed in these last times for you.

–1 Peter 1:17–20

DIG DEEPER

Not only did Jesus die in your place and save you from eternal death, but he also brought you into a new family. Check out Hebrews 2:11: "For the one who sanctifies and those who are sanctified all have one Father. That is why Jesus is not ashamed to call them brothers and sisters."

As a Christian, you're part of God's family. Congratulations! Take a minute to thank your heavenly Father for being a child of God.

Related Texts: Exodus 12–13; John 1:19–36; Hebrews 2:11–18; Revelation 13:8

Now at midnight the LORD struck every firstborn male in the land of Egypt, from the firstborn of Pharaoh who sat on his throne to the firstborn of the prisoner who was in the dungeon, and every firstborn of the livestock. During the night Pharaoh got up, he along with all his officials and all the Egyptians, and there was a loud wailing throughout Egypt because there wasn't a house without someone dead. He summoned Moses and Aaron during the night and said, "Get out immediately from among my people, both you and the Israelites, and go, worship the LORD as you have said. Take even your flocks and your herds as you asked and leave, and also bless me."

Now the Egyptians pressured the people in order to send them quickly out of the country, for they said, "We're all going to die!" So the people took their dough before it was leavened, with their kneading bowls wrapped up in their clothes on their shoulders.

The Israelites acted on Moses's word and asked the Egyptians for silver and gold items and for clothing. And the LORD gave the people such favor with the Egyptians that they gave them what they requested. In this way they plundered the Egyptians.

−Exodus 12:29−36

IN OTHER WORDS

The release of the Israelites is another example of how God remains faithful to his promises! No doubt the Israelites wanted God's help a lot earlier. They screamed, cried, complained, and prayed like crazy. But God had his own plans and demonstrated his goodness by protecting the Israelites' release from Egypt. He proved that he is God and that his timing is perfect.

Most people are a lot like the Israelites and want God to move faster than he does. But he is God, he is faithful, and his timing is always perfect.

That's plenty of reason to trust him and give him your life today—he keeps his promises.

Related Texts: Deuteronomy 16:1−8; Psalms 78:41−52; 105:26−38; 2 Thessalonians 1:5−10

The Egyptians — all Pharaoh's horses and chariots, his horsemen, and his army — chased after them and caught up with them as they camped by the sea beside Pi-hahiroth, in front of Baal-zephon.

As Pharaoh approached, the Israelites looked up and there were the Egyptians coming after them! The Israelites were terrified and cried out to the LORD for help. They said to Moses, "Is it because there are no graves in Egypt that you have taken us away to die in the wilderness? What have you done to us by bringing us out of Egypt? Isn't this what we told you in Egypt: Leave us alone so that we may serve the Egyptians? It would have been better for us to serve the Egyptians than to die in the wilderness."

But Moses said to the people, "Don't be afraid. Stand firm and see the LORD's salvation that he will accomplish for you today; for the Egyptians you see today, you will never see again. The LORD will fight for you, and you must be quiet."

The LORD said to Moses, "Why are you crying out to me? Tell the Israelites to break camp. As for you, lift up your staff, stretch out your hand over the sea, and divide it so that the Israelites can go through the sea on dry ground. As for me, I am going to harden the hearts of the Egyptians so that they will go in after them, and I will receive glory by means of Pharaoh, all his army, and his chariots and horsemen."

–Exodus 14:9–17

TAKE A SHOT

God saved the Israelites from their brutal captivity, and they still found reasons to complain. Write down three complaints you currently have about your life. How big are they? Can you change them on your own power? If so, what's keeping you? If not, beg God for his help and power. Also, be sure to express your thankfulness to God for saving you from the bondage of sin.

1.

2.

3.

Related Texts: Psalms 37:7; 46:10; Isaiah 59:1; Romans 9:14–24; Hebrews 11:1–2

Then Moses stretched out his hand over the sea. The LORD drove the sea back with a powerful east wind all that night and turned the sea into dry land. So the waters were divided, and the Israelites went through the sea on dry ground, with the waters like a wall to them on their right and their left.

The Egyptians set out in pursuit — all Pharaoh's horses, his chariots, and his horsemen — and went into the sea after them. During the morning watch, the LORD looked down at the Egyptian forces from the pillar of fire and cloud, and threw the Egyptian forces into confusion. He caused their chariot wheels to swerve and made them drive with difficulty. "Let's get away from Israel," the Egyptians said, "because the LORD is fighting for them against Egypt!"

Then the LORD said to Moses, "Stretch out your hand over the sea so that the water may come back on the Egyptians, on their chariots and horsemen." So Moses stretched out his hand over the sea, and at daybreak the sea returned to its normal depth. While the Egyptians were trying to escape from it, the LORD threw them into the sea. The water came back and covered the chariots and horsemen, plus the entire army of Pharaoh that had gone after them into the sea. Not even one of them survived.

—Exodus 14:21–28

WEIRD OR WHAT?

Today the Red Sea is known to have a total length of 1,200 miles and to range between 230 miles wide in the south and 130 miles wide in the north. The greatest depth of the Red Sea is about 7,200 feet. These numbers don't describe a little puddle! When God parted the Red Sea, he performed a major miracle.

God loves you so much that he's willing to part seas and open mountains to express his love and fulfill his promises. Count on God's power today!

Related Texts: Deuteronomy 11:1–4; Joshua 24:5–7; Psalms 114; 136:13–15; Hebrews 11:23–29

That day the LORD saved Israel from the power of the Egyptians, and Israel saw the Egyptians dead on the seashore. When Israel saw the great power that the LORD used against the Egyptians, the people feared the LORD and believed in him and in his servant Moses.

Then Moses and the Israelites sang this song to the LORD. They said:
I will sing to the LORD,
   for he is highly exalted;
he has thrown the horse
   and its rider into the sea.
The LORD is my strength
   and my song;
he has become my salvation.
This is my God,
   and I will praise him,
my father's God,
   and I will exalt him.
The LORD is a warrior;
   the LORD is his name.

He threw Pharaoh's chariots
and his army into the sea;
the elite of his officers
were drowned in the Red Sea. . . .

LORD, who is like you
   among the gods?
Who is like you, glorious
   in holiness,
revered with praises,
   performing wonders? . . .

The LORD will reign forever
   and ever!
   —*Exodus 14:30–31; 15:1–4,11,18*

TAKE A SHOT

Try writing a song or poem of praise describing the incredible saving power of God. (If you need help getting started, use some of the words from today's reading.)

*Related Texts: Psalm 136;
Ephesians 5:19–20; Revelation 15:2–4*

Give thanks to the LORD, call on
his name;
proclaim his deeds
    among the peoples.
Sing to him, sing praise to him;
tell about all his wondrous works!
Boast in his holy name;
let the hearts of those who seek
    the LORD rejoice.
Seek the LORD and his strength;
seek his face always.

Then he brought Israel out
    with silver and gold,
and no one among
    his tribes stumbled.
Egypt was glad when they left,
for the dread of Israel had fallen
    on them.
He spread a cloud as a covering
and gave a fire to light up
    the night.
They asked, and he brought quail
and satisfied them with bread
    from heaven.
He opened a rock, and water
    gushed out;
it flowed like a stream
    in the desert.
For he remembered
    his holy promise
to Abraham his servant.
He brought his people out
    with rejoicing,
his chosen ones with shouts of joy.
He gave them the lands
    of the nations,
and they inherited
what other peoples
    had worked for.

All this happened
so that they might keep
    his statutes
and obey his instructions.
Hallelujah!
                    —Psalm 105:1–4,37–45

TAKE A SHOT

Yesterday you wrote a song or poem
of praise describing God's power.
Today list one specific area in your
life where you need to experience
God's saving power. How can God
provide for this need?

"Seek the LORD and his strength;
seek his face always" (Ps 105:4).

_____

_____

_____

_____

_____

_____

_____

_____

_____

_____

_____

_____

_____

_____

_____

_____

_____

_____

Related Texts: Genesis 15;
Exodus 15:19–18:27; John 6;
Acts 7:36–38; 1 Corinthians 10:1–4

In the third month from the very day the Israelites left the land of Egypt, they came to the Sinai Wilderness. They traveled from Rephidim, came to the Sinai Wilderness, and camped in the wilderness. Israel camped there in front of the mountain.

Moses went up the mountain to God, and the LORD called to him from the mountain: "This is what you must say to the house of Jacob and explain to the Israelites: 'You have seen what I did to the Egyptians and how I carried you on eagles' wings and brought you to myself. Now if you will carefully listen to me and keep my covenant, you will be my own possession out of all the peoples, although the whole earth is mine, and you will be my kingdom of priests and my holy nation.' These are the words that you are to say to the Israelites."

After Moses came back, he summoned the elders of the people and set before them all these words that the LORD had commanded him. Then all the people responded together, "We will do all that the LORD has spoken." So Moses brought the people's words back to the LORD.

The LORD said to Moses, "I am going to come to you in a dense cloud, so that the people will hear when I speak with you and will always believe you." Moses reported the people's words to the LORD.

—Exodus 19:1–9

IN OTHER WORDS

On this mountain Moses received from God the Ten Commandments. Over the next ten days you will read these commandments. Take notice that the first four commandments provide direction on loving God. The next six commandments provide instructions on how to live with and relate to one another.

This is why Jesus summed up the Ten Commandments (Mt 22:37,39) by saying, "Love the Lord your God with all your heart, with all your soul, and with all your mind" (commandments 1–4). And, "Love your neighbor as you love yourself" (commandments 5–10).

Today, look for opportunities to love God, your friends (neighbors), and yourself.

Related Texts: Deuteronomy 4:1–20; Jeremiah 31:31–34; Hebrews 8

I am the LORD your God, who brought you out of the land of Egypt, out of the place of slavery. Do not have other gods besides me.

—Exodus 20:2–3

Let the whole earth sing to
　the LORD.
Proclaim his salvation from day
　to day.
Declare his glory
　among the nations,
his wondrous works
　among all peoples.

For the LORD is great
　and highly praised;
he is feared above all gods.
For all the gods of the peoples are
　worthless idols,
but the LORD made the heavens.
Splendor and majesty are
　before him;
strength and joy are in his place.
Ascribe to the LORD, families
　of the peoples,
ascribe to the LORD glory
　and strength.
Ascribe to the LORD the glory
　of his name;
bring an offering and come
　before him.
Worship the LORD
　in the splendor of his holiness;
let the whole earth tremble
　before him.

The world is firmly established;
it cannot be shaken.
Let the heavens be glad
　and the earth rejoice,
and let them say
　among the nations, "The LORD
　reigns!"

—1 Chronicles 16:23–31

WEIRD OR WHAT?

Idols were viewed as having god-like power. People believed the power of gods could be contained in an idol. This is one reason why God refused to allow any images (or idols) to be made of him.

God's presence and power cannot be limited to a human-made idol. Idols have no real power—they can be stolen or destroyed. God is living and not bound by a church, a temple, or a golden calf.

You'd search forever to find any book, person, or crystal ball that has anything like God's power. Today, pause and thank God that his power isn't limited to your imagination.

Related Texts: Exodus 18:8–10; Deuteronomy 4:32–39; 5:1–21; 13:1–16; Isaiah 37:15–20; Ephesians 4:4–6

Do not make an idol for yourself, whether in the shape of anything in the heavens above or on the earth below or in the waters under the earth. Do not bow in worship to them, and do not serve them; for I, the LORD your God, am a jealous God, bringing the consequences of the fathers' iniquity on the children to the third and fourth generations of those who hate me, but showing faithful love to a thousand generations of those who love me and keep my commands.

−Exodus 20:4−6

Not to us, LORD, not to us,
but to your name give glory
because of your faithful love,
    because of your truth.
Why should the nations say,
"Where is their God?"
Our God is in heaven
and does whatever he pleases.

Their idols are silver and gold,
made by human hands.
They have mouths
    but cannot speak,
eyes, but cannot see.
They have ears but cannot hear,
noses, but cannot smell.
They have hands but cannot feel,
feet, but cannot walk.
They cannot make a sound
    with their throats.
Those who make them are just
    like them,
as are all who trust in them.

−Psalm 115:1−8

BIG TIME WORD

An idol was a handmade item that became the object of worship. People may have worshiped a wooden pigeon, a golden calf, or a ceramic armadillo. The important thing wasn't what they worshiped but that they worshiped something other than the one true God.

Is idol worship even an issue today? No and yes. No, because you probably don't have friends bowing before foreign objects. But yes, it's an issue when you watch your friends value and worship material possessions and take their eyes off God.

How about you? Do you have any modern-day idols? Television? Clothes? Music? Boyfriend or girlfriend? Do you have other "gods" that are more important than God? If so, you may want to reread the last sentence in today's reading!

Related Texts: Deuteronomy 7; Isaiah 44:6−19; Jeremiah 10:1−16; 16:19−21; Matthew 6:19−24; 1 John 5:21

Do not misuse the name of the LORD your God, because the LORD will not leave anyone unpunished who misuses his name.

—Exodus 20:7

Now the son of an Israelite mother and an Egyptian father was among the Israelites. A fight broke out in the camp between the Israelite woman's son and an Israelite man. Her son cursed and blasphemed the Name, and they brought him to Moses. (His mother's name was Shelomith, a daughter of Dibri of the tribe of Dan.) They put him in custody until the LORD's decision could be made clear to them.

Then the LORD spoke to Moses: "Bring the one who has cursed to the outside of the camp and have all who heard him lay their hands on his head; then have the whole community stone him. And tell the Israelites: If anyone curses his God, he will bear the consequences of his sin. Whoever blasphemes the name of the LORD must be put to death; the whole community is to stone him. If he blasphemes the Name, he is to be put to death, whether the resident alien or the native."

—Leviticus 24:10–16

The name of the LORD is
    a strong tower;
the righteous run to it
    and are protected.

—Proverbs 18:10

ONE MINUTE MEMORY

"The name of the LORD is a strong tower; the righteous run to it and are protected" (Pr 18:10).

Related Texts: Exodus 3:13–15; Psalms 20; 86:5–12; Acts 4:5–12

Remember the Sabbath day, to keep it holy: You are to labor six days and do all your work, but the seventh day is a Sabbath to the LORD your God. You must not do any work — you, your son or daughter, your male or female servant, your livestock, or the resident alien who is within your city gates. For the LORD made the heavens and the earth, the sea, and everything in them in six days; then he rested on the seventh day. Therefore the LORD blessed the Sabbath day and declared it holy.

−Exodus 20:8−11

Moving on from there, he entered their synagogue. There he saw a man who had a shriveled hand, and in order to accuse him they asked him, "Is it lawful to heal on the Sabbath?"

He replied to them, "Who among you, if he had a sheep that fell into a pit on the Sabbath, wouldn't take hold of it and lift it out? A person is worth far more than a sheep; so it is lawful to do what is good on the Sabbath."

Then he told the man, "Stretch out your hand." So he stretched it out, and it was restored, as good as the other.

−Matthew 12:9−13

WEIRD OR WHAT?

For those faithful to Judaism, the Sabbath is a day when all work stops. Sabbath = no work.

During Old Testament times if someone broke Sabbath rules, the person was judged and possibly put to death (see Nm 15:32–36).

In modern times (like today) there is difficulty interpreting what is work when compared to Old Testament times. For example, the rule prohibiting anyone from making a fire on the Sabbath would be difficult to keep today. Some people would argue that even turning on a light switch on the Sabbath is a noncombustive type of burning similar to starting a fire. Actually, some faithful to Judaism are prohibited from turning on anything electrical because they believe it violates the Sabbath (they make an exception with the refrigerator and leave it on . . . or, leave it working).

Related Texts: Genesis 2:1−3;
Exodus 16:11−30; Psalm 62:1−5;
Mark 2:23−28; Hebrews 4:1−4

H onor your father and your mother so that you may have a long life in the land that the LORD your God is giving you....

"Whoever strikes his father or his mother must be put to death."
—*Exodus 20:12; 21:15*

"If anyone curses his father or mother, he must be put to death. He has cursed his father or mother; his death is his own fault."
—*Leviticus 20:9*

A wise son brings joy to his father, but a foolish son, heartache
   to his mother....

Listen to your father who gave
   you life,
and don't despise your mother
   when she is old.
Buy — and do not sell — truth, wisdom, instruction,
   and understanding.
The father of a righteous son
   will rejoice greatly,
and one who fathers a wise son
   will delight in him.
Let your father and mother
   have joy,
and let her who gave birth to you
   rejoice.
—*Proverbs 10:1; 23:22–25*

Children, obey your parents in the Lord, because this is right.
—*Ephesians 6:1*

HERE'S THE DEAL

Truth alert! There are no perfect families and no perfect parents. Parents don't have an easy job; it's one of the toughest responsibilities on earth. Parents don't receive a college degree in parenting, and there's no such thing as a professional parent. Parents live with a lot of pressure to care for their children, manage their careers, and navigate their own personal lives. In case you've forgotten, parents are also human, which means they've got real feelings and pain just like you.

One of the ways in which you can honor your parents is to allow them the freedom to fail. Like you, they're not perfect; and they need your love, forgiveness, and acceptance. Many parents are so accustomed to their child's greed—always wanting something—that they're shocked when greed is replaced with compassion. Give it a try. Honor your parents and watch for God's blessing on your life.

Related Texts: Malachi 4:5–6; Colossians 3:20–21; 2 Timothy 3:1–5; Titus 1:6–9

Do not murder.
—Exodus 20:13

Whoever sheds human blood,
by humans his blood will be shed,
for God made humans in
   his image.
—Genesis 9:6

"You have heard that it was said
to our ancestors, **Do not murder**,
and whoever murders will be
subject to judgment. But I tell you,
everyone who is angry with his
brother or sister will be subject
to judgment. Whoever insults his
brother or sister, will be subject
to the court. Whoever says, 'You
fool!' will be subject to hellfire."
—Matthew 5:21–22

For this is the message you have
heard from the beginning: We
should love one another, unlike
Cain, who was of the evil one and
murdered his brother. And why
did he murder him? Because his
deeds were evil, and his brother's
were righteous.
   Do not be surprised, brothers
and sisters, if the world hates you.
We know that we have passed
from death to life because we
love our brothers and sisters. The
one who does not love remains
in death. Everyone who hates his
brother or sister is a murderer,
and you know that no murderer
has eternal life residing in him.
—1 John 3:11–15

BIG TIME WORD

Murder is bad. Anger isn't bad.
Resentment is bad. Anger isn't
bad. Hate is bad. Anger isn't bad.
Revenge is bad. Anger isn't bad.
Bitterness is bad. Anger isn't bad.
Get the point? Anger isn't bad!

Anger comes and goes as a
quick and natural emotion. It
becomes negative when you allow
it to stay in your life, thoughts,
and hearts. When anger remains, it
transforms into resentment, which
then can lead to bitterness, hate,
and revenge.

Be careful your anger doesn't
lead to sin. The Bible gives
instruction that anger should be
dealt with before the sun goes
down (and the day ends). Deal
with your anger today so it doesn't
become resentment—you'll sleep a
lot better.

*Related Texts: Genesis 4:1–16;
Numbers 35:9–34; Matthew 15:10–20;
John 8:42–44; Romans 1:28–32*

Do not commit adultery.
—Exodus 20:14

Why, my son, would you
   lose yourself
with a forbidden woman
or embrace a wayward woman?
For a man's ways are before
   the LORD's eyes,
and he considers all his paths.
—Proverbs 5:20–21

Don't you know that the
unrighteous will not inherit
God's kingdom? Do not be
deceived: No sexually immoral
people, idolaters, adulterers,
or males who have sex with
males, no thieves, greedy people,
drunkards, verbally abusive
people, or swindlers will inherit
God's kingdom. And some of you
used to be like this. But you were
washed, you were sanctified,
you were justified in the name of
the Lord Jesus Christ and by the
Spirit of our God.
—1 Corinthians 6:9–11

Marriage is to be honored by
all and the marriage bed kept
undefiled, because God will
judge the sexually immoral and
adulterers.
—Hebrews 13:4

HERE'S THE DEAL

God wasn't big on setting up rules to frustrate people. A lot of people believe God is a type of cosmic killjoy who lives in heaven thinking of ways to squash fun. This couldn't be further from the truth! God created rules and guidelines to help people live life to its fullest.

When it comes to adultery or sex outside of marriage, God established this rule for our own good. God isn't down on sex. He created it. God is down on pain! And the pain from adultery is intense and usually results in broken families, destroyed lives, and terrible lifelong memories.

God wants his people to be sexually pure for the health, happiness, and goodness of his children. Sex is a beautiful gift from God, and he created it to be shared and experienced between a husband and wife. God gets really excited when life is lived as he designed it to be lived. Keep following him and you'll continue to discover how rich and full life was intended to be.

Related Texts: Proverbs 5:1–19;
6:20–35; Romans 1:18–27;
Ephesians 4:17–24; Colossians 3:1–7;
1 Thessalonians 4:3–8

Do not steal.

—Exodus 20:15

Place no trust in oppression
or false hope in robbery.
If wealth increases,
don't set your heart on it.

God has spoken once;
I have heard this twice:
strength belongs to God,
and faithful love belongs
    to you, LORD.
For you repay each according to
    his works.

—Psalm 62:10–12

Instruct those who are rich in the
present age not to be arrogant
or to set their hope on the
uncertainty of wealth, but on God,
who richly provides us with all
things to enjoy. Instruct them to
do what is good, to be rich in good
works, to be generous and willing
to share, storing up treasure for
themselves as a good foundation
for the coming age, so that they
may take hold of what is truly life.

—1 Timothy 6:17–19

Let the thief no longer steal.
Instead, he is to do honest work
with his own hands, so that he has
something to share with anyone
in need.

—Ephesians 4:28

TAKE A SHOT

What would you say to your very
best friend if you caught him or her
stealing? What about if that friend
stole something of yours? Would that
change the conversation?

*Related Texts: Proverbs 1:10–19;
10:2; Isaiah 10:1–4; Malachi 3:6–12;
Titus 2:9–10*

Do not give false testimony against your neighbor.

—Exodus 20:16

"If a malicious witness testifies against someone accusing him of a crime, the two people in the dispute are to stand in the presence of the LORD before the priests and judges in authority at that time. The judges are to make a careful investigation, and if the witness turns out to be a liar who has falsely accused his brother, you must do to him as he intended to do to his brother. You must purge the evil from you. Then everyone else will hear and be afraid, and they will never again do anything evil like this among you...."

—Deuteronomy 19:16–20

LORD, who can dwell in your tent?
Who can live on
   your holy mountain?

The one who lives blamelessly,
   practices righteousness,
and acknowledges the truth
   in his heart —
who does not slander
   with his tongue,
who does not harm his friend
or discredit his neighbor,

—Psalm 15:1–3

DIG DEEPER

Proverbs is an incredible book filled with wisdom and common sense. Here are a few verses on telling the truth:

"By rebellious speech an evil person is trapped, but a righteous person escapes from trouble" (Pr 12:13).

"Whoever speaks the truth declares what is right, but a false witness speaks deceit" (12:17).

"A person giving false testimony against his neighbor is like a club, a sword, or a sharp arrow" (25:18).

Jesus said, "Everyone who is of the truth listens to my voice" (Jn 18:37). Make it a goal to see that truth flows from your heart today!

Related Texts: Proverbs 12:17–18; 25:18; Isaiah 29:19–21; Matthew 15:10–20; Mark 14:53–64

Do not covet your neighbor's house. Do not covet your neighbor's wife, his male or female servant, his ox or donkey, or anything that belongs to your neighbor.

−Exodus 20:17

Do not owe anyone anything, except to love one another, for the one who loves another has fulfilled the law. The commandments, **Do not commit adultery; do not murder; do not steal; do not covet;** and any other commandment, are summed up by this commandment: **Love your neighbor as yourself.** Love does no wrong to a neighbor. Love, therefore, is the fulfillment of the law.

−Romans 13:8−10

But godliness with contentment is great gain. For we brought nothing into the world, and we can take nothing out. If we have food and clothing, we will be content with these.

−1 Timothy 6:6−8

Keep your life free from the love of money. Be satisfied with what you have, for he himself has said, **I will never leave you or aban**don you.

−Hebrews 13:5

ONE-MINUTE MEMORY

"Keep your life free from the love of money. Be satisfied with what you have, for he himself has said, 'I will never leave you or abandon you'" (Heb 13:5).

Related Texts: Deuteronomy 31:6; Proverbs 1:10−19; Philippians 4:11−12; 1 Timothy 6:9−11; James 4:1−3; 1 John 2:15−17

Listen, Israel: The Lord our God, the Lord is one. Love the Lord your God with all your heart, with all your soul, and with all your strength. These words that I am giving you today are to be in your heart. Repeat them to your children. Talk about them when you sit in your house and when you walk along the road, when you lie down and when you get up. Bind them as a sign on your hand and let them be a symbol on your forehead. Write them on the doorposts of your house and on your city gates."

–Deuteronomy 6:4–9

"Teacher, which command in the law is the greatest?"

He said to him, "**Love the Lord your God with all your heart, with all your soul, and with all your mind.** This is the greatest and most important command. The second is like it: **Love your neighbor as yourself.** All the Law and the Prophets depend on these two commands."

–Matthew 22:36–40

TAKE A SHOT

What does the command, "Love your neighbor as yourself" mean to you?

What is one action you can take today to bring the second greatest commandment into action in your life?

Related Texts: Leviticus 19:18,33–34; Micah 6:8; Mark 12:28–31; Luke 10:25–37; Acts 4:32–35; Romans 13:8–10; 2 Corinthians 8:13–15

You must not mistreat any widow or fatherless child. If you do mistreat them, they will no doubt cry to me, and I will certainly hear their cry. My anger will burn, and I will kill you with the sword; then your wives will be widows and your children fatherless."

—Exodus 22:22–24

Do not deny justice to a resident alien or fatherless child, and do not take a widow's garment as security. Remember that you were a slave in Egypt, and the LORD your God redeemed you from there. Therefore I am commanding you to do this.

"When you reap the harvest in your field, and you forget a sheaf in the field, do not go back to get it. It is to be left for the resident alien, the fatherless, and the widow, so that the LORD your God may bless you in all the work of your hands. When you knock down the fruit from your olive tree, do not go over the branches again. What remains will be for the resident alien, the fatherless, and the widow. When you gather the grapes of your vineyard, do not glean what is left. What remains will be for the resident alien, the fatherless, and the widow. Remember that you were a slave in the land of Egypt. Therefore I am commanding you to do this."

—Deuteronomy 24:17–22

Pure and undefiled religion before God the Father is this: to look after orphans and widows in their distress and to keep oneself unstained from the world.

—James 1:27

JUST A THOUGHT

God's presence and reflection will be evident in your life when you go out of your way to care for orphans and widows. Do you know someone who does this? Take delight in serving God by loving those who may need it the most.

Related Texts: Deuteronomy 10:17–20; Psalms 68:5; 146:9; 1 Timothy 5:3–16

When a man steals an ox or a sheep and butchers it or sells it, he must repay five cattle for the ox or four sheep for the sheep.... But if this happens after sunrise, the householder is guilty of bloodshed. A thief must make full restitution. If he is unable, he is to be sold because of his theft. If what was stolen — whether ox, donkey, or sheep — is actually found alive in his possession, he must repay double.

"When a man lets a field or vineyard be grazed in, and then allows his animals to go and graze in someone else's field, he must repay with the best of his own field or vineyard....

In any case of wrongdoing involving an ox, a donkey, a sheep, a garment, or anything else lost, and someone claims, 'That's mine,' the case between the two parties is to come before the judges. The one the judges condemn must repay double to his neighbor."

—Exodus 22:1,3–5,9

IN OTHER WORDS

Restitution means to pay back or to make equal. For example, if you stole something, you would need to pay that person back in order to restore his or her property and to restore the relationship.

Restoration, or bringing people back together, is a biblical theme. Jesus taught his followers to restore relationships. It was such a big deal to Jesus that he told them it was more important to leave a worship service and make things right with a person than to stay and worship God.

Jesus didn't give instructions to steal your joy, actually the opposite is true. Biblical instructions are given to help you live right and enjoy the friendships God has given you. Do you have any friends you need to forgive or be forgiven by today? Make plans to reconcile with them and you'll find yourself a happier person.

Related Texts: Numbers 5:5–8; Matthew 5:23–24; Luke 19:1–10; 1 Corinthians 6:1–11

W hen men get in a fight and hit a pregnant woman so that her children are born prematurely but there is no injury, the one who hit her must be fined as the woman's husband demands from him, and he must pay according to judicial assessment. If there is an injury, then you must give life for life, eye for eye, tooth for tooth, hand for hand, foot for foot, burn for burn, bruise for bruise, wound for wound."

—Exodus 21:22–25

"If a man kills anyone, he must be put to death. Whoever kills an animal is to make restitution for it, life for life. If any man inflicts a permanent injury on his neighbor, whatever he has done is to be done to him: fracture for fracture, eye for eye, tooth for tooth. Whatever injury he inflicted on the person, the same is to be inflicted on him. Whoever kills an animal is to make restitution for it, but whoever kills a person is to be put to death. You are to have the same law for the resident alien and the native, because I am the LORD your God."

— Leviticus 24:17–22

"You have heard that it was said, **An eye for an eye** and **a tooth for a tooth**. But I tell you, don't resist an evildoer. On the contrary, if anyone slaps you on your right cheek, turn the other to him also."

—Matthew 5:38–39

BIG TIME WORD

During Old Testament times the law permitted retaliation for an intentional injury (see Lv 24:19–21). For example, if you smack Tom in the face, he gets to hit you back. But in the New Testament, Jesus explained the essential meaning of the law. He instructed a new value—not to strike back. He challenged followers to live without seeking revenge.

Jesus said, "But I tell you, love your enemies and pray for those who persecute you. . . . For if you love those who love you, what reward will you have? Don't even the tax collectors do the same? And if you greet only your brothers and sisters, what are you doing out of the ordinary?" (Mt 5:44,46–47).

Jesus inspires followers to live different than the rest of the world. Next time you pass someone you don't like, pray for that person—see what happens.

Related Texts: Exodus 21:22–25; Deuteronomy 19:16–21; Psalm 103:8–12; Matthew 5:38–42

Whoever strikes a person so that he dies must be put to death....

"Whoever strikes his father or his mother must be put to death.

"Whoever kidnaps a person must be put to death, whether he sells him or the person is found in his possession...."

"Do not allow a sorceress to live.

"Whoever has sexual intercourse with an animal must be put to death."

"Observe the Sabbath, for it is holy to you. Whoever profanes it must be put to death. If anyone does work on it, that person must be cut off from his people."

−Exodus 21:12,15−16;
22:18−19; 31:14

"If anyone curses his father or mother, he must be put to death. He has cursed his father or mother; his death is his own fault.

"If a man commits adultery with a married woman — if he commits adultery with his neighbor's wife — both the adulterer and the adulteress must be put to death. If a man sleeps with his father's wife, he has violated the intimacy that belongs to his father. Both of them must be put to death; their death is their own fault. If a man sleeps with his daughter-in-law, both of them must be put to death. They have acted perversely; their death is their own fault. If a man sleeps with a man as with a woman, they have both committed a detestable act. They must be put to death; their death is their own fault."

−Leviticus 20:9−13

BIG TIME WORD

It's fairly clear from these Old Testament passages that a strong cultural view of the death penalty existed during those days. Today, capital punishment is more a political issue than a religious one. Though the death penalty isn't always enforced for killing someone, there usually is a consequence for crime.

The decisions you make today probably won't result in the death penalty, but the consequences may result in pain, broken relations, negative memories, and other difficulties. Decisions have consequences, and as a follower of Jesus, it's important to think through potential consequences prior to decisions. Jesus came so that followers would live life to its fullest. Today, think through your decisions and their consequences and stay alive for another day.

Related Texts: Genesis 9:6;
Leviticus 24:17−22; Deuteronomy 24:16;
Matthew 21:33−44

The Lord spoke to Moses and Aaron: "Tell the Israelites: You may eat all these kinds of land animals. You may eat any animal with divided hooves and that chews the cud. . . .

"This is what you may eat from all that is in the water: You may eat everything in the water that has fins and scales, whether in the seas or streams. But these are to be abhorrent to you: everything in the seas or streams that does not have fins and scales among all the swarming things and other living creatures in the water. They are to remain abhorrent to you; you must not eat any of their meat, and you must abhor their carcasses. . . .

"All winged insects that walk on all fours are to be abhorrent to you. But you may eat these kinds of all the winged insects that walk on all fours: those that have jointed legs above their feet for hopping on the ground. . . .

For I am the Lord your God, so you must consecrate yourselves and be holy because I am holy. Do not defile yourselves by any swarming creature that crawls on the ground. For I am the Lord, who brought you up from the land of Egypt to be your God, so you must be holy because I am holy."

—Leviticus 11:1–3,9–11, 20–21,44–45

BIBLICAL BIO

The Israelites were descendants of Abraham and were called "God's chosen people." They were special because of the promise God made to Abraham. Because of Abraham's faithfulness, God promised Abraham that his descendants would be blessed.

The Israelites' journey was an up-and-down one. They lived in slavery for four hundred years (down) before God delivered them from Egyptian bondage (up). God promised them a new home (up). But before they arrived there, they rebelled against God (down). God punished them by allowing them to wander in the desert for forty years (down) before fulfilling his promise and allowing them to enter into the promised land (up).

The Israelites' journey reveals God's character. (1) God is faithful to his promise. (2) God loves his people. (3) God hates sin. (4) God wants you to be faithful in your relationship with him. Which of these four truths do you need to learn today? It's more fun to live the "up" side than the "down" side. Wouldn't you agree?

Related Texts: Genesis 7:1–4; Matthew 15:1–20; Mark 7:1–23; Acts 10; Romans 14

Set aside the month of Abib and observe the Passover to the LORD your God, because the LORD your God brought you out of Egypt by night in the month of Abib. Sacrifice to the LORD your God a Passover animal from the herd or flock in the place where the LORD chooses to have his name dwell. . . . Eat unleavened bread for six days. On the seventh day there is to be a solemn assembly to the LORD your God; do not do any work.

"You are to count seven weeks, counting the weeks from the time the sickle is first put to the standing grain. You are to celebrate the Festival of Weeks to the LORD your God with a freewill offering that you give in proportion to how the LORD your God has blessed you. . . .

"You are to celebrate the Festival of Shelters for seven days when you have gathered in everything from your threshing floor and winepress. . . . You are to hold a seven-day festival for the LORD your God in the place he chooses, because the LORD your God will bless you in all your produce and in all the work of your hands, and you will have abundant joy.

"All your males are to appear three times a year before the LORD your God in the place he chooses: at the Festival of Unleavened Bread, the Festival of Weeks, and the Festival of Shelters. No one is to appear before the LORD empty-handed. Everyone must appear with a gift suited to his means, according to the blessing the LORD your God has given you."

—Deuteronomy 16:1–2,8–10, 13,15–17

HERE'S THE DEAL

The names of these festivals might seem a bit bizarre, but they were very important festivals to the people of Israel. The word *festival* is taken from a Hebrew word that means "to celebrate." God commanded the Israelites to take time from their busy schedules and give thanks to him through these celebrations.

Unfortunately, in today's world, there is an absence of celebration. There are plenty of parties that aren't true celebrations. Most parties don't honor God. Often parties honor the god of alcohol. They're celebrations in disguise—they provide momentary happiness. Once the party is over and the alcohol buzz wears off, people start to look for a new high the next day.

Followers of Jesus can celebrate in a new way. Celebration is giving thanks for all God is and all he has done. Create your own festivals and wake up each morning learning to thank God. This action will result in you becoming a different person and learning how to celebrate at the party that never ends—life.

Related Texts: Exodus 12; 23:14–17; Leviticus 23; Colossians 2:16–23

H onor your father and your mother, as the LORD your God has commanded you, so that you may live long and so that you may prosper in the land the LORD your God is giving you.

—Deuteronomy 5:16

Then Jesus was approached by Pharisees and scribes from Jerusalem, who asked, "Why do your disciples break the tradition of the elders? For they don't wash their hands when they eat."

He answered them, "Why do you break God's commandment because of your tradition? For God said: **Honor your father and your mother**; and, **Whoever speaks evil of father or mother must be put to death**. But you say, 'Whoever tells his father or mother, "Whatever benefit you might have received from me is a gift committed to the temple," he does not have to honor his father.' In this way, you have nullified the word of God because of your tradition. Hypocrites! Isaiah prophesied correctly about you when he said:

**This people honors me with their lips,
but their heart is far from me.
They worship me in vain,
teaching as doctrines human commands.**"

—Matthew 15:1–9

TAKE A SHOT

What are four qualities you appreciate about your mother?

You can show her great honor by taking the time to let her know what you admire about her. Through words or a letter you can give her a better gift than money could buy . . . and more memorable too!

Related Texts: Exodus 20:12; 21:15; Leviticus 20:9; Ephesians 6:1–2

S hout for joy, you heavens!
  Earth, rejoice!
Mountains break
    into joyful shouts!
For the LORD has comforted
  his people,
and will have compassion
    on his afflicted ones.

Zion says, "The LORD
    has abandoned me;
the Lord has forgotten me!"
"Can a woman forget
    her nursing child,
or lack compassion for the child
    of her womb?
Even if these forget,
  yet I will not forget you.
Look, I have inscribed you
    on the palms of my hands;
your walls are continually
    before me.
Your builders hurry;
those who destroy
    and devastate you
    will leave you.
Look up, and look around.
They all gather together;
    they come to you.
As I live" —
    this is the LORD's declaration —
"you will wear all your children
    as jewelry,
and put them on as a bride does.
For your waste and desolate places
and your land marked by ruins
will now be indeed too small
    for the inhabitants,
and those who swallowed you up
    will be far away."
               —Isaiah 49:13–19

JUST A THOUGHT

Moms are famous for the incredible love they show their children. They are nurturing and loving. But, since all love originates with God, just think how much more God loves you: "Dear friends, let us love one another, because love is from God, and everyone who loves has been born of God and knows God" (1Jn 4:7).

Related Texts: Psalm 51:1–9; 77:1–8; 103:1–18; Isaiah 66:12–14; Lamentations 3:22–33; Colossians 3:12–14

H allelujah!
Give praise, servants
of the LORD;
praise the name of the LORD.
Let the name of the LORD
be blessed
both now and forever.
From the rising of the sun
to its setting,
let the name of the LORD
be praised.

The LORD is exalted above
all the nations,
his glory above the heavens.
Who is like the LORD our God —
the one enthroned on high,
who stoops down to look
on the heavens and the earth?
He raises the poor from the dust
and lifts the needy
from the trash heap
in order to seat them
with nobles —
with the nobles of his people.
He gives the childless woman
a household,
making her the joyful mother
of children.
Hallelujah!

—Psalm 113

WEIRD OR WHAT?

Did you know that the Psalms were written to be sung? Like today, music was both popular and powerful during biblical times. Moses sang and taught his followers to sing—the Israelites sang on their way to the promised land. Jesus sang with his disciples. Paul sang in jail. Just imagine how great the singing will be in heaven!

Since God isn't concerned about the quality of your voice, try singing a song of thanksgiving to God for giving you another day to enjoy his love.

Related Texts: 1 Samuel 2:1–10; Job 42:12–16; Psalm 127:3–5; Proverbs 17:6; Isaiah 54:1–8; Luke 1

L isten, my son,
  to your father's instruction,
and don't reject
    your mother's teaching,
for they will be a garland of favor
    on your head
and pendants
    around your neck....

The words of King Lemuel,
a pronouncement that his mother
    taught him:

What should I say, my son?
What, son of my womb?
What, son of my vows?
Don't spend your energy
    on women
or your efforts on those
    who destroy kings.
It is not for kings, Lemuel,
it is not for kings to drink wine
or for rulers to desire beer.
Otherwise, he will drink,
forget what is decreed,
and pervert justice for all
    the oppressed.
Give beer to one who is dying
and wine to one whose life
    is bitter.
Let him drink so that he can forget
    his poverty
and remember his trouble
    no more.
Speak up for those who have
    no voice,
for the justice of all
    who are dispossessed.
Speak up, judge righteously,
and defend the cause of
    the oppressed and needy.
                    —*Proverbs 1:8–9; 31:1–9*

ONE-MINUTE MEMORY

"Listen, my son, to your father's instruction, and don't reject your mother's teaching, for they will be a garland of favor on your head and pendants around your neck" (Pr 1:8–9).

Related Texts: Exodus 2:1–9; Proverbs 6:20–24; 2 Timothy 1:5; 3:14–17

Who can find a wife
of noble character?
She is far more precious
than jewels.
The heart of her husband trusts
in her,
and he will not lack
anything good.
She rewards him with good,
not evil,
all the days of her life.
She selects wool and flax
and works with willing hands.
She is like the merchant ships,
bringing her food from far away.
She rises while it is still night
and provides food
for her household
and portions for
her female servants.
She evaluates a field and buys it;
she plants a vineyard
with her earnings.
She draws on her strength
and reveals that her arms
are strong.
She sees that her profits are good,
and her lamp never goes out
at night.
She extends her hands
to the spinning staff,
and her hands hold the spindle.
Her hands reach out to the poor,
and she extends her hands
to the needy.
—Proverbs 31:10–20

JUST A THOUGHT

A beautiful woman is easy to find, but a woman who loves God and celebrates life is a remarkable discovery.

Related Texts: Genesis 24; Acts 18:23–26; Romans 16:1–6

Who can find a wife
    of noble character?
She is far more precious
    than jewels....

She is not afraid for her household
    when it snows,
for all in her household
    are doubly clothed.
She makes her own bed coverings;
her clothing is fine linen and purple.
Her husband is known
    at the city gates,
where he sits among the elders
    of the land.
She makes and sells
    linen garments;
she delivers belts
    to the merchants.
Strength and honor are
    her clothing,
and she can laugh at the time
    to come.
Her mouth speaks wisdom,
and loving instruction is
    on her tongue.
She watches over the activities
    of her household
and is never idle.
Her children rise up
    and call her blessed;
her husband also praises her:
"Many women have done
    noble deeds,
but you surpass them all!"
Charm is deceptive and beauty
    is fleeting,
but a woman who fears the LORD
    will be praised.
Give her the reward of her labor,
and let her works praise her
    at the city gates....

A man who finds a wife finds
    a good thing
and obtains favor from the LORD.
        —*Proverbs 31:10,21–31; 18:22*

TAKE A SHOT

These verses describe a woman who possesses godly qualities that make her shine with a new type of beauty.

If you are female, write down three qualities from today's passage that you would like in your life. Next to each quality, write one goal that might help you develop the quality.

If you are male, write down three qualities you would like to see in the woman you marry. Then ask God to prepare you to be the kind of man who will bring out the inner beauty in your future wife.

Qualities	Goals
1.	
2.	
3.	

Related Texts: 1 Samuel 25:1–42;
Proverbs 19:14; Luke 1:26–55;
Ephesians 5:21–24; 1 Peter 3:1–6

R ejoice, childless one,
who did not give birth;
burst into song and shout,
you who have not been in labor!
For the children
    of the desolate one will be more
than the children
    of the married woman,"
says the LORD.

"Do not be afraid, for you will not
    be put to shame;
don't be humiliated,
    for you will not be disgraced.
For you will forget the shame
    of your youth,
and you will no longer remember
the disgrace of your widowhood.
Indeed, your husband is
    your Maker —
his name is the LORD of Armies —
and the Holy One of Israel is
    your Redeemer;
he is called the God of the
    whole earth.
For the LORD has called you,
like a wife deserted and wounded
    in spirit,
a wife of one's youth
    when she is rejected,"
says your God.
"I deserted you for a brief moment,
but I will take you back
    with abundant compassion.
In a surge of anger
I hid my face from you
    for a moment,
but I will have compassion on you
with everlasting love,"
says the LORD your Redeemer.
                    —Isaiah 54:1,4–8

DIG DEEPER

While you're alive, you will experience times of pain, emptiness, and sadness—everyone does. In the midst of pain, there is hope for those who have been promised eternal life. Check out the description of heaven from Rv 21:2–4:

I also saw the holy city, the new Jerusalem, coming down out of heaven from God, prepared like a bride adorned for her husband.

Then I heard a loud voice from the throne: Look, God's dwelling is with humanity, and he will live with them. They will be his peoples, and God himself will be with them and be their God. He will wipe away every tear from their eyes. Death will be no more; grief, crying, and pain will be no more, because the previous things have passed away.

God will be your everything. May this give you hope to keep living every day with the faith that someday you'll be in God's presence.

Related Texts: Psalm 45; Song of Songs 4; Isaiah 62:1–7; Revelation 19:5–9; 21:1–4

When a man sells his daughter as a concubine, she is not to leave as the male slaves do. If she is displeasing to her master, who chose her for himself, then he must let her be redeemed. He has no right to sell her to foreigners because he has acted treacherously toward her. Or if he chooses her for his son, he must deal with her according to the customary treatment of daughters. If he takes an additional wife, he must not reduce the food, clothing, or marital rights of the first wife. And if he does not do these three things for her, she may leave free of charge, without any payment."

−Exodus 21:7−11

"Do not debase your daughter by making her a prostitute, or the land will be prostituted and filled with depravity."

−Leviticus 19:29

"When brothers live on the same property and one of them dies without a son, the wife of the dead man may not marry a stranger outside the family. Her brother-in-law is to take her as his wife, have sexual relations with her, and perform the duty of a brother-in-law for her. The first son she bears will carry on the name of the dead brother, so his name will not be blotted out from Israel."

−Deuteronomy 25:5−6

IN OTHER WORDS

Women throughout the Bible are found in many different roles and situations. In ancient times, women weren't considered as important as men, so God made laws to protect women. Some of those laws sound very strange today. Both culture and the family system were very male-centered. During these times, the woman's place was in the fields or working long and hard hours at home doing the cooking, grinding grain, and drawing water. The Law shielded women from the abuse that was typical in this ancient society.

Within the Old Testament, there are some incredible examples of women. Exceptional women such as Miriam, Deborah, Huldah, and Esther were leaders who served and guided God's people.

Related Texts: Exodus 22:16−17; Numbers 27; 30; 36; Deuteronomy 21:10−17; 22:13−30; 25:7−10; Ruth 3−4; 1 Timothy 3:2,12

Now the first covenant also had regulations for ministry and an earthly sanctuary. For a tabernacle was set up, and in the first room, which is called the holy place, were the lampstand, the table, and the presentation loaves. Behind the second curtain was a tent called the most holy place. It had the gold altar of incense and the ark of the covenant, covered with gold on all sides, ...

With these things prepared like this, the priests enter the first room repeatedly, performing their ministry. But the high priest alone enters the second room, and he does that only once a year, and never without blood, which he offers for himself and for the sins the people had committed in ignorance ...

But Christ has appeared as a high priest of the good things that have come. In the greater and more perfect tabernacle not made with hands (that is, not of this creation), he entered the most holy place once for all time, not by the blood of goats and calves, but by his own blood, having obtained eternal redemption....

−Hebrews 9:1−4,6−7,11−12

IN OTHER WORDS

In the Old Testament, the high priest was the greatest of all priests who performed sacrifices to God on behalf of the people. In the New Testament, Jesus is given the title *high priest* because he sacrificed his life on behalf of all people.

When you understand the meaning of this title, you can better appreciate that Jesus destroyed the power of sin in your life by dying on the cross.

You can never thank God too many times for that ultimate sacrifice he made on your behalf. Go ahead and thank him one more time today.

Related Texts: Exodus 25−27; 35−40; Mark 15:37,38; Hebrews 9:13−28; 10:19−23

The LORD said to Aaron, "You, your sons, and your ancestral family will be responsible for iniquity against the sanctuary. You and your sons will be responsible for iniquity involving your priesthood. But also bring your relatives with you from the tribe of Levi, your ancestral tribe, so they may join you and assist you and your sons in front of the tent of the testimony. . . .

"You are to guard the sanctuary and the altar so that wrath may not fall on the Israelites again. Look, I have selected your fellow Levites from the Israelites as a gift for you, assigned by the LORD to work at the tent of meeting. But you and your sons will carry out your priestly responsibilities for everything concerning the altar and for what is inside the curtain, and you will do that work. I am giving you the work of the priesthood as a gift, but an unauthorized person who comes near the sanctuary will be put to death." . . .

"I give to you and to your sons and daughters all the holy contributions that the Israelites present to the LORD as a permanent statute. It is a permanent covenant of salt before the LORD for you as well as your offspring."

The LORD told Aaron, "You will not have an inheritance in their land; there will be no portion among them for you. I am your portion and your inheritance among the Israelites."

—*Numbers 18:1–2,5–7,19–20*

DIG DEEPER

One of the duties of the high priest was to present sacrifices. Today, Christians are called priests because followers of Jesus are still to present sacrifices. Christians are called to give their lives as living sacrifices. Check out Romans 12:1: "Therefore, brothers and sisters, in view of the mercies of God, I urge you to present your bodies as a living sacrifice, holy and pleasing to God; this is your true worship."

This lifestyle sacrifice requires you to present to God all that you are, into all that you know about God. A living sacrifice reveals that God is top priority in all parts of your life. It's not the easiest sacrifice to make, but it sure pleases God. Today, think about what a living sacrifice would mean with your life.

Related Texts: Leviticus 1–7; 21–22; Numbers 3; Hebrews 7–9; 1 Peter 2:4–10

When the Lord your God brings you into the land you are entering to possess, and he drives out many nations before you — the Hethites, Girgashites, Amorites, Canaanites, Perizzites, Hivites and Jebusites, seven nations more numerous and powerful than you — and when the Lord your God delivers them over to you and you defeat them, you must completely destroy them. Make no treaty with them and show them no mercy. You must not intermarry with them, and you must not give your daughters to their sons or take their daughters for your sons, because they will turn your sons away from me to worship other gods. Then the Lord's anger will burn against you, and he will swiftly destroy you. Instead, this is what you are to do to them: tear down their altars, smash their sacred pillars, cut down their Asherah poles, and burn their carved images. For you are a holy people belonging to the Lord your God. The Lord your God has chosen you to be his own possession out of all the peoples on the face of the earth.

"The Lord had his heart set on you and chose you, not because you were more numerous than all peoples, for you were the fewest of all peoples. But because the Lord loved you and kept the oath he swore to your ancestors, he brought you out with a strong hand and redeemed you from the place of slavery, from the power of Pharaoh king of Egypt."

—Deuteronomy 7:1–8

IN OTHER WORDS

These types of Bible passages make it difficult to imagine God possessing mercy, compassion, and love. But consider this: during that time other nations served other gods — just like today.

Israel traveled through nations that served other gods. When one nation conquered another, it was proof their nation's god was more powerful. War was common, and if Israel didn't kill other nations, they would have been killed or taken as slaves.

Today those who believe in Jesus are considered a nation. There will come a day when our nation will be taken to heaven and made like Jesus. We are God's children, God's nation, God's army. God is a God of love, mercy, and compassion, but there will come a time when he will judge all who are not his nation, his people, his kingdom. What kingdom are you a citizen of?

Related Texts: Deuteronomy 8:18–9:5; Judges 2:10–23; 2 Corinthians 6:14–7:1; Colossians 4:4–6; 1 Peter 2:1–12

This command that I give you today is certainly not too difficult or beyond your reach. It is not in heaven so that you have to ask, 'Who will go up to heaven, get it for us, and proclaim it to us so that we may follow it?' And it is not across the sea so that you have to ask, 'Who will cross the sea, get it for us, and proclaim it to us so that we may follow it?' But the message is very near you, in your mouth and in your heart, so that you may follow it. See, today I have set before you life and prosperity, death and adversity. For I am commanding you today to love the LORD your God, to walk in his ways, and to keep his commands, statutes, and ordinances, so that you may live and multiply, and the LORD your God may bless you in the land you are entering to possess. But if your heart turns away and you do not listen and you are led astray to bow in worship to other gods and serve them, I tell you today that you will certainly perish and will not prolong your days in the land you are entering to possess across the Jordan. I call heaven and earth as witnesses against you today that I have set before you life and death, blessing and curse. Choose life so that you and your descendants may live, love the LORD your God, obey him, and remain faithful to him. For he is your life, and he will prolong your days as you live in the land the LORD swore to give to your ancestors Abraham, Isaac, and Jacob."

—Deuteronomy 30:11–20

ONE MINUTE MEMORY

"Love the LORD your God, obey him, and remain faithful to him. For he is your life" (Dt 30:20).

Related Texts: Deuteronomy 7:9–15; 10:12–13; Micah 6:6–8; John 14:15; Romans 10:5–13; 1 John 5:3

When he saw the crowds, he went up on the mountain, and after he sat down, his disciples came to him. Then he began to teach them, saying:

"Blessed are the poor in spirit,
for the kingdom of heaven
is theirs.
Blessed are those who mourn,
for they will be comforted.
Blessed are the humble,
for they will inherit the earth.
Blessed are those who hunger
and thirst for righteousness,
for they will be filled.
Blessed are the merciful,
for they will be shown mercy.
Blessed are the pure in heart,
for they will see God.
Blessed are the peacemakers,
for they will be called
sons of God.
Blessed are those who are
persecuted because
of righteousness,
for the kingdom of heaven
is theirs."

—Matthew 5:1–10

BIG TIME WORD

Being gentle in today's world is not often seen as a strength. And yet Jesus said a gentle person will be blessed and will inherit the earth. Wow! That's quite a promise just for being gentle. What's the big deal about being gentle? Aren't gentle people just quiet, shy, and weak? Not at all!

A gentle person has a proper perspective of himself before God and other people. Gentleness isn't a sign of weakness; actually it's the opposite—gentleness is a symbol of strength. Gentle people understand that they don't have to be obnoxious and bring attention to themselves to gain attention. A gentle person is secure in who he was created to be and understands the true greatness of God. Therefore, he doesn't need to seek out attention.

Spend some time thinking about your life and how you could be more gentle with others. Keep your eyes open for examples of gentleness and be ready to learn from gentle people. You might as well—since they will inherit the earth.

Related Texts: Genesis 12:1–3; Psalms 1; 84; Luke 6:17–26; 11:27–28; John 20:24–29

You are the salt of the earth. But if the salt should lose its taste, how can it be made salty? It's no longer good for anything but to be thrown out and trampled under people's feet.

"You are the light of the world. A city situated on a hill cannot be hidden. No one lights a lamp and puts it under a basket, but rather on a lampstand, and it gives light for all who are in the house. In the same way, let your light shine before others, so that they may see your good works and give glory to your Father in heaven."

–Matthew 5:13–16

Let no one deceive you with empty arguments, for God's wrath is coming on the disobedient because of these things. Therefore, do not become their partners. For you were once darkness, but now you are light in the Lord. Walk as children of light — for the fruit of the light consists of all goodness, righteousness, and truth — testing what is pleasing to the Lord.

–Ephesians 5:6–10

JUST A THOUGHT

Don't hide it! The world is filled with darkness and needs you to be a bright light today. Let your life shine!

Related Texts: Proverbs 13:9; Mark 9:50; Luke 14:34–35; 1 Peter 4:12–19

Don't think that I came to abolish the Law or the Prophets. I did not come to abolish but to fulfill. For truly I tell you, until heaven and earth pass away, not the smallest letter or one stroke of a letter will pass away from the law until all things are accomplished. Therefore, whoever breaks one of the least of these commands and teaches others to do the same will be called least in the kingdom of heaven. But whoever does and teaches these commands will be called great in the kingdom of heaven. For I tell you, unless your righteousness surpasses that of the scribes and Pharisees, you will never get into the kingdom of heaven."

−Matthew 5:17−20

Therefore, there is now no condemnation for those in Christ Jesus, because the law of the Spirit of life in Christ Jesus has set you free from the law of sin and death. For what the law could not do since it was weakened by the flesh, God did. He condemned sin in the flesh by sending his own Son in the likeness of sinful flesh as a sin offering, in order that the law's requirement would be fulfilled in us who do not walk according to the flesh but according to the Spirit.

−Romans 8:1−4

BIBLICAL BIO

The Pharisees were a very respected and influential group of Jewish religious leaders. They were known for their strict commitment to following the law exactly as it was written.

They focused so much on displaying the right behavior that they missed the Scripture's revelation that Jesus was the Messiah. They began with good intentions, but they became blind to what Jesus had to say. Jesus focused on the heart, and the Pharisees focused on actions. Jesus constantly battled with them over their external focus. He even called them "whitewashed tombs" because they looked good on the outside (by doing the right actions), but they were dead on the inside (their heart in the wrong place).

You can fool anyone with your spirituality—well, anyone except God. God knows your heart, and he knows the real you.

If you're a modern-day Pharisee, take off your mask, get your heart right with God, and start living a life that values the inner world.

Related Texts: Psalm 119:161−176; Matthew 22:34−40; Romans 3:21− 31; 7−8

TAKE A SHOT

You have heard that it was said to our ancestors, **Do not murder**, and whoever murders will be subject to judgment. But I tell you, everyone who is angry with his brother or sister will be subject to judgment. Whoever insults his brother or sister, will be subject to the court. Whoever says, 'You fool!' will be subject to hellfire. So if you are offering your gift on the altar, and there you remember that your brother or sister has something against you, leave your gift there in front of the altar. First go and be reconciled with your brother or sister, and then come and offer your gift. Reach a settlement quickly with your adversary while you're on the way with him to the court, or your adversary will hand you over to the judge, and the judge to the officer, and you will be thrown into prison. Truly I tell you, you will never get out of there until you have paid the last penny."

—Matthew 5:21–26

The one who says he is in the light but hates his brother or sister is in the darkness until now. The one who loves his brother or sister remains in the light, and there is no cause for stumbling in him. But the one who hates his brother or sister is in the darkness, walks in the darkness, and doesn't know where he's going, because the darkness has blinded his eyes.

—1 John 2:9–11

If you were to try to follow the teachings in today's reading, what should you be doing with your enemies or those you don't like?

What are the results of disliking another person according to 1Jn 2:9–11?

Related Texts: Exodus 20:13; Proverbs 8:12–13; Matthew 5:38–48; Luke 6:22–36

You have heard that it was said, **Do not commit adultery.** But I tell you, everyone who looks at a woman lustfully has already committed adultery with her in her heart. If your right eye causes you to sin, gouge it out and throw it away. For it is better that you lose one of the parts of your body than for your whole body to be thrown into hell. And if your right hand causes you to sin, cut it off and throw it away. For it is better that you lose one of the parts of your body than for your whole body to go into hell.

"It was also said, **Whoever divorces his wife must give her a written notice of divorce.** But I tell you, everyone who divorces his wife, except in a case of sexual immorality, causes her to commit adultery. And whoever marries a divorced woman commits adultery."

—Matthew 5:27–32

For this is God's will, your sanctification: that you keep away from sexual immorality, that each of you knows how to control his own body in holiness and honor, not with lustful passions, like the Gentiles, who don't know God. This means one must not transgress against and take advantage of a brother or sister in this manner, because the Lord is an avenger of all these offenses, as we also previously told and warned you. For God has not called us to impurity but to live in holiness. Consequently, anyone who rejects this does not reject man, but God, who gives you his Holy Spirit.

—1 Thessalonians 4:3–8

WEIRD OR WHAT?

The Old Testament was originally written in the Hebrew language (and a little in Aramaic). The Hebrew word used to describe sex outside of the marriage relationship (or fornication) is *zanah*. This word is used ninety-nine times in the Old Testament. In the New Testament that same word is translated in the Greek language as *porneia* (from which we get the root for the word *pornography*).

The Bible has a lot to say about sex. Whether it's in Hebrew, Greek, or translated to English, it stays the same message: God created sex as good and intended it for marriage. Sex in any language says the same thing: Wait until you're married.

Related Texts: Deuteronomy 24:1–4; Proverbs 5; Malachi 2:10–16; Matthew 19:3–12; 1 Corinthians 7

You have heard that it was said, **An eye for an eye** and **a tooth for a tooth.** But I tell you, don't resist an evildoer. On the contrary, if anyone slaps you on your right cheek, turn the other to him also. As for the one who wants to sue you and take away your shirt, let him have your coat as well. And if anyone forces you to go one mile, go with him two. Give to the one who asks you, and don't turn away from the one who wants to borrow from you.

"You have heard that it was said, **Love your neighbor** and hate your enemy. But I tell you, love your enemies and pray for those who persecute you, so that you may be children of your Father in heaven. For he causes his sun to rise on the evil and the good, and sends rain on the righteous and the unrighteous. For if you love those who love you, what reward will you have? Don't even the tax collectors do the same? And if you greet only your brothers and sisters, what are you doing out of the ordinary? Don't even the Gentiles do the same? Be perfect, therefore, as your heavenly Father is perfect."

—Matthew 5:38–48

Dear friends, let us love one another, because love is from God, and everyone who loves has been born of God and knows God. The one who does not love does not know God, because God is love.

—1 John 4:7–8

IN OTHER WORDS

In Jesus's famous sermon (the Sermon on the Mount in Matthew 5–7), Jesus enhanced the Old Testament law that people were familiar with. He challenged people to take the law one step further, and these steps are no baby steps—they are huge jumps! Jesus does this six times in Matthew 5. Here are two examples in addition to the two in today's reading (see if you can find the other two on your own).

The Law: "Do not murder" (v. 21).
Jesus's Command: "But I tell you, everyone who is angry with his brother or sister will be subject to judgment" (v. 22).

The Law: "Do not commit adultery" (v. 27).
Jesus's Command: "But I tell you, everyone who looks at a woman lustfully has already committed adultery with her in his heart" (v. 28).

Jesus is concerned with your heart, and any actions that don't display the proper motives of the heart are empty actions. Check yourself today, and if you need a little help, ask God to perform "heart surgery" on you.

Related Texts: Genesis 12:1–3; Leviticus 24:17–20; Luke 6:27–37; Romans 12:14–18

Be careful not to practice your righteousness in front of others to be seen by them. Otherwise, you have no reward with your Father in heaven. So whenever you give to the poor, don't sound a trumpet before you, as the hypocrites do in the synagogues and on the streets, to be applauded by people. Truly I tell you, they have their reward. But when you give to the poor, don't let your left hand know what your right hand is doing, so that your giving may be in secret. And your Father who sees in secret will reward you....

"Don't store up for yourselves treasures on earth, where moth and rust destroy and where thieves break in and steal. But store up for yourselves treasures in heaven, where neither moth nor rust destroys, and where thieves don't break in and steal. For where your treasure is, there your heart will be also.

"The eye is the lamp of the body. If your eye is healthy, your whole body will be full of light. But if your eye is bad, your whole body will be full of darkness. So if the light within you is darkness, how deep is that darkness!

"No one can serve two masters, since either he will hate one and love the other, or he will be devoted to one and despise the other. You cannot serve both God and money."

—Matthew 6:1–4,19–24

HERE'S THE DEAL

Churches and Christian ministries wouldn't have to waste their time raising money if the followers of Jesus would give graciously. Rather, ministries could spend their fund-raising time and effort trying to change the world. But, since the world is filled with more takers than givers, money is often an issue for ministries.

During the Old Testament times the Israelites were required by law to give a portion (called a tithe) of their money to support God's work. But in the New Testament, Jesus emphasizes the attitude of the heart more than the amount during giving. A tithe that is given with a bad heart has no meaning for the giver. God wants followers of Jesus to learn to give freely and cheerfully (see 2Co 9:7).

Giving your money demonstrates your obedience to God. Be guaranteed that God will honor your giving, your faithfulness, and your heart. He will take care of you—you can't ever outgive God.

Related Texts: Proverbs 11:24–25;
Mark 10:17–31; Luke 6:38; 12:32–34;
Acts 20:32–35; 2 Corinthians 9:6–15

Whenever you pray, you must not be like the hypocrites, because they love to pray standing in the synagogues and on the street corners to be seen by people. Truly I tell you, they have their reward. But when you pray, go into your private room, shut your door, and pray to your Father who is in secret. And your Father who sees in secret will reward you. When you pray, don't babble like the Gentiles, since they imagine they'll be heard for their many words. Don't be like them, because your Father knows the things you need before you ask him.

Therefore, you should pray like this:

Our Father in heaven,
your name be honored as holy.
Your kingdom come.
Your will be done
on earth as it is in heaven.
Give us today our daily bread.
And forgive us our debts,
as we also have forgiven
    our debtors.
And do not bring us
    into temptation,
but deliver us from the evil one.

"For if you forgive others their offenses, your heavenly Father will forgive you as well. But if you don't forgive others, your Father will not forgive your offenses."
—Matthew 6:5–15

JUST A THOUGHT

If you don't know what to say or how to pray, don't worry. Talk to God like a friend. He hears your prayers, and he doesn't give you a grade on how good your prayer sounds. Your words directed toward God will always make sense to him.

Related Texts: Psalm 5; Mark 11:22–26; Luke 11:1–13; 18:1–14; James 5:13–20

Whenever you fast, don't be gloomy like the hypocrites. For they disfigure their faces so that their fasting is obvious to people. Truly I tell you, they have their reward. But when you fast, put oil on your head and wash your face, so that your fasting isn't obvious to others but to your Father who is in secret. And your Father who sees in secret will reward you.

—Matthew 6:16–18

Now John's disciples and the Pharisees were fasting. People came and asked him, "Why do John's disciples and the Pharisees' disciples fast, but your disciples do not fast?"

Jesus said to them, "The wedding guests cannot fast while the groom is with them, can they? As long as they have the groom with them, they cannot fast. But the time will come when the groom will be taken away from them, and then they will fast on that day. No one sews a patch of unshrunk cloth on an old garment. Otherwise, the new patch pulls away from the old cloth, and a worse tear is made. And no one puts new wine into old wineskins. Otherwise, the wine will burst the skins, and the wine is lost as well as the skins. No, new wine is put into fresh wineskins."

—Mark 2:18–22

IN OTHER WORDS

Fasting is going without food or drink for a period of time. During biblical times fasting was done for a variety of reasons. Today the most common description of fasting is related to a spiritual habit or discipline. The discipline is to spend extra time focusing on God and giving him priority over food. People who fast may spend time in prayer during the times when they would normally eat.

Before you try to fast, discuss it further with your parents or pastor to better understand the spiritual benefit as well as the health precautions. Whether or not you fast, be reminded that Jesus cares deeply about the motives of your heart.

He knows your heart. He knows the real you!

Related Texts: Esther 3–4; Isaiah 58; Jonah 3; Zechariah 7–8; Acts 14:21–23

Therefore I tell you: Don't worry about your life, what you will eat or what you will drink; or about your body, what you will wear. Isn't life more than food and the body more than clothing? Consider the birds of the sky: They don't sow or reap or gather into barns, yet your heavenly Father feeds them. Aren't you worth more than they? Can any of you add one moment to his life span by worrying? And why do you worry about clothes? Observe how the wildflowers of the field grow: They don't labor or spin thread. Yet I tell you that not even Solomon in all his splendor was adorned like one of these. If that's how God clothes the grass of the field, which is here today and thrown into the furnace tomorrow, won't he do much more for you — you of little faith? So don't worry, saying, 'What will we eat?' or 'What will we drink?' or 'What will we wear?' For the Gentiles eagerly seek all these things, and your heavenly Father knows that you need them. But seek first the kingdom of God and his righteousness, and all these things will be provided for you. Therefore don't worry about tomorrow, because tomorrow will worry about itself. Each day has enough trouble of its own.

—Matthew 6:25–34

ONE-MINUTE MEMORY

"Therefore, don't worry about tomorrow, because tomorrow will worry about itself. Each day has enough trouble of its own" (Mt 6:34).

Related Texts: Proverbs 12:25; Mark 13:11; Luke 12:11–34; Philippians 4:6–7

Do not judge, so that you won't be judged. For you will be judged by the same standard with which you judge others, and you will be measured by the same measure you use. Why do you look at the splinter in your brother's eye but don't notice the beam of wood in your own eye? Or how can you say to your brother, 'Let me take the splinter out of your eye,' and look, there's a beam of wood in your own eye? Hypocrite! First take the beam of wood out of your eye, and then you will see clearly to take the splinter out of your brother's eye. Don't give what is holy to dogs or toss your pearls before pigs, or they will trample them under their feet, turn, and tear you to pieces.

"Ask, and it will be given to you. Seek, and you will find. Knock, and the door will be opened to you. For everyone who asks receives, and the one who seeks finds, and to the one who knocks, the door will be opened. Who among you, if his son asks him for bread, will give him a stone? Or if he asks for a fish, will give him a snake? If you then, who are evil, know how to give good gifts to your children, how much more will your Father in heaven give good things to those who ask him. Therefore, whatever you want others to do for you, do also the same for them, for this is the Law and the Prophets."

—Matthew 7:1–12

WEIRD OR WHAT?

The word *hypocrite* means to "act out the part of a character in a play."

In ancient times actors covered their faces with masks, representing the characters they were playing.

Today, a hypocrite is known as one who covers or hides his real self and "acts out" as a different person. This person would be considered a fake.

Anyone can always fool an "audience," but God isn't fooled. God wrote the ultimate script, created the characters, and knows everything about the play. God created you just as he wants you to be. If you're wearing a mask, consider asking God for the courage to take it off. You'll enjoy life a lot better when you show the real you.

Related Texts: John 16:24; Romans 14:1–13; 1 Corinthians 5; James 4:1–3; 1 John 3:21–22

Enter through the narrow gate. For the gate is wide and the road broad that leads to destruction, and there are many who go through it. How narrow is the gate and difficult the road that leads to life, and few find it. . . .

"Not everyone who says to me, 'Lord, Lord,' will enter the kingdom of heaven, but only the one who does the will of my Father in heaven. On that day many will say to me, 'Lord, Lord, didn't we prophesy in your name, drive out demons in your name, and do many miracles in your name?' Then I will announce to them, 'I never knew you. **Depart from me, you lawbreakers!**'

"Therefore, everyone who hears these words of mine and acts on them will be like a wise man who built his house on the rock. The rain fell, the rivers rose, and the winds blew and pounded that house. Yet it didn't collapse, because its foundation was on the rock. But everyone who hears these words of mine and doesn't act on them will be like a foolish man who built his house on the sand. The rain fell, the rivers rose, the winds blew and pounded that house, and it collapsed. It collapsed with a great crash."

—Matthew 7:13–14,21–27

JUST A THOUGHT

When Jesus finished speaking, the crowds were amazed! People came from everywhere to hear him speak, and he continually amazed them.

Today, he amazes people still. Is he amazing to you?

Related Texts: Proverbs 14:11–12; Luke 13:22–30; John 10:1–10; Ephesians 2:13–22

When the people saw that Moses delayed in coming down from the mountain, they gathered around Aaron and said to him, "Come, make gods for us who will go before us because this Moses, the man who brought us up from the land of Egypt — we don't know what has happened to him!"

Aaron replied to them, "Take off the gold rings that are on the ears of your wives, your sons, and your daughters and bring them to me." So all the people took off the gold rings that were on their ears and brought them to Aaron. He took the gold from them, fashioned it with an engraving tool, and made it into an image of a calf.

Then they said, "Israel, these are your gods, who brought you up from the land of Egypt!"

When Aaron saw this, he built an altar in front of it and made an announcement: "There will be a festival to the LORD tomorrow." Early the next morning they arose, offered burnt offerings, and presented fellowship offerings. The people sat down to eat and drink, and got up to party.

The LORD spoke to Moses: "Go down at once! For your people you brought up from the land of Egypt have acted corruptly.

The LORD also said to Moses, "I have seen this people, and they are indeed a stiff-necked people. Now leave me alone, so that my anger can burn against them and I can destroy them. Then I will make you into a great nation."

–Exodus 32:1–7,9–10

HERE'S THE DEAL

Moses was an amazing leader! He accomplished astonishing results with a group of people who weren't good at playing follow-the-leader.

Today, the world is in desperate need of quality leaders! But, unfortunately, we have accepted and embraced poor definitions of leadership. Stereotypes describe effective leaders as being men or women who possess charisma or display outgoing and opinionated personalities. But these descriptions limit leadership to those who feel comfortable in front of a crowd.

Effective leaders can be quiet and stay completely behind the scenes. There are good leaders in your church whom you may not ever see. They may set up chairs, straighten the church building, or cut out paper figures for the Sunday School class. These people are leaders because they're serving God in ways that don't bring them a lot of attention. They're leading through serving.

Jesus left everyone with a new standard for leadership when he arrived on the world's scene. He revealed the true heart of leadership—serving. When you serve others, you are displaying leadership gifts. God's work needs all kinds of leaders, especially servant-leaders. One of those servant leaders looks just like you.

Related Texts: Deuteronomy 9:7–15; Nehemiah 9:16–19; Psalm 106:19–22; Acts 7:37–41

But Moses sought the favor of the Lord his God: "Lord, why does your anger burn against your people you brought out of the land of Egypt with great power and a strong hand? Why should the Egyptians say, 'He brought them out with an evil intent to kill them in the mountains and eliminate them from the face of the earth'? Turn from your fierce anger and relent concerning this disaster planned for your people. Remember your servants Abraham, Isaac, and Israel — you swore to them by yourself and declared, 'I will make your offspring as numerous as the stars of the sky and will give your offspring all this land that I have promised, and they will inherit it forever.'" So the Lord relented concerning the disaster he had said he would bring on his people.

Then Moses turned and went down the mountain with the two tablets of the testimony in his hands.

As he approached the camp and saw the calf and the dancing, Moses became enraged and threw the tablets out of his hands, smashing them at the base of the mountain. He took the calf they had made, burned it up, and ground it to powder. He scattered the powder over the surface of the water and forced the Israelites to drink the water.

—Exodus 32:11–15,19–20

BIG TIME WORD

When Moses begged God on behalf of the Israelites, he was praying or pleading for their own good. Today, this type of prayer is referred to as intercessory prayer. Intercessory prayer is when you pray for someone else. You've probably done that before and didn't know it had such a big time name. Also, did you know that the Holy Spirit intercedes on your behalf? Check it out:

"In the same way the Spirit also helps us in our weakness, because we do not know what to pray for as we should, but the Spirit himself intercedes for us with inexpressible groanings. And he who searches our hearts knows the mind of the Spirit, because he intercedes for the saints according to the will of God" (Rm 8:26–27).

God hears your prayers on behalf of the people you pray for, and God hears the prayers of the Holy Spirit, who pleads for you. Put God's ears to the test today on behalf of someone you know and care for.

Related Texts: Genesis 15:1–5; 22:15–18; 26:2–4; Deuteronomy 9:16–21; Psalm 106:23; Jonah 3; Acts 7:40–42

Now I do not want you to be unaware, brothers and sisters, that our ancestors were all under the cloud, all passed through the sea, . . . They all ate the same spiritual food, and all drank the same spiritual drink. For they drank from the spiritual rock that followed them, and that rock was Christ. Nevertheless God was not pleased with most of them, since they were struck down in the wilderness. . . .

These things happened to them as examples, and they were written for our instruction, on whom the ends of the ages have come. So, whoever thinks he stands must be careful not to fall. No temptation has come upon you except what is common to humanity. But God is faithful; he will not allow you to be tempted beyond what you are able, but with the temptation he will also provide the way out so that you may be able to bear it.

—1 Corinthians 10:1,3–5,11–13

ONE-MINUTE MEMORY

"No temptation has come upon you except what is common to humanity. But God is faithful; he will not allow you to be tempted beyond what you are able, but with the temptation he will also provide the way out so that you may be able to bear it" (1Co 10:13).

Related Texts: Exodus 14; 17:1–7; 32; John 6; Hebrews 2:9–18; James 1:12–15

The LORD said to Moses, "Cut two stone tablets like the first ones, and I will write on them the words that were on the first tablets, which you broke. . . .

The LORD came down in a cloud, stood with him there, and proclaimed his name, "the LORD." The LORD passed in front of him and proclaimed:

The LORD — the LORD is a compassionate and gracious God, slow to anger and abounding in faithful love and truth, maintaining faithful love to a thousand generations, forgiving iniquity, rebellion, and sin. But he will not leave the guilty unpunished, bringing the consequences of the fathers' iniquity on the children and grandchildren to the third and fourth generation.

Moses immediately knelt low on the ground and worshiped. Then he said, "My Lord, if I have indeed found favor with you, my Lord, please go with us (even though this is a stiff-necked people), forgive our iniquity and our sin, and accept us as your own possession."

And the LORD responded, "Look, I am making a covenant. In the presence of all your people I will perform wonders that have never been done in the whole earth or in any nation. All the people you live among will see the LORD's work, for what I am doing with you is awe-inspiring.
    —*Exodus 34:1,5–10*

IN OTHER WORDS

The word *repent* means to confess to God that you know you've messed up (sinned) and then to change your mind so you won't commit that sin again. Repentance is bigger than mere confession, it means changing the direction of your life and stopping the sins you've confessed.

In John 8 you will see that Jesus forgave a woman who was caught in the act of adultery. As she left his presence, Jesus said to her, "Go, and from now on do not sin anymore" (Jn 8:11). Her personal repentance required more than simply receiving forgiveness; it also included a radical change in her lifestyle.

Do you have an area of your life where you need to repent? It's "confess" and "change"—because you're sorry enough about your sin to stop sinning!

Related Texts: Psalms 86:15; 103:8; 145:8; John 3:16–21; 1 John 1:9

Don't be like your ancestors and your brothers who were unfaithful to the LORD, the God of their ancestors so that he made them an object of horror as you yourselves see. Don't become obstinate now like your ancestors did. Give your allegiance to the LORD, and come to his sanctuary that he has consecrated forever. Serve the LORD your God so that he may turn his burning anger away from you, for when you return to the LORD, your brothers and your sons will receive mercy in the presence of their captors and will return to this land. For the LORD your God is gracious and merciful; he will not turn his face away from you if you return to him."

–2 Chronicles 30:7–9

The LORD is gracious
    and compassionate,
slow to anger and great
    in faithful love.
The LORD is good to everyone;
his compassion rests
    on all he has made.

–Psalm 145:8–9

Blessed be the God and Father of our Lord Jesus Christ, the Father of mercies and the God of all comfort. He comforts us in all our affliction, so that we may be able to comfort those who are in any kind of affliction, through the comfort we ourselves receive from God. For just as the sufferings of Christ overflow to us, so also through Christ our comfort overflows.

–2 Corinthians 1:3–5

JUST A THOUGHT

When it comes to temptation, God won't allow more to be put "on you" than he puts "in you" to deal with the temptation.

Related Texts: Exodus 33:19; 2 Chronicles 30:7–9; Nehemiah 9:16–19; Psalm 103; Lamentations 3:19–23; Colossians 3:12–14

Who is a God like you,
  forgiving iniquity
  and passing over rebellion
for the remnant
  of his inheritance?
He does not hold on
  to his anger forever
because he delights
  in faithful love.
He will again have compassion
  on us;
he will vanquish our iniquities.
You will cast all our sins
into the depths of the sea.
You will show loyalty to Jacob
and faithful love to Abraham,
as you swore to our ancestors
from days long ago.

—Micah 7:18–20

This is the message we have heard from him and declare to you: God is light, and there is absolutely no darkness in him. If we say, "We have fellowship with him," and yet we walk in darkness, we are lying and are not practicing the truth. If we walk in the light as he himself is in the light, we have fellowship with one another, and the blood of Jesus his Son cleanses us from all sin. If we say, "We have no sin," we are deceiving ourselves, and the truth is not in us. If we confess our sins, he is faithful and righteous to forgive us our sins and to cleanse us from all unrighteousness. If we say, "We have not sinned," we make him a liar, and his word is not in us.

—1 John 1:5–10

HERE'S THE DEAL

There are few things more mind-blowing than God's forgiveness. Did you know God forgives you over and over? Do you ever wonder why he doesn't get tired of forgiving just you? Well, add the times he's forgiven you to the times he's forgiven forty billion other people over the years—that's a lot of forgiveness.

In addition to God's forgiveness, he instructs his followers to forgive and keep forgiving. This is difficult! But you can't expect God to forgive you if you aren't willing to forgive others. Jesus said, "For if you forgive others their offenses, your heavenly Father will forgive you as well. But if you don't forgive others, your Father will not forgive your offenses" (Mt 6:14–15).

It's clear cut! If you want to be forgiven by God, you must forgive others.

After you've confessed your sins to God, rest in the truth that he delights in forgiving and forgetting your sins. There's great freedom and hope in him forgetting your sins (as long as you've forgiven others, right?). Do you have any forgiving you need to do today?

Related Texts: Numbers 14:1–35; 1 Kings 8:27–53; Psalm 32:1–5; Daniel 9:1–19; Matthew 6:14–15; 18:21–35

The LORD is gracious
and righteous;
our God is compassionate.
The LORD guards
the inexperienced;
I was helpless, and he saved me.
Return to your rest, my soul,
for the LORD has been good to you.
—Psalm 116:5–7

But God, who is rich in mercy, because of his great love that he had for us, made us alive with Christ even though we were dead in trespasses. You are saved by grace! He also raised us up with him and seated us with him in the heavens in Christ Jesus, so that in the coming ages he might display the immeasurable riches of his grace through his kindness to us in Christ Jesus. For you are saved by grace through faith, and this is not from yourselves; it is God's gift — not from works, so that no one can boast. For we are his workmanship, created in Christ Jesus for good works, which God prepared ahead of time for us to do.
—Ephesians 2:4–9

IN OTHER WORDS

The word *grace* is one of the greatest words you could ever learn as a follower of Jesus. Grace is best defined by the words undeserved gift. The undeserved gift is God's love. His love never stops! This gift of love keeps giving.

There is nothing you have done or can do to deserve God's grace. You can't work for it, earn it, achieve it, or buy it. All you can do is receive it. It's free! What a great gift!

When you sense God's love today, stop for a moment and thank him for his free gift of grace.

Related Texts: Numbers 6:24–26; Proverbs 3:33–35; Romans 5:12–21

For I am the LORD, who brought you up from the land of Egypt to be your God, so you must be holy because I am holy.

—Leviticus 11:45

In the year that King Uzziah died, I saw the Lord seated on a high and lofty throne, and the hem of his robe filled the temple. Seraphim were standing above him; they each had six wings: with two they covered their faces, with two they covered their feet, and with two they flew. And one called to another:

Holy, holy, holy is the LORD
of Armies;
his glory fills the whole earth. . . .

For the High and Exalted One,
who lives forever, whose name
is holy, says this:
"I live in a high and holy place,
and with the oppressed
and lowly of spirit,
to revive the spirit of the lowly
and revive the heart
of the oppressed.
For I will not accuse you forever,
and I will not always be angry;
for then the spirit
would grow weak before me,
even the breath,
which I have made.

—Isaiah 6:1–3; 57:15–16

As obedient children, do not be conformed to the desires of your former ignorance. But as the one who called you is holy, you also are to be holy in all your conduct; for it is written, **Be holy, because I am holy.**

—1 Peter 1:14–16

IN OTHER WORDS

It's a wild truth to think about the fact that God wants you to be holy as he is holy. Luckily, he has promised you his Holy Spirit to help out! God calls you to be holy or "set apart" or "be different" from the world. For example, if your friends plan to do something bad and you're pursuing holiness, you wouldn't take part in their negative plans. Instead, you would set yourself apart from them and be different.

Holiness is learning to hate that which is evil and trying to live a life that is pleasing to God. Ask God to help you live a life that is set apart today.

Related Texts: Exodus 15:11; Leviticus 22:31–33; Psalm 99; Revelation 4; 15:2–4

I lift my eyes to you,
  the one enthroned in heaven.
Like a servant's eyes
  on his master's hand,
like a servant girl's eyes
  on her mistress's hand,
so our eyes are on the LORD
  our God
until he shows us favor.

Show us favor, LORD,
  show us favor,
for we've had more than enough
  contempt.
We've had more than enough
scorn from the arrogant
and contempt from the proud.
–Psalm 123:1–4

And you were dead in your
trespasses and sins in which you
previously walked according to
the ways of this world, according
to the ruler of the power of
the air, the spirit now working
in the disobedient. We too all
previously lived among them in
our fleshly desires, carrying out
the inclinations of our flesh and
thoughts, and we were by nature
children under wrath as the
others were also. But God, who is
rich in mercy, because of his great
love that he had for us, made us
alive with Christ even though we
were dead in trespasses. You are
saved by grace!
–Ephesians 2:1–5

BIBLICAL BIO

Yahweh is the personal name by
which God revealed himself during
Old Testament times. It is related
to the Hebrew verb that means "to
be." Thus, God is self-existent. In
other words, he alone is the Creator
who depends on no one else. As he
said to Moses, "I AM WHO I AM"
(Ex 3:14). In English Bibles, the
name "Yahweh" is usually expressed
as LORD (with small capital letters).

  God is given other names
throughout the Bible as well, such
as Almighty, Rock, Most High,
Father, and more. These names
express his character, his abilities,
and the ways in which he loves
you. These truths are worthy of your
celebration today!

*Related Texts: Exodus 33:19;
Deuteronomy 4:31; Nehemiah 9:29–31;
Micah 7:18–20; Romans 9:11–18*

Then Job replied to the LORD:
I know that you can do
    anything
and no plan of yours
    can be thwarted.

—Job 42:1—2

Ascribe power to God.
His majesty is over Israel;
his power is among the clouds.
God, you are awe-inspiring
    in your sanctuaries.
The God of Israel gives power
    and strength to his people.
Blessed be God!

—Psalm 68:34—35

Oh, Lord GOD! You yourself
made the heavens and earth by
your great power and with your
outstretched arm. Nothing is too
difficult for you!

—Jeremiah 32:17

Our Lord and God,
you are worthy to receive
glory and honor and power,
because you have created
    all things,
and by your will
they exist and were created.

—Revelation 4:11

TAKE A SHOT

God is worthy of your honor and praise. List five "creations of God" that you are currently thankful for or appreciate.

1.

2.

3.

4.

5.

Related Texts: Genesis 18:14; Exodus 15:1—18; Psalm 29; Mark 4:35—41

W here can I go to escape
your Spirit?
Where can I flee
from your presence?
If I go up to heaven, you are there;
if I make my bed in Sheol,
you are there.
If I fly on the wings of the dawn
and settle down on
the western horizon,
even there your hand will lead me;
your right hand will hold on to me.
If I say, "Surely the darkness
will hide me,
and the light around me
will be night" —
even the darkness is not dark
to you.
The night shines like the day;
darkness and light are alike
to you.

—Psalm 139:7–12

"Am I a God who is only near" —
this is the LORD's declaration —
"and not a God who is far away?
Can a person hide in secret places
where I cannot see him?" — the
LORD's declaration. "Do I not fill
the heavens and the earth?" —
the LORD's declaration.

—Jeremiah 23:23–24

Jesus came near and said to them,
"All authority has been given to
me in heaven and on earth. Go,
therefore, and make disciples of
all nations, baptizing them in the
name of the Father and of the Son
and of the Holy Spirit, teaching
them to observe everything I have
commanded you. And remember,
I am with you always, to the end
of the age."

—Matthew 28:18–20

JUST A THOUGHT

Have you ever played hide-and-seek
and hidden so well that your friends
gave up looking for you? Well there
is nowhere you could go and hide
from the love of God.

Related Texts: Deuteronomy 4:7;
1 Kings 8:27; John 1:45–49; 14:16–17

L ORD, you have searched me
and known me.
You know when I sit down
and when I stand up;
you understand my thoughts
from far away.
You observe my travels
and my rest;
you are aware of all my ways.
Before a word is on my tongue,
you know all about it, LORD.
You have encircled me;
you have placed your hand on me.
This wondrous knowledge is
beyond me.
It is lofty; I am unable to reach it.
–Psalm 139:1–6

Oh, the depth of the riches
and the wisdom and the
knowledge of God!
How unsearchable his judgments
and untraceable his ways!
**For who has known the mind
of the Lord?** . . .
To him be the glory forever. Amen.
–Romans 11:33–34,36

For the word of God is living and
effective and sharper than any
double-edged sword, penetrating
as far as the separation of soul
and spirit, joints and marrow.
It is able to judge the thoughts
and intentions of the heart. No
creature is hidden from him, but
all things are naked and exposed
to the eyes of him to whom we
must give an account.
–Hebrews 4:12–13

ONE-MINUTE MEMORY

"For the word of God is living and effective and sharper than any double-edged sword, penetrating as far as the separation of soul and spirit, joints and marrow. It is able to judge the thoughts and intentions of the heart" (Heb 4:12).

*Related Texts: Psalm 94:1–11;
Proverbs 5:21; 1 Chronicles 1:18–25;
2 Chronicles 16:9; John 3:19–20*

L isten, Israel: The LORD our
God, the LORD is one.
—Deuteronomy 6:4

On that day the LORD will become
King over the whole earth — the
LORD alone, and his name alone.
—Zechariah 14:9

Or is God the God of Jews only?
Is he not the God of Gentiles too?
Yes, of Gentiles too, since there
is one God who will justify the
circumcised by faith and the
uncircumcised through faith.
—Romans 3:29–30

For even if there are so-called
gods, whether in heaven or on
earth — as there are many "gods"
and many "lords" — yet for us
there is one God, the Father. All
things are from him, and we
exist for him. And there is one
Lord, Jesus Christ. All things
are through him, and we exist
through him.
—1 Corinthians 8:5–6

There is one body and one Spirit
— just as you were called to one
hope at your calling — one Lord,
one faith, one baptism, one God
and Father of all, who is above all
and through all and in all.
—Ephesians 4:4–6

DIG DEEPER

When Jesus was asked which
command was the most important,
he answered, "The most important
is 'Listen, Israel! The Lord our God,
The Lord is one. Love the Lord your
God with all your heart, with all your
soul, with all your mind, and with all
your strength." (Mk 12:29–30).

There's no question about the
importance of loving God and loving
only God. This may be contrary to
the religious beliefs of some of your
friends, but the Bible is very clear
in its instructions about loving only
God. Check out Isaiah 44:6,8: "I
am the first and I am the last. There
is no God but me. . . . You are my
witnesses! Is there any God but me?
There is no other Rock; I do not
know any."

This is an important truth for you
as a follower of Jesus. When you
talk to God today, talk to him as
your only God.

Related Texts: Isaiah 44:6–8;
Malachi 2:10; Matthew 19:16–17;
23:1–10; Mark 12:28–34

A wake for me;
you have ordained
a judgment.
Let the assembly of peoples gather
around you;
take your seat on high over it.
The LORD judges the peoples;
vindicate me, LORD,
according to my righteousness
and my integrity.

Let the evil of the wicked come
to an end,
but establish the righteous.
The one who examines
the thoughts and emotions
is a righteous God.
—Psalm 7:6–9

"Look, the days are coming" —
this is the LORD's declaration —
"when I will raise up a Righteous
Branch for David.
He will reign wisely as king
and administer justice and
righteousness in the land.
In his days Judah will be saved,
and Israel will dwell securely.
This is the name he will be called:
The LORD Is Our Righteousness.
—Jeremiah 23:5–6

My little children, I am writing
you these things so that you may
not sin. But if anyone does sin, we
have an advocate with the Father
— Jesus Christ the righteous
one. He himself is the atoning
sacrifice for our sins, and not only
for ours, but also for those of the
whole world.
—1 John 2:1–2

BIBLICAL BIO

David was a man with many great
strengths who made some big and
serious mistakes.

David had a lot going for him. He
was used by God to kill Goliath and
claim victory for Israel. He displayed
great acts of friendship with
Jonathan. He was the most loved
king of Israel, and he wrote many of
the psalms in the Bible.

But just like everyone who has
strengths, David had weaknesses
too. David was disobedient to God
when he chose to have sex with
Bathsheba—the wife of one of
his soldiers. Then, he chose to
arrange for her husband's death so
Bathsheba could become his wife.
These were not minor choices!

Though David's life was not
perfect, God chose to use David's
family-line as the one through which
Jesus would be born. When you read
about Jesus being born through the
Davidic line, you will now know that
David was an ancestor of Jesus.

*Related Texts: Ezra 9; Psalm 36:5–10;
71; Daniel 9:1–19; Matthew 6:28–33;
Acts 3:12–16*

For through faith you are all sons of God in Christ Jesus. For those of you who were baptized into Christ have been clothed with Christ. There is no Jew or Greek, slave or free, male and female; since you are all one in Christ Jesus. And if you belong to Christ, then you are Abraham's seed, heirs according to the promise. . . . Instead, he is under guardians and trustees until the time set by his father. In the same way we also, when we were children, were in slavery under the elements of the world. When the time came to completion, God sent his Son, born of a woman, born under the law, to redeem those under the law, so that we might receive adoption as sons. And because you are sons, God sent the Spirit of his Son into our hearts, crying, "*Abba*, Father!" So you are no longer a slave but a son, and if a son, then God has made you an heir.

—Galatians 3:26–29; 4:2–7

See what great love the Father has given us that we should be called God's children — and we are! The reason the world does not know us is that it didn't know him. Dear friends, we are God's children now, and what we will be has not yet been revealed.

—1 John 3:1–2

JUST A THOUGHT

Every day can be Father's Day when you focus on God as your heavenly Father and rejoice over the fact that he loves you and accepts you just as you are.

Related Texts: Deuteronomy 32:6; Psalm 2; Isaiah 9:1–7; John 1:12–13; Romans 8; Hebrews 12:1–14

H onor your father and your
mother so that you may have
a long life in the land that the
LORD your God is giving you.

—Exodus 20:12

A man fathers a fool
    to his own sorrow;
the father of a fool has no joy....

My son, if your heart is wise,
my heart will indeed rejoice.
My innermost being will celebrate
when your lips say
    what is right....

Listen, my son, and be wise;
keep your mind
    on the right course.

—Proverbs 17:21; 23:15–16,19

Let the word of Christ dwell
richly among you, in all wisdom
teaching and admonishing one
another through psalms, hymns,
and spiritual songs, singing to God
with gratitude in your hearts. And
whatever you do, in word or in
deed, do everything in the name
of the Lord Jesus, giving thanks to
God the Father through him.

Wives, submit yourselves to
your husbands, as is fitting in the
Lord. Husbands, love your wives
and don't be bitter toward them.
Children, obey your parents in
everything, for this pleases the
Lord. Fathers, do not exasperate
your children, so that they won't
become discouraged.

—Colossians 3:16–21

HERE'S THE DEAL

There is a way to celebrate Father's
Day every day. It's a different type of
celebration, for it doesn't celebrate
earthly fathers but, instead, the one
and only heavenly Father.

You can . . .

1. **Celebrate** God the Father as your
   Creator. God made the delicate,
   inner parts of your body and knit
   you together in your mother's
   womb.
2. **Celebrate** God the Father as your
   Comforter. God will never let you
   down. People will always let
   you down, but God promises to
   comfort and care for you in every
   situation.
3. **Celebrate** God the Father as your
   Challenger. God doesn't want you
   to get stuck in a rut. He wants
   you to grow, change, and mature.

You can do this every day:

1. **Rejoice** in your **creation** by
   thanking God for your unique
   design and accepting yourself as
   he created you.
2. **Relax** in God's **comfort**. God loves
   you more than you love yourself.
3. **Run** with the **challenge** by taking
   baby steps toward spiritual
   maturity.

Celebrate this week by rejoicing,
relaxing, and running with God.

_____

_____

_____

Related Texts: Exodus 21:15;
Leviticus 19:3; Proverbs 10:1; 23:22–
25; Ephesians 6:1–3

Listen, sons,
to a father's discipline,
and pay attention so that
   you may gain understanding,
for I am giving you
   good instruction.
Don't abandon my teaching.
When I was a son with my father,
tender and precious to my mother,
he taught me and said,
"Your heart must hold on
   to my words.
Keep my commands and live.
Get wisdom, get understanding;
don't forget or turn away
   from the words from my mouth.
Don't abandon wisdom,
   and she will watch over you;
love her, and she will guard you.
Wisdom is supreme —
   so get wisdom.
And whatever else you get,
   get understanding.
Cherish her, and she will exalt you;
if you embrace her, she will
   honor you.
She will place a garland of favor
   on your head;
she will give you a crown
   of beauty."

Listen, my son. Accept my words,
and you will live many years.
I am teaching you the way
   of wisdom;
I am guiding you on straight paths.
When you walk, your steps
   will not be hindered;
when you run,
   you will not stumble.
                    —*Proverbs 4:1–12*

DIG DEEPER

The Proverbs are filled with very practical common-sense wisdom. The following two selections from Proverbs have to do with the wisdom your parents provide you:

   "Listen, my son, to your father's instruction, and don't reject your mother's teaching, for they will be a garland of favor on your head and pendants around your neck" (1:8–9).

   "My son, keep your father's command, and don't reject your mother's teaching. Always bind them to your heart; tie them around your neck. When you walk here and there, they will guide you; when you lie down, they will watch over you; when you wake up, they will talk to you" (6:20–22).

   You may not like to hear this, but God gave you parents to guide and direct you. They'll never be perfect, but you'll please God and honor your parents when you listen to their wisdom.

   Keep listening.

Related Texts: Deuteronomy 6:1–9; Proverbs 1:8; 6:20–24; 31:1–9; 2 Timothy 1:2–3

In struggling against sin, you have not yet resisted to the point of shedding your blood. And you have forgotten the exhortation that addresses you as sons:

> My son, do not take the Lord's discipline lightly
> or lose heart when you are reproved by him,
> for the Lord disciplines the one he loves
> and punishes every son he receives.

Endure suffering as discipline: God is dealing with you as sons. For what son is there that a father does not discipline? But if you are without discipline — which all receive — then you are illegitimate children and not sons. Furthermore, we had human fathers discipline us, and we respected them. Shouldn't we submit even more to the Father of spirits and live? For they disciplined us for a short time based on what seemed good to them, but he does it for our benefit, so that we can share his holiness. No discipline seems enjoyable at the time, but painful. Later on, however, it yields the peaceful fruit of righteousness to those who have been trained by it.

—*Hebrews 12:4–11*

BIG TIME WORD

The word used in today's selection is *discipline*. Another word commonly used in this context is *correct*. God corrects or disciplines those he loves. Discipline means correction.

God's discipline is to move you toward spiritual maturity, to correct you so you might be holy. Proverbs 10:17 provides this instruction, "The one who follows instruction is on the path to life, but the one who rejects correction goes astray."

God loves you so much that he wants you to gain understanding and learn to celebrate life to its fullest. You can open yourself to God's correction through reading the Bible, listening to God's Spirit, and learning from other followers of Jesus. Don't turn your back on correction. Here's why: "Poverty and disgrace come to those who ignore discipline, but the one who accepts correction will be honored" (Pr 13:18)

Related Texts: Deuteronomy 8:5; 1 Samuel 2:12–36; Proverbs 3:11–12; 15:5; Revelation 3:14–20

My son, pay attention
to my wisdom;
listen closely to my understanding
so that you may maintain
    discretion
and your lips safeguard knowledge.
Though the lips
    of the forbidden woman
    drip honey
and her words are
    smoother than oil,
in the end she's as bitter
    as wormwood
and as sharp as a double-
    edged sword....

Drink water
    from your own cistern,
water flowing from your own well.
Should your springs flow
    in the streets,
streams in the public squares?
They should be for you alone
and not for you to share
    with strangers.
Let your fountain be blessed,
and take pleasure in the wife
    of your youth.
A loving deer, a graceful doe —
let her breasts always satisfy you;
be lost in her love forever.
Why, my son, would you
    lose yourself
with a forbidden woman
or embrace a wayward woman?
For a man's ways are before
    the LORD's eyes,
and he considers all his paths.
A wicked man's iniquities will
    trap him;
he will become tangled
    in the ropes of his own sin.
He will die because there is
    no discipline,
and be lost because of
    his great stupidity.
                —*Proverbs 5:1–4,15–23*

TAKE A SHOT

Today's reading includes a father's wisdom to his son. The father advises his son to be careful and faithful in his relationship to his wife.

If you are male, write down three qualities you would like to have in your life before you are a husband. Next to each quality write a goal that will help you develop that quality.

Male
    Qualities   Goals

1.

2.

3.

If you are female, write down three qualities you would like to see in the man you marry. Then ask God to prepare you to be the kind of woman who will love and be faithful to her future husband.

Female
    Qualities

1.

2.

3.

_____

_____

_____

*Related Texts: Exodus 20:14;
Leviticus 20:10; Proverbs 2:16–22;
6:23–35; 7; Ephesians 5:1–3*

Like an apricot tree
among the trees of the forest,
so is my love
    among the young men.
I delight to sit in his shade,
and his fruit is sweet to my taste.
He brought me to the banquet hall,
and he looked on me with love.
Sustain me with raisins;
refresh me with apricots,
for I am lovesick.
May his left hand be
    under my head,
and his right arm embrace me. . . .

Listen! My love is approaching.
Look! Here he comes,
leaping over the mountains,
bounding over the hills.
My love is like a gazelle
or a young stag.
See, he is standing
    behind our wall,
gazing through the windows,
peering through the lattice.
My love calls to me:

Arise, my darling.
Come away, my beautiful one.
For now the winter is past;
the rain has ended and gone away.
The blossoms appear
    in the countryside.
The time of singing has come,
and the turtledove's cooing
    is heard in our land.
The fig tree ripens its figs;
the blossoming vines give off
    their fragrance.
Arise, my darling.
Come away, my beautiful one.
            —Song of Songs 2:3–6,8–13

WEIRD OR WHAT?

Song of Songs can be one of
the most confusing and widely
interpreted books in the Bible. It
contains sexual lyrics, a mysterious
religious meaning, and an
intriguing plot.

Song of Songs illustrates the
power of human love. This love
is a special gift from God. The
book is filled with a lot of sexual
imagery that will definitely grab
your attention. Read it with an open
mind and a heart to experience
God's radical yet tender love for you.

Related Texts: Psalm 45;
Song of Songs 1–8; 2 Corinthians
11:2–3; 1 Peter 3:1–6

H usbands, love your wives, just as Christ loved the church and gave himself for her to make her holy, cleansing her with the washing of water by the word. He did this to present the church to himself in splendor, without spot or wrinkle or anything like that, but holy and blameless. In the same way, husbands are to love their wives as their own bodies. He who loves his wife loves himself. For no one ever hates his own flesh but provides and cares for it, just as Christ does for the church, since we are members of his body. . . . To sum up, each one of you is to love his wife as himself, and the wife is to respect her husband.

—Ephesians 5:25–30,33

Husbands, in the same way, live with your wives in an understanding way, as with a weaker partner, showing them honor as coheirs of the grace of life, so that your prayers will not be hindered.

—1 Peter 3:7

JUST A THOUGHT

Imagine what families would be like if husbands and wives loved each other as much as Jesus loves his children.

Related Texts: Genesis 2:18–25; Hosea 3:1–3; Malachi 2:13–16; Colossians 3:19; Revelation 21:1–4

On the day the tabernacle was set up, the cloud covered the tabernacle, the tent of the testimony, and it appeared like fire above the tabernacle from evening until morning. It remained that way continuously: the cloud would cover it, appearing like fire at night. Whenever the cloud was lifted up above the tent, the Israelites would set out; at the place where the cloud stopped, there the Israelites camped. At the LORD's command the Israelites set out, and at the LORD's command they camped. As long as the cloud stayed over the tabernacle, they camped.

Even when the cloud stayed over the tabernacle many days, the Israelites carried out the LORD's requirement and did not set out. Sometimes the cloud remained over the tabernacle for only a few days. They would camp at the LORD's command and set out at the LORD's command. Sometimes the cloud remained only from evening until morning; when the cloud lifted in the morning, they set out. Or if it remained a day and a night, they moved out when the cloud lifted. Whether it was two days, a month, or longer, the Israelites camped and did not set out as long as the cloud stayed over the tabernacle. But when it was lifted, they set out. They camped at the LORD's command, and they set out at the LORD's command. They carried out the LORD's requirement according to his command through Moses.

—*Numbers 9:15–23*

IN OTHER WORDS

The tabernacle was a portable sanctuary—basically, it was easily moved.

Its purpose was to serve as a place where the Israelites could go to worship God and make sacrifices. It was a place where they could store the ark containing the Ten Commandments.

In Ex 25:8 God said, "They are to make a sanctuary for me so that I may dwell among them." The tabernacle became a visual symbol of God's presence for the Israelites. The cloud and fire described in today's reading were a physical reminder and testimony to the Israelites that God was with them.

Today God has given believers his Holy Spirit to express his presence in their lives. There won't be clouds and fire following you, but God's presence is still available in a portable sanctuary—your body. Spend time today thinking about yourself as God's temple.

Related Texts: Exodus 13:22,33; 40:34–38; Numbers 14:11–14; 1 Corinthians 10:1–2

They deliberately tested God,
  demanding the food
    they craved.
They spoke against God, saying,
"Is God able to provide food
    in the wilderness?
Look! He struck the rock
    and water gushed out;
torrents overflowed.
But can he also provide bread
or furnish meat for his people?"
Therefore, the LORD heard
    and became furious;
then fire broke out against Jacob,
and anger flared up against Israel
because they did not believe God
or rely on his salvation.
He gave a command
    to the clouds above
and opened the doors of heaven.
                    —Psalm 78:18–23

DIG DEEPER

This attitude of unthankfulness, unfaithfulness, and complaining wasn't limited to the Israelites. Thousands of years later, James wrote to Christians about the same type of problem:

> You desire and do not have. You murder and covet and cannot obtain. You fight and war. You do not have because you do not ask. You ask and don't receive because you ask with wrong motives, so that you may spend it on your pleasures.
>
> You adulteress people! Don't you know that friendship with the world is hostility toward God? So whoever wants to be the friend of the world becomes the enemy of God (Jms 4:2–4).

Today, a few thousand years later, this type of attitude remains a problem. Although God continues to show himself faithful, most still complain about things they don't have.

If you had to choose between being God's friend or enemy, you'd want to run from the evil pleasures of the world and be thankful God has given you what you have. What you have is more than most of the world will ever possess.

Related Texts: Numbers 11;
Psalm 106:1–15; Luke 4:1–13;
James 4:1–4

The LORD spoke to Moses: "Send men to scout out the land of Canaan I am giving to the Israelites.

At the end of forty days they returned from scouting out the land.

The men went back to Moses, Aaron, and the entire Israelite community in the Wilderness of Paran at Kadesh. They brought back a report for them and the whole community, and they showed them the fruit of the land. They reported to Moses, "We went into the land where you sent us. Indeed it is flowing with milk and honey, and here is some of its fruit. However, the people living in the land are strong, and the cities are large and fortified. . . .

Then Caleb quieted the people in the presence of Moses and said, "Let's go up now and take possession of the land because we can certainly conquer it!"

But the men who had gone up with him responded, "We can't attack the people because they are stronger than we are!". . .

Then the whole community broke into loud cries, and the people wept that night. All the Israelites complained about Moses and Aaron, and the whole community told them, "If only we had died in the land of Egypt, or if only we had died in this wilderness! Why is the LORD bringing us into this land to die by the sword? Our wives and children will become plunder. Wouldn't it be better for us to go back to Egypt?" So they said to one another, "Let's appoint a leader and go back to Egypt."

—Numbers 13:1–2,25–28,
30–31; 14:1–4

HERE'S THE DEAL

With all of God's provisions, you wouldn't think that the Israelites would whine and complain. Think about it! God gave the Israelites a leader—Moses. God saved them from slavery—in Egypt. God directed them to a new place to live—the promised land. How quickly they forgot his blessings.

Can you relate to forgetfulness over God's blessings in your life? It's easy to read about the Israelites and make fun of how unfaithful they were, but in reality, you may not be that much different from them. God has provided for you over and over. Do you still complain when you don't get what you want?

Being faithful is tough, but it's not impossible! Spend time today thinking of all the different ways God has shown himself faithful to you. Then, promise to trust him a little more today than you did yesterday.

Joshua 23:14; Psalms 103; 136; Isaiah 12; Luke 7:36-50

T hen Moses and Aaron fell facedown in front of the whole assembly of the Israelite community. Joshua son of Nun and Caleb son of Jephunneh, who were among those who scouted out the land, tore their clothes and said to the entire Israelite community, "The land we passed through and explored is an extremely good land. If the LORD is pleased with us, he will bring us into this land, a land flowing with milk and honey, and give it to us. Only don't rebel against the LORD, and don't be afraid of the people of the land, for we will devour them. Their protection has been removed from them, and the LORD is with us. Don't be afraid of them!" . . .

Then the LORD spoke to Moses and Aaron: "How long must I endure this evil community that keeps complaining about me? I have heard the Israelites' complaints that they make against me. Tell them: As I live — this is the LORD's declaration — I will do to you exactly as I heard you say. Your corpses will fall in this wilderness — all of you who were registered in the census, the entire number of you twenty years old or more — because you have complained about me. I swear that none of you will enter the land I promised to settle you in, except Caleb son of Jephunneh and Joshua son of Nun. . . .

—Numbers 14:5−9,26−30

What, then, are we to say about these things? If God is for us, who is against us?

—Romans 8:31

ONE MINUTE MEMORY

"If God is for us, who is against us?" (Rm 8:31).

Related Texts: Joshua 5:1−6;
John 6:48−51; 1 Corinthians 10:1−6;
Hebrews 3:7−4:7

Therefore, as the Holy Spirit says:
Today, if you hear his voice,
do not harden your hearts
as in the rebellion,
on the day of testing
in the wilderness,
where your ancestors
tested me, tried me,
and saw my works
for forty years.
Therefore I was provoked to
anger with that generation
and said, "They always
go astray in their hearts,
and they have not known
my ways."
So I swore in my anger,
"They will not enter my rest."
Watch out, brothers and sisters,
so that there won't be in any of
you an evil, unbelieving heart
that turns away from the living
God. But encourage each other
daily, while it is still called **today**,
so that none of you is hardened
by sin's deception. For we have
become participants in Christ if
we hold firmly until the end the
reality that we had at the start. As
it is said:
Today, if you hear his voice,
do not harden your hearts
as in the rebellion.
—Hebrews 3:7–15

TAKE A SHOT

A person with a hardened heart is someone who has become closed to truth, teachings, and the ways of God. What are three things you can do today to ensure that your heart doesn't become hardened and that you continue to grow in your faith and in your love of God?

1.

2.

3.

Related Texts: Psalm 95;
Matthew 17:1–5; John 14:15–24;
Acts 3:19–23; Hebrews 4

Now Korah son of Izhar, son of Kohath, son of Levi, with Dathan and Abiram, sons of Eliab, and On son of Peleth, sons of Reuben, took two hundred fifty prominent Israelite men who were leaders of the community and representatives in the assembly, and they rebelled against Moses. They came together against Moses and Aaron and told them, "You have gone too far! Everyone in the entire community is holy, and the LORD is among them. Why then do you exalt yourselves above the LORD's assembly?"

When Moses heard this, he fell facedown. Then he said to Korah and all his followers, "Tomorrow morning the LORD will reveal who belongs to him, who is set apart, and the one he will let come near him. He will let the one he chooses come near him. . . .

After Korah assembled the whole community against them at the entrance to the tent of meeting, the glory of the LORD appeared to the whole community. . . .

The earth opened its mouth and swallowed them and their households, all Korah's people, and all their possessions. They went down alive into Sheol with all that belonged to them. The earth closed over them, and they vanished from the assembly.

—Numbers 16:1–5,19,32–33

JUST A THOUGHT

Anytime you take a position of leadership, you can be confident there will be someone who doesn't like or appreciate you—if you want an example of this truth, look at what happened to Moses and Aaron.

Related texts: Psalm 106:16–17; Hebrews 10:26–31; 12:23–29; 2 Peter 1:16–2:22; Jude 11

The entire Israelite community entered the Wilderness of Zin in the first month, and they settled in Kadesh. . . .

There was no water for the community, so they assembled against Moses and Aaron. . . . Why have you brought the LORD's assembly into this wilderness for us and our livestock to die here? Why have you led us up from Egypt to bring us to this evil place? " . . .

Then Moses and Aaron went from the presence of the assembly to the doorway of the tent of meeting. They fell facedown, and the glory of the LORD appeared to them. The LORD spoke to Moses, "Take the staff and assemble the community. You and your brother Aaron are to speak to the rock while they watch, and it will yield its water. You will bring out water for them from the rock and provide drink for the community and their livestock."

So Moses took the staff from the LORD's presence just as he had commanded him. Moses and Aaron summoned the assembly in front of the rock, and Moses said to them, "Listen, you rebels! Must we bring water out of this rock for you? " Then Moses raised his hand and struck the rock twice with his staff, so that abundant water gushed out, and the community and their livestock drank.

But the LORD said to Moses and Aaron, "Because you did not trust me to demonstrate my holiness in the sight of the Israelites, you will not bring this assembly into the land I have given them."

—*Numbers 20:1,2,4–5,6–12*

WEIRD OR WHAT?

It seems strange that after all Moses and Aaron had done for God that they wouldn't be allowed to enter and enjoy the promised land. What went wrong? Well, when Moses and Aaron got water from the rock by striking it, they tried to improve on God's unimprovable plan. God could not reward them for being unfaithful to what he asked of them. Moses and Aaron learned a hard lesson that day: No one is exempt from the consequences of disobeying God.

Being faithful is an ongoing, everyday battle. Try to win that battle today and know that God will be pleased with your victory and your obedience. The more you do it, the easier obedience becomes.

Related Texts: Exodus 7:19–21; 8:16–17; 17:1–6; Deuteronomy 4:20–22; Acts 5:1–11

Then they set out from Mount Hor by way of the Red Sea to bypass the land of Edom, but the people became impatient because of the journey. The people spoke against God and Moses: "Why have you led us up from Egypt to die in the wilderness? There is no bread or water, and we detest this wretched food!" Then the LORD sent poisonous snakes among the people, and they bit them so that many Israelites died.

The people then came to Moses and said, "We have sinned by speaking against the LORD and against you. Intercede with the LORD so that he will take the snakes away from us." And Moses interceded for the people.

Then the LORD said to Moses, "Make a snake image and mount it on a pole. When anyone who is bitten looks at it, he will recover." So Moses made a bronze snake and mounted it on a pole. Whenever someone was bitten, and he looked at the bronze snake, he recovered.

—Numbers 21:4–9

"Just as Moses lifted up the snake in the wilderness, so the Son of Man must be lifted up, so that everyone who believes in him may have eternal life. For God loved the world in this way: He gave his one and only Son, so that everyone who believes in him will not perish but have eternal life. For God did not send his Son into the world to condemn the world, but to save the world through him.

—John 3:14–17

ONE MINUTE MEMORY

"For God did not send his Son into the world to condemn the world, but to save the world through him" (Jn 3:17).

Related Texts: Exodus 16:6–12; Numbers 14:26–37; 2 Kings 18:1–4; Lamentations 3:25–40; 1 Corinthians 10:1–11

The Israelites traveled on and camped in the plains of Moab near the Jordan across from Jericho. Now Balak son of Zippor saw all that Israel had done to the Amorites. Moab was terrified of the people because they were numerous, and Moab dreaded the Israelites. So the Moabites said to the elders of Midian, "This horde will devour everything around us like an ox eats up the green plants in the field."

Since Balak son of Zippor was Moab's king at that time, he sent messengers to Balaam son of Beor at Pethor, which is by the Euphrates in the land of his people. Balak said to him, "Look, a people has come out of Egypt; they cover the surface of the land and are living right across from me. Please come and put a curse on these people for me because they are more powerful than I am. I may be able to defeat them and drive them out of the land, for I know that those you bless are blessed and those you curse are cursed."

—Numbers 22:1–6

No Ammonite or Moabite may enter the LORD's assembly; none of their descendants, even to the tenth generation, may ever enter the LORD's assembly. This is because they did not meet you with food and water on the journey after you came out of Egypt, and because Balaam son of Beor from Pethor in Aram-naharaim was hired to curse you. Yet the LORD your God would not listen to Balaam, but he turned the curse into a blessing for you because the LORD your God loves you.

—Deuteronomy 23:3–5

BIBLICAL BIO

Balaam is an interesting character because he's famous for the strange way God got his attention—through a donkey.

One day Balaam was riding a donkey, and an angel appeared before them. Balaam didn't see the angel, but the donkey got spooked and went crazy. Three times the donkey went wild, and all three times Balaam beat the animal. God then caused the donkey to speak, saying, "What have I done to you that you have beaten me these three times?" (Nm 22:28). Now Balaam went crazy.

God was trying to stop Balaam's direction by speaking through a donkey. Balaam finally figured it out and responded with repentance.

Does God have your full attention? Ask him today if you're heading in the right direction with your life.

Related Texts: Genesis 12:1–3; Numbers 22–24; Joshua 24:8–10; 2 Peter 2:15–16

S ince Balaam saw that it
pleased the LORD to bless
Israel, he did not go to seek
omens as on previous occasions,
but turned toward the wilderness.
When Balaam looked up and saw
Israel encamped tribe by tribe,
the Spirit of God came on him,
and he proclaimed his poem:
> The oracle of Balaam son of Beor,
> the oracle of the man
>   whose eyes are opened,
> the oracle of one who hears
>   the sayings of God,
> who sees a vision
>   from the Almighty,
> who falls into a trance
>   with his eyes uncovered:
> How beautiful are your tents,
>   Jacob,
> your dwellings, Israel.
> They stretch out like river valleys,
> like gardens beside a stream,
> like aloes the LORD has planted,
> like cedars beside the water.
> Water will flow from his buckets,
> and his seed will be
>   by abundant water.
> His king will be greater
>   than Agag,
> and his kingdom will be exalted.
> God brought him out of Egypt;
> he is like the horns of a wild ox
>   for them.
> He will feed on enemy nations
> and gnaw their bones;
> he will strike them
>   with his arrows.
> He crouches, he lies down
>   like a lion
> or a lioness — who dares
>   to rouse him?
> Those who bless you
>   will be blessed,
> and those who curse you
>   will be cursed.

–*Numbers 24:1–9*

IN OTHER WORDS

Oracle is an odd word. One that might be more familiar to you is the word *prophecy*. These terms are used to describe a vision, a truth, a burden, or a word from God that is spoken by a person called an oracle or prophet. Prophets were messengers who were authorized to speak for God. Prophecies are often descriptions of what is to happen in the future. Many of the prophecies in the Bible have been coming true for thousands of years. When you read prophecies, you can be confident that God is unfolding history in his timing, and he will fulfill all prophecies! This is good news for those who believe God's ways. Take a moment to thank God for your future that he already knows.

Related Texts: Genesis 12:1–3; 22:15–18; 27:26–29; Deuteronomy 23:3–5; Joshua 13:22; 24:8–10; Revelation 2:12–14

While Israel was staying in the Acacia Grove, the people began to prostitute themselves with the women of Moab. The women invited them to the sacrifices for their gods, and the people ate and bowed in worship to their gods. So Israel aligned itself with Baal of Peor, and the LORD's anger burned against Israel. The LORD said to Moses, "Take all the leaders of the people and execute them in broad daylight before the LORD so that his burning anger may turn away from Israel."

So Moses told Israel's judges, "Kill each of the men who aligned themselves with Baal of Peor."
—Numbers 25:1–5

Flee sexual immorality! Every other sin a person commits is outside the body, but the person who is sexually immoral sins against his own body. Don't you know that your body is a temple of the Holy Spirit who is in you, whom you have from God? You are not your own, for you were bought at a price. So glorify God with your body.
—1 Corinthians 6:18–20

ONE-MINUTE MEMORY

"You are not your own, for you were bought at a price. So glorify God with your body" (1Co 6:19–20).

Related Texts: Deuteronomy 4:1–4; Joshua 22:16–20; Psalm 106:28–31; Hosea 9:10; 1 Corinthians 10:1–8

The LORD spoke to Moses, "Execute vengeance for the Israelites against the Midianites. After that, you will be gathered to your people."

So Moses spoke to the people, "Equip some of your men for war. They will go against Midian to inflict the LORD's vengeance on them. Send one thousand men to war from each Israelite tribe." So one thousand were recruited from each Israelite tribe out of the thousands in Israel — twelve thousand equipped for war. . . .

They waged war against Midian, as the LORD had commanded Moses, and killed every male. Along with the others slain by them, they killed the Midianite kings — Evi, Rekem, Zur, Hur, and Reba, the five kings of Midian. They also killed Balaam son of Beor with the sword. The Israelites took the Midianite women and their dependents captive, and they plundered all their cattle, flocks, and property. Then they burned all the cities where the Midianites lived, as well as all their encampments, . . .

Moses, the priest Eleazar, and all the leaders of the community went to meet them outside the camp. But Moses became furious with the officers, the commanders of thousands and commanders of hundreds, who were returning from the military campaign. "Have you let every female live?" he asked them. "Yet they are the ones who, at Balaam's advice, incited the Israelites to unfaithfulness against the LORD in the Peor incident, so that the plague came against the LORD's community.

–Numbers 31:1–5,7–10,13–16

DIG DEEPER

The battles that took place between Israel and other nations were necessary in order for the Israelites to occupy the promised land as God commanded. The victorious battles served as one way to prove that God was the only God.

The New Testament teaches Christians, "Do not repay anyone evil for evil. Give careful thought to do what is honorable in everyone's eyes. If possible, as far as it depends on you, live at peace with everyone" (Rm 12:17–18).

The key words to consider today are "if possible." It's tough not to fight and quarrel . . . but, accept the challenge of doing less of it today than you did yesterday—if possible. Then, celebrate your progress and your spiritual maturity.

Related Texts: Numbers 25; Deuteronomy 21:10–14; Joshua 13:16–22; Judges 6–8; Romans 12:16–21

This is the command — the statutes and ordinances — the LORD your God has commanded me to teach you, so that you may follow them in the land you are about to enter and possess. Do this so that you may fear the LORD your God all the days of your life by keeping all his statutes and commands I am giving you, your son, and your grandson, and so that you may have a long life. Listen, Israel, and be careful to follow them, so that you may prosper and multiply greatly, because the LORD, the God of your ancestors, has promised you a land flowing with milk and honey.

"Listen, Israel: The LORD our God, the LORD is one. Love the LORD your God with all your heart, with all your soul, and with all your strength. These words that I am giving you today are to be in your heart. Repeat them to your children. Talk about them when you sit in your house and when you walk along the road, when you lie down and when you get up. Bind them as a sign on your hand and let them be a symbol on your forehead. Write them on the doorposts of your house and on your city gates.

–Deuteronomy 6:1–9

I have seen a limit to all perfection, but your command is
  without limit.
How I love your instruction!
It is my meditation all day long.
–Psalm 119:96–97

HERE'S THE DEAL

If you've been reading the daily selections, you've probably noticed that God is serious when he commands us to love him and follow his instructions. Today's passage shows you the result of following him: "so that you may have a long life" (Dt 6:2). God's instructions were for you to live better and longer. That's worth underlining!

Think about this: if you built a house, you would know everything about it. You'd know the location of all the wires, the minor flaws, the strong areas, the depth of the foundation. You'd know it all! Then, with this knowledge, you could adequately inform the homeowners on how best to operate and live in their house. Right? You built it! This same principle works with God and his creations. God built you. He knows you the best—he knows your heart, thoughts, and plans. If you follow his instructions, you'll live life to its fullest. Thankfully, these instructions are in God's love-letter: the Bible.

It's your choice; you can either live the way you want and risk damaging your life, or you can live as God wants and celebrate life. Which sounds better to you?

Related Texts: Deuteronomy 10:12–16; 11:18–21; Psalm 1; 119; Proverbs 22:6; Mark 12:28–34; Luke 10:25–28; 1 John 5:1–4

Then Moses continued to speak these words to all Israel, saying, "I am now 120 years old; I can no longer act as your leader. The LORD has told me, 'You will not cross the Jordan.' The LORD your God is the one who will cross ahead of you. He will destroy these nations before you, and you will drive them out. Joshua is the one who will cross ahead of you, as the LORD has said. The LORD will deal with them as he did Sihon and Og, the kings of the Amorites, and their land when he destroyed them. The LORD will deliver them over to you, and you must do to them exactly as I have commanded you. Be strong and courageous; don't be terrified or afraid of them. For the LORD your God is the one who will go with you; he will not leave you or abandon you."

Moses then summoned Joshua and said to him in the sight of all Israel, "Be strong and courageous, for you will go with this people into the land the LORD swore to give to their ancestors. You will enable them to take possession of it. The LORD is the one who will go before you. He will be with you; he will not leave you or abandon you. Do not be afraid or discouraged."

Moses wrote down this law and gave it to the priests, the sons of Levi, who carried the ark of the LORD's covenant, and to all the elders of Israel.

—Deuteronomy 31:1–9

BIBLICAL BIO

Moses sent twelve spies into the promised land to evaluate the land's occupants. Joshua was one of the two spies who returned with a positive outlook and a strong faith that God would lead the Israelites into the promised land.

Joshua displayed confidence in God and leadership. He was such a strong leader that God appointed him to replace Moses. His leadership proved capable as he conquered enemies and led the Israelites into their inheritance.

Joshua's faithfulness allowed him to be used to fulfill God's prophecy and promise. There's that word again: faithfulness.

Does that come close to describing you?

Related Texts: Numbers 21:21–35; Deuteronomy 2:24–3:17; 1 Kings 8:54– 57; Hebrews 13:5–6

After the death of Moses the Lord's servant, the Lord spoke to Joshua son of Nun, Moses's assistant: "Moses my servant is dead. Now you and all the people prepare to cross over the Jordan to the land I am giving the Israelites. I have given you every place where the sole of your foot treads, just as I promised Moses. Your territory will be from the wilderness and Lebanon to the great river, the Euphrates River — all the land of the Hittites — and west to the Mediterranean Sea. No one will be able to stand against you as long as you live. I will be with you, just as I was with Moses. I will not leave you or abandon you.

"Be strong and courageous, for you will distribute the land I swore to their ancestors to give them as an inheritance. Above all, be strong and very courageous to observe carefully the whole instruction my servant Moses commanded you. Do not turn from it to the right or the left, so that you will have success wherever you go. This book of instruction must not depart from your mouth; you are to meditate on it day and night so that you may carefully observe everything written in it. For then you will prosper and succeed in whatever you do. Haven't I commanded you: be strong and courageous? Do not be afraid or discouraged, for the Lord your God is with you wherever you go."

—Joshua 1:1–9

BIG TIME WORD

It's an easy choice to be a coward and hide your feelings and beliefs and simply go along with the crowd. Being courageous is tough! Courageous people stand their ground and accept comments directed at them. They are willing to say "no," even when all their friends are saying "yes."

Courageous people aren't afraid of the jeers, laughter, or put-downs they might receive. If you're courageous, it doesn't mean you enjoy the attacks; rather, you aren't afraid of receiving them.

Being a follower of Jesus, in today's world, takes courage. If that doesn't describe you, give it a shot today and try standing up for what you believe is right.

Related Texts: Deuteronomy 11:22–25; Psalms 1; 19; 119; 1 Corinthians 16:13–14; Hebrews 3:1–6

J oshua son of Nun secretly sent two men as spies from the Acacia Grove, saying, "Go and scout the land, especially Jericho." So they left, and they came to the house of a prostitute named Rahab, and stayed there.

The king of Jericho was told, "Look, some of the Israelite men have come here tonight to investigate the land." Then the king of Jericho sent word to Rahab and said, "Bring out the men who came to you and entered your house, for they came to investigate the entire land."

But the woman had taken the two men and hidden them. So she said, "Yes, the men did come to me, but I didn't know where they were from. At nightfall, when the city gate was about to close, the men went out, and I don't know where they were going. Chase after them quickly, and you can catch up with them!" But she had taken them up to the roof and hidden them among the stalks of flax that she had arranged on the roof....

So the two men went into the hill country and stayed there three days until the pursuers had returned. They searched all along the way, but did not find them. Then the men returned, came down from the hill country, and crossed the Jordan. They went to Joshua son of Nun and reported everything that had happened to them. They told Joshua, "The LORD has handed over the entire land to us. Everyone who lives in the land is also panicking because of us."

—Joshua 2:1–6,22–24

JUST A THOUGHT

If God is willing to use a prostitute to help others, don't you think he can use you to do great things as well?

Related Texts: Matthew 1:1–6; Hebrews 11:31; James 2:25

Now Jericho was strongly fortified because of the Israelites — no one leaving or entering. The LORD said to Joshua, "Look, I have handed Jericho, its king, and its best soldiers over to you. March around the city with all the men of war, circling the city one time. Do this for six days. Have seven priests carry seven ram's-horn trumpets in front of the ark. But on the seventh day, march around the city seven times, while the priests blow the ram's horns. When there is a prolonged blast of the horn and you hear its sound, have all the troops give a mighty shout. Then the city wall will collapse, and the troops will advance, each man straight ahead." . . .

So the troops shouted, and the ram's horns sounded. When they heard the blast of the ram's horn, the troops gave a great shout, and the wall collapsed. The troops advanced into the city, each man straight ahead, and they captured the city. They completely destroyed everything in the city with the sword — every man and woman, both young and old, and every ox, sheep, and donkey. . . .

However, Joshua spared Rahab the prostitute, her father's family, and all who belonged to her, because she hid the messengers Joshua had sent to spy on Jericho, and she still lives in Israel today.

—Joshua 6:1–5,20–21,25

HERE'S THE DEAL

This story of how God wanted Israel to attack Jericho reveals that God's plans are often different from ours. It's good to be reminded of that truth!

Imagine the Israelites' military headquarters. The trained soldiers were reviewing their plan on how to conquer Jericho. In walks Joshua—their leader. He proceeds to tell them to scrap the logical attack plans and instead march around the city, play their trumpets, and shout loudly so the city walls will crumble. Can you imagine the soldiers' response? "Yeah, right, Joshua. What drugs have you been taking?" His plan would have seemed ridiculous if God wasn't in control.

When God is in charge of your life, you may find his ways and plans are different from yours. Next time you're faced with a problem, ask God to reveal his plan to you. And don't be surprised if his plan doesn't happen as you thought it would. Go grab your trumpet and get ready for God to work in your life!

Related Texts: Numbers 10:1–10; Judges 7:1–22; Matthew 1:1–6

Just as the LORD had commanded his servant Moses, Moses commanded Joshua. That is what Joshua did, leaving nothing undone of all that the LORD had commanded Moses.

So Joshua took all this land — the hill country, all the Negev, all the land of Goshen, the foothills, the Arabah, and the hill country of Israel with its foothills — from Mount Halak, which ascends to Seir, as far as Baal-gad in the Valley of Lebanon at the foot of Mount Hermon. He captured all their kings and struck them down, putting them to death. Joshua waged war with all these kings for a long time. No city made peace with the Israelites except the Hivites who inhabited Gibeon; all of them were taken in battle. For it was the LORD's intention to harden their hearts, so that they would engage Israel in battle, be completely destroyed without mercy, and be annihilated, just as the LORD had commanded Moses. . . .

So Joshua took the entire land, in keeping with all that the LORD had told Moses. Joshua then gave it as an inheritance to Israel according to their tribal allotments. After this, the land had rest from war.

—Joshua 11:15–20,23

TAKE A SHOT

The Israelites went through a lot of pain, suffering, wandering, and disobedience before reaching the promise land. God proved himself faithful by fulfilling his promise to the Israelites. He brought them into their inheritance!

God is faithful! Does God's faithfulness mean anything to you? If yes, what does it mean? Can God rely on your faithfulness?

Related Texts: Deuteronomy 7; 9:1–6; 18:9–14; 20:16–18; Joshua 7–10

Therefore, fear the LORD and worship him in sincerity and truth. Get rid of the gods your ancestors worshiped beyond the Euphrates River and in Egypt, and worship the LORD. But if it doesn't please you to worship the LORD, choose for yourselves today: Which will you worship — the gods your ancestors worshiped beyond the Euphrates River or the gods of the Amorites in whose land you are living? As for me and my family, we will worship the LORD."

The people replied, "We will certainly not abandon the LORD to worship other gods! For the LORD our God brought us and our ancestors out of the land of Egypt, out of the place of slavery, and performed these great signs before our eyes. He also protected us all along the way we went and among all the peoples whose lands we traveled through. The LORD drove out before us all the peoples, including the Amorites who lived in the land. We too will worship the LORD, because he is our God."

But Joshua told the people, "You will not be able to worship the LORD, because he is a holy God. He is a jealous God; he will not forgive your transgressions and sins. If you abandon the LORD and worship foreign gods, he will turn against you, harm you, and completely destroy you, after he has been good to you."

"No!" the people answered Joshua. "We will worship the LORD."

—Joshua 24:14–21

HERE'S THE DEAL

Before he died, Joshua repeatedly challenged the Israelites to turn from their idols and love God. Doesn't it seem strange for the Israelites to continue to worship idols and other gods after all they had seen God do for them? Talk about short-term memory loss!

Do you ever act like the Israelites? You probably do—everyone does! God has done a lot for you. He sent Jesus to die in your place. What more could he do? And yet unfaithfulness creeps in when you turn your back on him and make other "gods" higher priorities. You can point to the Israelites and say, "How could they be so stupid?" Unfortunately, they might be able to make the same comments about your unfaithfulness.

Don't allow the day to end without taking a reflective journey of your own faith and commitment to God. God has proven himself to be faithful over and over. Can you say the same thing the Israelites eventually said: "We will worship the LORD" (Jos 24:21)? If so, tell God your desire right now.

Related Texts: Exodus 24:3–8; Leviticus 26; Romans 6; Hebrews 3–4

The he people worshiped the LORD throughout Joshua's lifetime and during the lifetimes of the elders who outlived Joshua. They had seen all the LORD's great works he had done for Israel.

Joshua son of Nun, the servant of the LORD, died at the age of 110. They buried him in the territory of his inheritance, in Timnath-heres, in the hill country of Ephraim, north of Mount Gaash. That whole generation was also gathered to their ancestors. After them another generation rose up who did not know the LORD or the works he had done for Israel.

The Israelites did what was evil in the LORD's sight. They worshiped the Baals ...

The LORD's anger burned against Israel, and he handed them over to marauders who raided them. He sold them to the enemies around them, and they could no longer resist their enemies ...

The LORD raised up judges, who saved them from the power of their marauders, ...Whenever the LORD raised up a judge for the Israelites, the LORD was with him and saved the people from the power of their enemies while the judge was still alive. The LORD was moved to pity whenever they groaned because of those who were oppressing and afflicting them. Whenever the judge died, the Israelites would act even more corruptly than their ancestors, following other gods to serve them and bow in worship to them. They did not turn from their evil practices or their obstinate ways.
—*Judges 2:7–11,14,16,18–19*

IN OTHER WORDS

During Old Testament times, judges were very different from today's court judges. Old Testament judges were appointed by God to lead the Israelites after they occupied the promised land. They judged disputes and provided spiritual and military leadership.

Even though the Israelites had a designated person to act as judge, God was and is the ultimate and only qualified true Judge. It's written in Jms 4:12: "There is one lawgiver and judge who is able to save and to destroy. But who are you to judge your neighbor?"

Stop playing judge of others today and see if it makes any difference in your life. It's best to let God play that role.

You won't miss anything if you stop judging.

Related Texts: Deuteronomy 4:1–10; 11:18–25; Judges 2:19–3:31; Psalm 78:1–6; Ephesians 2:1–10

The Israelites again did what was evil in the sight of the LORD after Ehud had died. So the LORD sold them to King Jabin of Canaan, who reigned in Hazor. The commander of his army was Sisera who lived in Harosheth of the Nations. Then the Israelites cried out to the LORD, because Jabin had nine hundred iron chariots, and he harshly oppressed them twenty years.

Deborah, a prophetess and the wife of Lappidoth, was judging Israel at that time. She would sit under the palm tree of Deborah between Ramah and Bethel in the hill country of Ephraim, and the Israelites went up to her to settle disputes.

She summoned Barak son of Abinoam from Kedesh in Naphtali and said to him, "Hasn't the LORD, the God of Israel, commanded you, 'Go, deploy the troops on Mount Tabor, and take with you ten thousand men from the Naphtalites and Zebulunites? Then I will lure Sisera commander of Jabin's army, his chariots, and his infantry at the Wadi Kishon to fight against you, and I will hand him over to you.'"

Barak said to her, "If you will go with me, I will go. But if you will not go with me, I will not go."

"I will gladly go with you," she said, "but you will receive no honor on the road you are about to take, because the LORD will sell Sisera to a woman."

—Judges 4:1–9

BIBLICAL BIO

Deborah was a judge who is best known for leading a victorious battle over Sisera. Prior to this battle she was confident that God had already planned and prepared the victory. When she told one of her military leaders to begin the battle, he requested her presence by saying, "If you will go with me, I will go" (Jdg 4:8).

Deborah's faith in God gave her the confidence to say: "Go! This is the day the LORD has handed Sisera over to you" (4:14). Deborah is another example of someone who possessed faithfulness and confidence that God is who he claims to be.

How might you be more confident that God will provide for you?

_____

_____

_____

_____

_____

_____

_____

_____

_____

_____

_____

_____

_____

_____

_____

_____

Related Texts: Exodus 15:19–21;
Judges 5:1–12; 2 Kings 22:11–20;
2 Chronicles 34:19–28; Luke 2:21–38

Then Deborah said to Barak, "Go! This is the day the LORD has handed Sisera over to you. Hasn't the LORD gone before you?" So Barak came down from Mount Tabor with ten thousand men following him.

The LORD threw Sisera, all his charioteers, and all his army into a panic before Barak's assault. Sisera left his chariot and fled on foot. Barak pursued the chariots and the army as far as Harosheth of the Nations, and the whole army of Sisera fell by the sword; not a single man was left.

Meanwhile, Sisera had fled on foot to the tent of Jael, the wife of Heber the Kenite, because there was peace between King Jabin of Hazor and the family of Heber the Kenite. Jael went out to greet Sisera and said to him, "Come in, my lord. Come in with me. Don't be afraid." So he went into her tent, and she covered him with a blanket. He said to her, "Please give me a little water to drink for I am thirsty." She opened a container of milk, gave him a drink, and covered him again. Then he said to her, "Stand at the entrance to the tent. If a man comes and asks you, 'Is there a man here?' say, 'No.'" While he was sleeping from exhaustion, Heber's wife, Jael, took a tent peg, grabbed a hammer, and went silently to Sisera. She hammered the peg into his temple and drove it into the ground, and he died.

—Judges 4:14–21

WEIRD OR WHAT?

Even though the Israelites had several different judges over the years, they experienced similar results during the time of each judge. These can be seen in five stages:

Stage 1: ***Sin***—the Israelites returned to worship idols and left God.

Stage 2: ***Oppression***—because of their sin, God allowed surrounding nations to rule over the Israelites.

Stage 3: ***Repent***—because of the oppression and pain, the Israelites would repent and turn back to God.

Stage 4: ***Saved***—after they repented, God would provide a judge to save them from the ruling nations.

Stage 5: ***Peace***—then there was a time of peace when the Israelites would worship God and stay out of trouble.

But, before long, the people would return to stage 1 and sin.

Do you have any destructive cycles that begin with sin? If so, is there anyone in your life who can help you break that cycle?

Related Texts: Judges 3:12–30; 5:13–31; 1 Samuel 12:8–11; Hebrews 11:32–34

The Israelites again did what was evil in the Lord's sight, so the Lord handed them over to the Philistines forty years. There was a certain man from Zorah, from the family of Dan, whose name was Manoah; his wife was unable to conceive and had no children. The angel of the Lord appeared to the woman and said to her, "Although you are unable to conceive and have no children, you will conceive and give birth to a son. Now please be careful not to drink wine or beer, or to eat anything unclean; for indeed, you will conceive and give birth to a son. You must never cut his hair, because the boy will be a Nazirite to God from birth, and he will begin to save Israel from the power of the Philistines." ...

So the woman gave birth to a son and named him Samson. The boy grew, and the Lord blessed him. Then the Spirit of the Lord began to stir him in the Camp of Dan, between Zorah and Eshtaol.

And he judged Israel twenty years in the days of the Philistines.

—Judges 13:1–5,24–25; 15:20

DIG DEEPER

When an angel appeared to Samson's mother and told her she was going to have a special son, it wasn't going to be the last time God used this technique to announce a unique birth. Hundreds of years later an angel told the virgin Mary that she was going to have a child unlike anyone the world had ever seen. God used Mary to bring his Son into this world:

"Then the angel told her, 'Do not be afraid, Mary, for you have found favor with God. Now listen: You will conceive and give birth to a son, and you will name him Jesus. He will be great and will be called the Son of the Most High, and the Lord God will give him the throne of his father David'" (Lk 1:30–32).

The world hasn't been the same since that historic moment. There's a big difference between Samson and Jesus. One was only a man; the other, the God-Man. Take a minute to thank God for choosing to enter the world. Because God arrived as a human being, he understands everything about your humanity!

Related Texts: Genesis 25:21–24; Numbers 6:1–21; Judges 14–15; Luke 1

Some time later, he fell in love with a woman named Delilah, who lived in the Sorek Valley. The Philistine leaders went to her and said, "Persuade him to tell you where his great strength comes from, so we can overpower him, tie him up, and make him helpless. Each of us will then give you 1,100 pieces of silver."

So Delilah said to Samson, "Please tell me, where does your great strength come from? How could someone tie you up and make you helpless?"

Samson told her, "If they tie me up with seven fresh bowstrings that have not been dried, I will become weak and be like any other man."

The Philistine leaders brought her seven fresh bowstrings that had not been dried, and she tied him up with them. While the men in ambush were waiting in her room, she called out to him, "Samson, the Philistines are here!" But he snapped the bowstrings as a strand of yarn snaps when it touches fire. The secret of his strength remained unknown.

—Judges 16:4–9

BIBLICAL BIO

Samson is known for being a man with great strength and unique abilities. Why God chose to bless his strength by the length of his hair is a wild mystery. But it's not unique that God chooses to work in strange ways—it's seen several times in the Bible.

As you read today and will read tomorrow, Samson hung out with and confided in the wrong person. Delilah broke his trust, and it resulted in Samson losing his hair, his strength, and his leadership.

Samson's life can provide a powerful learning example. God gave him many gifts that came with a potential for greatness. But Samson made bad decisions and aligned himself with the wrong people. Think about your life for a minute—who do you hang around and are they a positive influence or are they keeping you from using God's gift in your life? If so, you know the right decision to make.

Related Texts: Judges 14–15;
Proverbs 5; 6:20–7:27; 31:1–3;
2 Timothy 2:20–23

H ow can you say, 'I love you,'" she told him, "when your heart is not with me? This is the third time you have mocked me and not told me what makes your strength so great!"

Because she nagged him day after day and pleaded with him until she wore him out, he told her the whole truth and said to her, "My hair has never been cut, because I am a Nazirite to God from birth. If I am shaved, my strength will leave me, and I will become weak and be like any other man."

When Delilah realized that he had told her the whole truth, she sent this message to the Philistine leaders: "Come one more time, for he has told me the whole truth." The Philistine leaders came to her and brought the silver with them.

Then she let him fall asleep on her lap and called a man to shave off the seven braids on his head. In this way, she made him helpless, and his strength left him. Then she cried, "Samson, the Philistines are here!" When he awoke from his sleep, he said, "I will escape as I did before and shake myself free." But he did not know that the LORD had left him.

The Philistines seized him and gouged out his eyes. They brought him down to Gaza and bound him with bronze shackles, and he was forced to grind grain in the prison.

—Judges 16:15–21

HERE'S THE DEAL

After reading about Delilah's manipulation, it sure doesn't seem as though the tactics have changed very much over a few thousand years. Her line is still famous: "If you love me you'll . . ." This obvious and manipulating line has caused a lot of pain over the years.

Unfortunately, the line may win for the manipulator, but the person who gives in usually loses. In Samson's case, he lost big time. You will lose too if you feel pressured to do something you don't want to do. If you ever hear this, "If you really love me you'll . . . steal for me . . . have sex with me . . lie for me . . . whatever," beware! True love for another person doesn't pursue selfish advantage. If someone really loves you, he or she will respect and honor your feelings. Being used is no fun.

Evaluate your relationships. Are you being used? Are you using anyone? What can you do to put a stop to it today?

Related Texts: Numbers 6:2–21; 30:1–2; Proverbs 11:13; 20:19; Ecclesiastes 5:4–6; Luke 12:47–48

N ow the Philistine leaders gathered together to offer a great sacrifice to their god Dagon. They rejoiced and said:

Our god has handed over
our enemy Samson to us.

When they were in good spirits, they said, "Bring Samson here to entertain us." So they brought Samson from prison, and he entertained them. They had him stand between the pillars.

Samson said to the young man who was leading him by the hand, "Lead me where I can feel the pillars supporting the temple, so I can lean against them." The temple was full of men and women; all the leaders of the Philistines were there, and about three thousand men and women were on the roof watching Samson entertain them. He called out to the LORD, "Lord GOD, please remember me. Strengthen me, God, just once more. With one act of vengeance, let me pay back the Philistines for my two eyes." Samson took hold of the two middle pillars supporting the temple and leaned against them, one on his right hand and the other on his left. Samson said, "Let me die with the Philistines." He pushed with all his might, and the temple fell on the leaders and all the people in it. And those he killed at his death were more than those he had killed in his life.

–Judges 16:23,25–30

WEIRD OR WHAT?

Samson is written about in the Bible more than any of the other judges, but he was the least likely of all judges to be morally qualified for his leadership position. Also, he was the only judge who didn't bring the Israelites any lasting relief from their painful and oppressed condition.

So why does Samson get so much attention? It's not known why there is so much more about Samson than Ibzan (Jdg 12:8–10), but it's good to know that God uses people who don't have it all together. Does that sound like you?

You're not perfect, but God can still do great things in and through your life.

Related Texts: Psalm 3; Isaiah 1:24;
Jeremiah 5:7–9,29; 9:9;
Hebrews 11:32–34

During the time of the judges, there was a famine in the land. A man left Bethlehem in Judah with his wife and two sons to stay in the territory of Moab for a while. The man's name was Elimelech, and his wife's name was Naomi. The names of his two sons were Mahlon and Chilion. They were Ephrathites from Bethlehem in Judah. They entered the fields of Moab and settled there. Naomi's husband, Elimelech, died, and she was left with her two sons. Her sons took Moabite women as their wives: one was named Orpah and the second was named Ruth. After they lived in Moab about ten years, both Mahlon and Chilion also died, and the woman was left without her two children and without her husband.

She and her daughters-in-law set out to return from the territory of Moab, because she had heard in Moab that the Lord had paid attention to his people's need by providing them food. She left the place where she had been living, accompanied by her two daughters-in-law, and traveled along the road leading back to the land of Judah.

Naomi said to them, "Each of you go back to your mother's home. May the Lord show kindness to you as you have shown to the dead and to me. . . .

But Ruth replied:
Don't plead with me
    to abandon you
or to return and not follow you.
For wherever you go, I will go,
and wherever you live,
    I will live;
your people will be my people,
and your God will be my God.
Where you die, I will die,
and there I will be buried.
May the Lord punish me,
and do so severely,
if anything but death
    separates you and me.
So Naomi came back from the territory of Moab with her daughter-in-law Ruth the Moabitess. They arrived in Bethlehem at the beginning of the barley harvest.

—Ruth 1:1–8,16–17,22

JUST A THOUGHT

Be on the lookout for God's reward in your life. He rewards faithfulness—loving him and expressing love to others.

Related Texts: 2 Samuel 3:14–16; Proverbs 20:6; Song of Songs 8:6–7; 1 Corinthians 13

Now Naomi had a relative on her husband's side. He was a prominent man of noble character from Elimelech's family. His name was Boaz.

Ruth the Moabitess asked Naomi, "Will you let me go into the fields and gather fallen grain behind someone with whom I find favor?"

Naomi answered her, "Go ahead, my daughter." So Ruth left and entered the field to gather grain behind the harvesters. She happened to be in the portion of the field belonging to Boaz, who was from Elimelech's family. . . .

Then Boaz said to Ruth, "Listen, my daughter. Don't go and gather grain in another field, and don't leave this one, but stay here close to my female servants. . . .

She fell facedown, bowed to the ground, and said to him, "Why have I found favor with you, so that you notice me, although I am a foreigner?"

Boaz answered her, "Everything you have done for your mother-in-law since your husband's death has been fully reported to me: how you left your father and mother and your native land, and how you came to a people you didn't previously know. May the LORD reward you for what you have done, and may you receive a full reward from the LORD God of Israel, under whose wings you have come for refuge."

—Ruth 2:1–3,8,10–12

WEIRD OR WHAT?

Gleaning was the term used when someone would gather food left from a harvest. Gleaners would follow the field workers and pick up dropped or leftover food. During Old Testament times, they made it a law that poor people and visiting travelers could glean the fallen food or grain. God always wanted provisions made for those who were less fortunate or didn't have the availability to own or buy.

God has given you many gifts and abilities that you could share with people in need. How can you distribute some of your excess to those who are not as fortunate as you? That's a big question—give it some serious thought.

Related Texts: Leviticus 25:25–27,49–50; Psalm 91; Jeremiah 32:6–14

Ruth's mother-in-law Naomi said to her, "My daughter, shouldn't I find rest for you, so that you will be taken care of? Now isn't Boaz our relative? Haven't you been working with his female servants? This evening he will be winnowing barley on the threshing floor. Wash, put on perfumed oil, and wear your best clothes. Go down to the threshing floor, but don't let the man know you are there until he has finished eating and drinking. When he lies down, notice the place where he's lying, go in and uncover his feet, and lie down. Then he will explain to you what you should do." ...

After Boaz ate, drank, and was in good spirits, he went to lie down at the end of the pile of barley, and she came secretly, uncovered his feet, and lay down.

At midnight, Boaz was startled, turned over, and there lying at his feet was a woman! So he asked, "Who are you?"

"I am Ruth, your servant," she replied. "Take me under your wing, for you are a family redeemer."

Then he said, "May the LORD bless you, my daughter. You have shown more kindness now than before, because you have not pursued younger men, whether rich or poor. Now don't be afraid, my daughter. I will do for you whatever you say, since all the people in my town know that you are a woman of noble character.

–Ruth 3:1–4,7–11

BIBLICAL BIO

As you can tell by your reading, Ruth was a true and loyal friend. She was unselfish and deeply committed to Naomi. She loved Naomi and enjoyed her company, and their relationship serves as a great example of biblical friendship.

As you read about Ruth and Naomi, you might think about your relationships and the commitments you and your friends make to one another. Is there depth beyond the fun you have together? Would a degree of pain devastate your relationships? Take an inventory of your friendships and see what you need from a friend and how you can become a better friend.

Related Texts: Genesis 38:8–10; Deuteronomy 25:5–10; Hebrews 13:4

Boaz said to the elders and all the people, "You are witnesses today that I am buying from Naomi everything that belonged to Elimelech, Chilion, and Mahlon. I have also acquired Ruth the Moabitess, Mahlon's widow, as my wife, to perpetuate the deceased man's name on his property, so that his name will not disappear among his relatives or from the gate of his hometown. You are witnesses today."

All the people who were at the city gate, including the elders, said, "We are witnesses. May the LORD make the woman who is entering your house like Rachel and Leah, who together built the house of Israel. May you be powerful in Ephrathah and your name well known in Bethlehem. May your house become like the house of Perez, the son Tamar bore to Judah, because of the offspring the LORD will give you by this young woman."

Boaz took Ruth and she became his wife. He slept with her, and the LORD granted conception to her, and she gave birth to a son. The women said to Naomi, "Blessed be the LORD, who has not left you without a family redeemer today. May his name become well known in Israel. He will renew your life and sustain you in your old age. Indeed, your daughter-in-law, who loves you and is better to you than seven sons, has given birth to him."

—Ruth 4:9–15

TAKE A SHOT

Ruth was a woman who expressed kindness. This quality of kindness is rare in today's world. List three specific acts of kindness you can do today to make a difference in someone's life.

1.

2.

3.

Related Texts: Genesis 29:31–30:4; 38; Micah 5:2; Matthew 1:1–6

What sign, then, are you going to do so that we may see and believe you? " they asked. "What are you going to perform? Our ancestors ate the manna in the wilderness, just as it is written: **He gave them bread from heaven to eat.**"

Jesus said to them, "Truly I tell you, Moses didn't give you the bread from heaven, but my Father gives you the true bread from heaven. For the bread of God is the one who comes down from heaven and gives life to the world."

Then they said, "Sir, give us this bread always."

"I am the bread of life," Jesus told them. "No one who comes to me will ever be hungry, and no one who believes in me will ever be thirsty again. But as I told you, you've seen me, and yet you do not believe. Everyone the Father gives me will come to me, and the one who comes to me I will never cast out. For I have come down from heaven, not to do my own will, but the will of him who sent me. This is the will of him who sent me: that I should lose none of those he has given me but should raise them up on the last day. For this is the will of my Father: that everyone who sees the Son and believes in him will have eternal life, and I will raise him up on the last day."

—John 6:30–40

IN OTHER WORDS

Eternal life is timeless and has no beginning and no end. Since God is eternal he created the earth and human beings—both of which have a beginning and an end.

Eternal life is the life with God after your life on earth ends. This life is promised to those who, by faith, believe Jesus's death on the cross paid for their sins and made them right with God. Those made right will experience eternal life with God and eternal life is longer than you could ever imagine.

The question for those who don't believe isn't, "How long is eternal?" Rather, "Doesn't eternal life in the presence of God sound a lot better than eternal life separated from God?" That would be hell!

What do you think?

Related Texts: Deuteronomy 8:2; Proverbs 30:7–9; John 6:25–59; 1 Corinthians 10:16–17; Revelation 2:17

Jesus spoke to them again: "I am the light of the world. Anyone who follows me will never walk in the darkness but will have the light of life." . . .

As he was passing by, he saw a man blind from birth. His disciples asked him, "Rabbi, who sinned, this man or his parents, that he was born blind?"

"Neither this man nor his parents sinned," Jesus answered. "This came about so that God's works might be displayed in him. We must do the works of him who sent me while it is day. Night is coming when no one can work. As long as I am in the world, I am the light of the world."

After he said these things he spit on the ground, made some mud from the saliva, and spread the mud on his eyes. "Go," he told him, "wash in the pool of Siloam" (which means "Sent"). So he left, washed, and came back seeing.

In him was life, and that life was the light of men. That light shines in the darkness, and yet the darkness did not overcome it.
—John 8:12; 9:1–7; 1:4–5

JUST A THOUGHT

Don't be blind to what God can do in and through your life. Here's a good principle to remember: You do the possible with faith so that God will do the impossible.

Related Texts: Psalm 27:1; John 1:1–14; 3:19–22; 12:44–46; 1 John 1:1–7; Revelation 21:2–27

Truly I tell you, anyone who doesn't enter the sheep pen by the gate but climbs in some other way is a thief and a robber. The one who enters by the gate is the shepherd of the sheep. The gatekeeper opens it for him, and the sheep hear his voice. He calls his own sheep by name and leads them out. When he has brought all his own outside, he goes ahead of them. The sheep follow him because they know his voice. They will never follow a stranger; instead they will run away from him, because they don't know the voice of strangers." Jesus gave them this figure of speech, but they did not understand what he was telling them.

Jesus said again, "Truly I tell you, I am the gate for the sheep. All who came before me are thieves and robbers, but the sheep didn't listen to them. I am the gate. If anyone enters by me, he will be saved and will come in and go out and find pasture. A thief comes only to steal and kill and destroy. I have come so that they may have life and have it in abundance.

—John 10:1–10

ONE MINUTE MEMORY

"A thief comes only to steal and kill and destroy. I have come so that they may have life and have it in abundance" (Jn 10:10).

Related Texts: Psalm 118:17–21; Matthew 7:13–14; 25:1–13; Luke 13:23–29; John 14

I am the good shepherd. The good shepherd lays down his life for the sheep. The hired hand, since he is not the shepherd and doesn't own the sheep, leaves them and runs away when he sees a wolf coming. The wolf then snatches and scatters them. This happens because he is a hired hand and doesn't care about the sheep.

"I am the good shepherd. I know my own, and my own know me, just as the Father knows me, and I know the Father. I lay down my life for the sheep. But I have other sheep that are not from this sheep pen; I must bring them also, and they will listen to my voice. Then there will be one flock, one shepherd. This is why the Father loves me, because I lay down my life so that I may take it up again. No one takes it from me, but I lay it down on my own. I have the right to lay it down, and I have the right to take it up again. I have received this command from my Father."

—John 10:11–18

He himself bore our sins in his body on the tree; so that, having died to sins, we might live for righteousness. **By his wounds you have been healed.** For you **were like sheep going astray,** but you have now returned to the Shepherd and Overseer of your souls.

—1 Peter 2:24–25

WEIRD OR WHAT?

There are many animals mentioned throughout the Bible. Sheep appear more frequently than any other animal—over seven hundred times.

So why do sheep get a lot of publicity in the Bible when they're not smart animals? Have you ever seen one doing tricks in a circus? No! They're dumb. They are helpless animals in need of a shepherd to lead them to their water and food. Wait! Maybe that's why they're mentioned a lot . . . because humans resemble sheep. Sometimes we're dumb and get ourselves into trouble and have a need for a shepherd. Jesus described himself as the good shepherd (Jn 10:11). He takes care of his sheep . . . that means ewe . . . which isn't baaaad news.

You're a whole lot smarter than sheep if you follow the shepherd today.

Related Texts: Psalm 23; Isaiah 40:10–11; Zechariah 11:4–17; Matthew 25:31–46; Luke 15:3–7; Hebrews 13:20–21

Now a man was sick, Lazarus from Bethany, the village of Mary and her sister Martha. Mary was the one who anointed the Lord with perfume and wiped his feet with her hair, and it was her brother Lazarus who was sick. So the sisters sent a message to him: "Lord, the one you love is sick."

When Jesus heard it, he said, "This sickness will not end in death but is for the glory of God, so that the Son of God may be glorified through it." . . .

When Jesus arrived, he found that Lazarus had already been in the tomb four days. . . .

Then Martha said to Jesus, "Lord, if you had been here, my brother wouldn't have died. Yet even now I know that whatever you ask from God, God will give you."

"Your brother will rise again," Jesus told her.

Martha said to him, "I know that he will rise again in the resurrection at the last day."

Jesus said to her, "I am the resurrection and the life. The one who believes in me, even if he dies, will live. Everyone who lives and believes in me will never die. Do you believe this?"

"Yes, Lord," she told him, "I believe you are the Messiah, the Son of God, who comes into the world." . . .

After he said this, he shouted with a loud voice, "Lazarus, come out!" The dead man came out bound hand and foot with linen strips and with his face wrapped in a cloth. Jesus said to them, "Unwrap him and let him go."
—John 11:1–4,17,21–27,43–44

IN OTHER WORDS

In today's reading you'll see the word *Messiah*. During Old Testament times people believed that God would send Israel a deliverer who would rule as king, restore the divided kingdom, and explain God's plan. This special person would be called the Messiah.

Today, Christians accept Jesus as God's Son and the promised Messiah. But during Jesus's time, people didn't believe he fit the prophesied description of the Messiah. Because of this, Jesus was charged with blasphemy, rejected by the Jewish leaders, and put to death by hanging on a cross.

Most present-day Jewish people still don't believe Jesus was the Messiah and are still waiting for the promised Messiah. How about you? What are you waiting for? Do you believe Jesus was who he claimed to be? God's Son? The Messiah? Or just another good teacher?

Related Texts: Deuteronomy 32:39; John 5:19–26; Romans 5–6; 2 Timothy 1:8–10; 1 John 1:1–3

Don't let your heart be troubled. Believe in God; believe also in me. In my Father's house are many rooms. If it were not so, would I have told you that I am going to prepare a place for you? If I go away and prepare a place for you, I will come again and take you to myself, so that where I am you may be also. You know the way to where I am going."

"Lord," Thomas said, "we don't know where you're going. How can we know the way?"

Jesus told him, "I am the way, the truth, and the life. No one comes to the Father except through me. If you know me, you will also know my Father. From now on you do know him and have seen him."

"Lord," said Philip, "show us the Father, and that's enough for us."

Jesus said to him, "Have I been among you all this time and you do not know me, Philip? The one who has seen me has seen the Father. How can you say, 'Show us the Father'?

—John 14:1–9

ONE-MINUTE MEMORY

"Jesus told him, 'I am the way, the truth, and the life. No one comes to the Father except through me'" (Jn 14:6).

Related Texts: Psalm 96; John 1:1–18; 3:13–16; Acts 4:12; Hebrews 10:19–22

I am the true vine, and my Father is the gardener. Every branch in me that does not produce fruit he removes, and he prunes every branch that produces fruit so that it will produce more fruit. You are already clean because of the word I have spoken to you. Remain in me, and I in you. Just as a branch is unable to produce fruit by itself unless it remains on the vine, neither can you unless you remain in me. I am the vine; you are the branches. The one who remains in me and I in him produces much fruit, because you can do nothing without me. If anyone does not remain in me, he is thrown aside like a branch and he withers. They gather them, throw them into the fire, and they are burned. If you remain in me and my words remain in you, ask whatever you want and it will be done for you. My Father is glorified by this: that you produce much fruit and prove to be my disciples.

"As the Father has loved me, I have also loved you. Remain in my love. If you keep my commands you will remain in my love, just as I have kept my Father's commands and remain in his love.

"I have told you these things so that my joy may be in you and your joy may be complete.

—John 15:1–11

BIG TIME WORD

In order to keep God's commandments, you must obey God's ways. The Bible is filled with incredible examples of people who obeyed God. Abraham obeyed God and as a result the Israelites, as unfaithful as they were, were God's special nation. All because Abraham obeyed. He wasn't perfect, but he sought after obedience.

God loves obedience. Obedience is living according to God's plans. God is delighted when you choose to obey him. Obedience is more than knowing the Bible; it's living every day by faith that God is ultimately in control and knows what's best for your life. That's obedience! Try pleasing God today by obeying one of his instructions.

Related Texts: Psalm 80:8–19; Isaiah 5:1–7; 27:2–6; Luke 6:43–45; Galatians 5:22–23; Colossians 1:3–12

There was a man from Ramathaim-zophim in the hill country of Ephraim. His name was Elkanah son of Jeroham, son of Elihu, son of Tohu, son of Zuph, an Ephraimite. He had two wives, the first named Hannah and the second Peninnah. Peninnah had children, but Hannah was childless. This man would go up from his town every year to worship and to sacrifice to the LORD of Armies at Shiloh, where Eli's two sons, Hophni and Phinehas, were the LORD's priests.

Whenever Elkanah offered a sacrifice, he always gave portions of the meat to his wife Peninnah and to each of her sons and daughters. But he gave a double portion to Hannah, for he loved her even though the LORD had kept her from conceiving. Her rival would taunt her severely just to provoke her, because the LORD had kept Hannah from conceiving. . . .

On one occasion, Hannah got up after they ate and drank at Shiloh. The priest Eli was sitting on a chair by the doorpost of the LORD's temple. Deeply hurt, Hannah prayed to the LORD and wept with many tears. Making a vow, she pleaded, "LORD of Armies, if you will take notice of your servant's affliction, remember and not forget me, and give your servant a son, I will give him to the LORD all the days of his life, and his hair will never be cut."

−1 Samuel 1:1−6,9−11

TAKE A SHOT

Hannah asked God for something that seemed impossible. Write one prayer request that might seem impossible for God to answer. Let God know the desires within your heart.

It seems impossible, but, God, please . . .

Related Texts: Genesis 11:29−30; 25:21; 29:31; Psalm 113:9; Isaiah 54:1; Luke 1:4−22; 23:28−30; Hebrews 11:11

The next morning Elkanah and Hannah got up early to worship before the LORD. Afterward, they returned home to Ramah. Then Elkanah was intimate with his wife Hannah, and the LORD remembered her. After some time, Hannah conceived and gave birth to a son. She named him Samuel, because she said, "I requested him from the LORD."

When Elkanah and all his household went up to make the annual sacrifice and his vow offering to the LORD, Hannah did not go and explained to her husband, "After the child is weaned, I'll take him to appear in the LORD's presence and to stay there permanently." ...

"Do what you think is best, and stay here until you've weaned him. May the LORD confirm your word." So Hannah stayed there and nursed her son until she weaned him. When she had weaned him, she took him with her to Shiloh, as well as a three-year-old bull, half a bushel of flour, and a clay jar of wine. Though the boy was still young, she took him to the LORD's house at Shiloh. Then they slaughtered the bull and brought the boy to Eli.

"Please, my lord," she said, "as surely as you live, my lord, I am the woman who stood here beside you praying to the LORD. I prayed for this boy, and since the LORD gave me what I asked him for, I now give the boy to the LORD. For as long as he lives, he is given to the LORD." Then he worshiped the LORD there.

—1 Samuel 1:19–22,23–28

TAKE A SHOT

It's not uncommon to ask God for something and then not thank him for answering the prayer. Hannah expressed her thankfulness by giving Samuel back to God for his service.

If any of your prayers have been answered, thank God for hearing your prayers and responding. Express your thanksgiving in a letter to God.

Dear God:

Related Texts: Genesis 8:1; 19:29; 30:22; Exodus 2:24; Luke 1:23–45; Acts 10:25–31; Revelation 16:19; 18:5

Eli's sons were wicked men; they did not respect the LORD ...

Samuel served in the LORD's presence — this mere boy was dressed in the linen ephod. Each year his mother made him a little robe and took it to him when she went with her husband to offer the annual sacrifice. Eli would bless Elkanah and his wife: "May the LORD give you children by this woman in place of the one she has given to the LORD." Then they would go home.

The LORD paid attention to Hannah's need, and she conceived and gave birth to three sons and two daughters. Meanwhile, the boy Samuel grew up in the presence of the LORD....

Samuel grew. The LORD was with him, and he fulfilled everything Samuel prophesied. All Israel from Dan to Beer-sheba knew that Samuel was a confirmed prophet of the LORD. The LORD continued to appear in Shiloh, because there he revealed himself to Samuel by his word....

Samuel judged Israel throughout his life. Every year he would go on a circuit to Bethel, Gilgal, and Mizpah and would judge Israel at all these locations. Then he would return to Ramah because his home was there, he judged Israel there, and he built an altar to the LORD there.

−1 Samuel 2:12,18−21;
3:19−21; 7:15−17

JUST A THOUGHT

You're never too young to love God and learn to grow up in his ways.

Related Texts: Genesis 4:25−26;
Deuteronomy 18:15−19; Joshua 21:45;
Luke 1:13−17

When Samuel grew old, he appointed his sons as judges over Israel. His firstborn son's name was Joel and his second was Abijah. They were judges in Beer-sheba. However, his sons did not walk in his ways — they turned toward dishonest profit, took bribes, and perverted justice.

So all the elders of Israel gathered together and went to Samuel at Ramah. They said to him, "Look, you are old, and your sons do not walk in your ways. Therefore, appoint a king to judge us the same as all the other nations have."

When they said, "Give us a king to judge us," Samuel considered their demand wrong, so he prayed to the LORD. But the LORD told him, "Listen to the people and everything they say to you. They have not rejected you; they have rejected me as their king. They are doing the same thing to you that they have done to me, since the day I brought them out of Egypt until this day, abandoning me and worshiping other gods. Listen to them, but solemnly warn them and tell them about the customary rights of the king who will reign over them."

Samuel told all the LORD's words to the people who were asking him for a king. . . .

The people refused to listen to Samuel. "No!" they said. "We must have a king over us. Then we'll be like all the other nations: our king will judge us, go out before us, and fight our battles."

Samuel listened to all the people's words and then repeated them to the LORD. "Listen to them," the LORD told Samuel. "Appoint a king for them."

–1 Samuel 8:1–10,19–22

HERE'S THE DEAL

Samuel's sons seem to do what so many others do. They fail to follow God's ways. Taking bribes and gaining from others in a dishonest way not only reveals a sinful heart but, more specifically, a greedy heart.

Throughout the Bible the display of greed is seen as an action that hurts people and keeps one from pursing godliness. Greed takes one's eyes off of God and puts them on the object of the greed. For example, if you are greedy for money, you will think more about money and how to get it than you will think about God. Obviously, God would find something wrong with that.

Right now, identify the object of your greed. Really! Pause and think about what you're typically greedy for. Do you have it in your mind? Good. Now, take a minute to consider its value in comparison to eternity with God. The object of your greed will eventually burn on earth. No matter how great it is now, it's not worth taking your eyes off God. The real value is in being right with God. Don't let greed get in your way and become another story like Samuel's sons.

Related Texts: Deuteronomy 17:14–20; 1 Samuel 8:11–18; Isaiah 9:6; Jeremiah 10:1–10; 1 Timothy 1:17

S amuel summoned the people to the LORD at Mizpah and said to the Israelites, "This is what the LORD, the God of Israel, says: 'I brought Israel out of Egypt, and I rescued you from the power of the Egyptians and all the kingdoms that were oppressing you.' But today you have rejected your God, who saves you from all your troubles and afflictions. You said to him, 'You must set a king over us.' Now therefore present yourselves before the LORD by your tribes and clans."

Samuel had all the tribes of Israel come forward, and the tribe of Benjamin was selected. Then he had the tribe of Benjamin come forward by its clans, and the Matrite clan was selected. Finally, Saul son of Kish was selected. But when they searched for him, they could not find him. They again inquired of the LORD, "Has the man come here yet?"

The LORD replied, "There he is, hidden among the supplies."

They ran and got him from there. When he stood among the people, he stood a head taller than anyone else. Samuel said to all the people, "Do you see the one the LORD has chosen? There is no one like him among the entire population."

And all the people shouted, "Long live the king!"

Samuel proclaimed to the people the rights of kingship. He wrote them on a scroll, which he placed in the presence of the LORD. Then Samuel sent all the people home.

—1 Samuel 10:17–25

BIBLICAL BIO

One of the many reasons that Samuel was unique was because he was the last of the judges and the first of the prophets. His mother, Hannah, asked God for a child and Samuel was her gift. His name actually means "asked of God."

As a young child, Samuel got the privilege of being in God's presence. It was obvious that God wanted to use him in great ways. Eli, a priest, was instrumental in helping Samuel learn God's standards.

It's great to see an example where God prepared a child to do his work. Consider this—you're never too young for God to begin working in your life. Spend a minute and ask God to send the right person to train and help you grow stronger in your faith.

Related Texts: Deuteronomy 17:14–20; 1 Samuel 9:1–10:16,21–24; John 12:12–15

S amuel told Saul, "The LORD sent me to anoint you as king over his people Israel. Now, listen to the words of the LORD. This is what the LORD of Armies says: 'I witnessed what the Amalekites did to the Israelites when they opposed them along the way as they were coming out of Egypt. Now go and attack the Amalekites and completely destroy everything they have. . . .'"

Then Saul struck down the Amalekites from Havilah all the way to Shur, which is next to Egypt. . . . Saul and the troops spared Agag, and the best of the sheep, goats, cattle, and choice animals, as well as the young rams and the best of everything else. They were not willing to destroy them, but they did destroy all the worthless and unwanted things.

Then the word of the LORD came to Samuel, "I regret that I made Saul king, for he has turned away from following me and has not carried out my instructions." . . .

When Samuel came to him, Saul said, "May the LORD bless you. I have carried out the LORD's instructions." . . .

Then Samuel said:
Does the LORD take pleasure
   in burnt offerings
   and sacrifices
as much as in obeying the LORD?

Look: to obey is better
   than sacrifice,
to pay attention is better
   than the fat of rams.
For rebellion is like the sin
   of divination,

and defiance is like wickedness
   and idolatry.
Because you have rejected
   the word of the LORD,
he has rejected you as king.
    −1 Samuel 15:1−3,7,9−11,
    13,22−23

HERE'S THE DEAL

God places a higher level of moral responsibility on Christian leaders. Don't miss this truth: God wants all his followers to live right and follow him, but he wants his leaders to be godly examples. God doesn't expect leaders to be perfect; he knows better. But God also knows that leaders are watched by followers; leadership demands responsibility. For example, Saul, who was chosen to be king and leader, lied to Samuel. This disobedience made God angry.

A strong leader will make attempts to live his/her life to obey and please God. If you are a leader in your youth group or church, be reminded that you are a model to others of what it looks like to follow Jesus with your life. Whether or not you like it, people judge Christianity by its leaders. God wants you to be a faithful leader today, and you're not too young to serve God with your life.

Related Texts: Exodus 17:8−16; Deuteronomy 25:17−19; Micah 6:6−8; Luke 16:10−13

The LORD said to Samuel, "How long are you going to mourn for Saul, since I have rejected him as king over Israel? Fill your horn with oil and go. I am sending you to Jesse of Bethlehem because I have selected for myself a king from his sons."...

When they arrived, Samuel saw Eliab and said, "Certainly the LORD's anointed one is here before him."

But the LORD said to Samuel, "Do not look at his appearance or his stature because I have rejected him. Humans do not see what the LORD sees, for humans see what is visible, but the LORD sees the heart."...

Then Jesse presented Shammah, but Samuel said, "The LORD hasn't chosen this one either." After Jesse presented seven of his sons to him, Samuel told Jesse, "The LORD hasn't chosen any of these." Samuel asked him, "Are these all the sons you have?"

"There is still the youngest," he answered, "but right now he's tending the sheep." Samuel told Jesse, "Send for him. We won't sit down to eat until he gets here." So Jesse sent for him. He had beautiful eyes and a healthy, handsome appearance.

Then the LORD said, "Anoint him, for he is the one." So Samuel took the horn of oil and anointed him in the presence of his brothers, and the Spirit of the LORD came powerfully on David from that day forward. Then Samuel set out and went to Ramah.

−1 Samuel 16:1,6−7,9−13

ONE-MINUTE MEMORY

"Humans do not see what the LORD sees, for humans sees what is visible, but the LORD sees the heart" (1Sm 16:7).

Related Texts: Psalm 78:70−72; Matthew 5:8; 12:33−35; Luke 6:43−45; Acts 13:21−23

The Philistines gathered their forces for war at Socoh in Judah and camped between Socoh and Azekah in Ephes-dammim. Saul and the men of Israel gathered and camped in the Valley of Elah; then they lined up in battle formation to face the Philistines.

The Philistines were standing on one hill, and the Israelites were standing on another hill with a ravine between them. Then a champion named Goliath, from Gath, came out from the Philistine camp. He was nine feet, nine inches tall and wore a bronze helmet and bronze scale armor that weighed one hundred twenty-five pounds. There was bronze armor on his shins, and a bronze javelin was slung between his shoulders. His spear shaft was like a weaver's beam, and the iron point of his spear weighed fifteen pounds. In addition, a shield-bearer was walking in front of him.

He stood and shouted to the Israelite battle formations, "Why do you come out to line up in battle formation?" He asked them, "Am I not a Philistine and are you not servants of Saul? Choose one of your men and have him come down against me. If he wins in a fight against me and kills me, we will be your servants. But if I win against him and kill him, then you will be our servants and serve us." Then the Philistine said, "I defy the ranks of Israel today. Send me a man so we can fight each other!" When Saul and all Israel heard these words from the Philistine, they lost their courage and were terrified.

—1 Samuel 17:1–11

WEIRD OR WHAT?

The armor that Goliath wore weighed more than David's entire body. David's victory over the giant is another example of how huge obstacles can be overcome when God is involved.

Related Texts: Numbers 13:26–33; Deuteronomy 11:22–25; Psalm 15; Proverbs 14:27; 15:33; 29:25

David said to Saul, "Don't let anyone be discouraged by him; your servant will go and fight this Philistine!"

But Saul replied, "You can't go fight this Philistine. You're just a youth, and he's been a warrior since he was young."

David answered Saul, "Your servant has been tending his father's sheep. Whenever a lion or a bear came and carried off a lamb from the flock, I went after it, struck it down, and rescued the lamb from its mouth. If it reared up against me, I would grab it by its fur, strike it down, and kill it. Your servant has killed lions and bears; this uncircumcised Philistine will be like one of them, for he has defied the armies of the living God." Then David said, "The LORD who rescued me from the paw of the lion and the paw of the bear will rescue me from the hand of this Philistine."

Saul said to David, "Go, and may the LORD be with you." . . .

Instead, he took his staff in his hand and chose five smooth stones from the wadi and put them in the pouch, in his shepherd's bag. Then, with his sling in his hand, he approached the Philistine.

−1 Samuel 17:32−37,40

DIG DEEPER

A lot of people want to tell students they are the church of tomorrow. They believe God will use you when you're older. Here's the problem with that statement: You're the church of today! God can and will use you right now! God never gives a command to follow him tomorrow or assigns a specific age for obedience. God has used young people (like David) in the past, and he will continue to use those who want to live for him. Check out what Paul told young Timothy: "Don't let anyone despise your youth, but set an example for the believers in speech, in conduct, in love, in faith, and in purity" (1Tm 4:12).

Your age may be a problem for some but not for God.

Thank him for your age and ask him to do something great with your life today.

Related Texts: Psalms 31:11−18; 97:10; 144; Ephesians 6:10−18; 1 Timothy 4:12

The Philistine came closer and closer to David, with the shield-bearer in front of him. When the Philistine looked and saw David, he despised him because he was just a youth, healthy and handsome. He said to David, "Am I a dog that you come against me with sticks?" Then he cursed David by his gods. . . .

David said to the Philistine, "You come against me with a sword, spear, and javelin, but I come against you in the name of the LORD of Armies, the God of the ranks of Israel — you have defied him. Today, the LORD will hand you over to me. Today, I'll strike you down, remove your head, and give the corpses of the Philistine camp to the birds of the sky and the wild creatures of the earth. Then all the world will know that Israel has a God, and this whole assembly will know that it is not by sword or by spear that the LORD saves, for the battle is the LORD's. He will hand you over to us."

When the Philistine started forward to attack him, David ran quickly to the battle line to meet the Philistine. David put his hand in the bag, took out a stone, slung it, and hit the Philistine on his forehead. The stone sank into his forehead, and he fell facedown to the ground.

—1 Samuel 17:41–43, 45–49

JUST A THOUGHT

A little stone with big faith can conquer a big giant with a little god.

Related Texts: 2 Samuel 21:15–22; Psalm 27; Hebrews 11:32–34

When David had finished speaking with Saul, Jonathan was bound to David in close friendship, and loved him as much as he loved himself. Saul kept David with him from that day on and did not let him return to his father's house.

Jonathan made a covenant with David because he loved him as much as himself. Then Jonathan removed the robe he was wearing and gave it to David, along with his military tunic, his sword, his bow, and his belt.

David marched out with the army and was successful in everything Saul sent him to do. Saul put him in command of the fighting men, which pleased all the people and Saul's servants as well.

As the troops were coming back, when David was returning from killing the Philistine, the women came out from all the cities of Israel to meet King Saul, singing and dancing with tambourines, with shouts of joy, and with three-stringed instruments. As they danced, the women sang:

Saul has killed his thousands,
but David his tens of thousands.

Saul was furious and resented this song. "They credited tens of thousands to David," he complained, "but they only credited me with thousands. What more can he have but the kingdom?" So Saul watched David jealously from that day forward.

—1 Samuel 18:1–9

BIBLICAL BIO

Jonathan was an example of loyalty. He was loyal to God and to his friends. His friendship with David is one of the great models for friendship found within the Bible. Jonathan's ultimate loyalty began with God, but because of his strong relationship with God, Jonathan was able to gain God's wisdom.

Jonathan is a great example for anyone to follow. He was unselfish and set a high standard for friendship. A friend like Jonathan is difficult to find. If you have a friend who isn't selfish and is loyal to you, be sure to express your appreciation today.

A loyal friendship is definitely worth fighting for!

Related Texts: Proverbs 27:4; Acts 5:12–19; 7:9–10; Romans 13:12–14; 2 Corinthians 11:2; Galatians 5:19–20

S aul ordered his son Jonathan and all his servants to kill David. But Saul's son Jonathan liked David very much, so he told him, "My father, Saul, intends to kill you. Be on your guard in the morning and hide in a secret place and stay there. I'll go out and stand beside my father in the field where you are and talk to him about you. When I see what he says, I'll tell you."

Jonathan spoke well of David to his father, Saul. He said to him, "The king should not sin against his servant David. He hasn't sinned against you; in fact, his actions have been a great advantage to you. He took his life in his hands when he struck down the Philistine, and the LORD brought about a great victory for all Israel. You saw it and rejoiced, so why would you sin against innocent blood by killing David for no reason?"

Saul listened to Jonathan's advice and swore an oath: "As surely as the LORD lives, David will not be killed." So Jonathan summoned David and told him all these words. Then Jonathan brought David to Saul, and he served him as he did before....

Now an evil spirit sent from the LORD came on Saul as he was sitting in his palace holding a spear. David was playing the lyre, and Saul tried to pin David to the wall with the spear. As the spear struck the wall, David eluded Saul, ran away, and escaped that night ...

—1 Samuel 19:1–7,9–10

TAKE A SHOT

List three qualities you look for in a friend. Next to each of the qualities, come up with an action plan of how you can improve those qualities in your own life. Be specific about what you need to do and when you're going to start working on them. If you expect those qualities in others, you should have them in your own life as well.

1.

2.

3.

*Related Texts: 1 Samuel 19–30;
Psalms 52; 54; 57; 59; James 1:13–15*

The Philistines fought against Israel, and Israel's men fled from them. Many were killed on Mount Gilboa. The Philistines pursued Saul and his sons and killed his sons Jonathan, Abinadab, and Malchishua. When the battle intensified against Saul, the archers spotted him and severely wounded him. Then Saul said to his armor-bearer, "Draw your sword and run me through with it, or these uncircumcised men will come and torture me." But his armor-bearer would not do it because he was terrified. Then Saul took his sword and fell on it. When his armor-bearer saw that Saul was dead, he also fell on his own sword and died. So Saul and his three sons died — his whole house died together.

When all the men of Israel in the valley saw that the army had fled and that Saul and his sons were dead, they abandoned their cities and fled. So the Philistines came and settled in them. . . .

Saul died for his unfaithfulness to the Lord because he did not keep the Lord's word. He even consulted a medium for guidance, but he did not inquire of the Lord. So the Lord put him to death and turned the kingdom over to David son of Jesse.

—1 Chronicles 10:1–7,13–14

JUST A THOUGHT

In Saul's situation, disobedience resulted in a quick death. What might be the consequences of disobedience in your life?

Related Texts: 1 Samuel 28; 31; 2 Samuel 1; 16:15–17:23; Matthew 27:1–5; Acts 16:22–28

When the king had settled into his palace and the LORD had given him rest on every side from all his enemies, the king said to the prophet Nathan, "Look, I am living in a cedar house while the ark of God sits inside tent curtains."

So Nathan told the king, "Go and do all that is on your mind, for the LORD is with you."

But that night the word of the LORD came to Nathan: . . .

"So now this is what you are to say to my servant David: 'This is what the LORD of Armies says: I took you from the pasture, from tending the flock, to be ruler over my people Israel. I have been with you wherever you have gone, and I have destroyed all your enemies before you. I will make a great name for you like that of the greatest on the earth. . . .

" 'The LORD declares to you: The LORD himself will make a house for you. When your time comes and you rest with your ancestors, I will raise up after you your descendant, who will come from your body, and I will establish his kingdom. He is the one who will build a house for my name, and I will establish the throne of his kingdom forever. I will be his father, and he will be my son. When he does wrong, I will discipline him with a rod of men and blows from mortals. But my faithful love will never leave him as it did when I removed it from Saul, whom I removed from before you. Your house and kingdom will endure before me forever, and your throne will be established forever.' "

—2 Samuel 7:1–4,8–9,11–16

IN OTHER WORDS

In today's reading you can see God promising great things through David's family. This is one of the prophesies that refers to the birth of Jesus. God promised that a great king would be born through David's family. This king would live forever and build an eternal kingdom. Sound familiar?

The Bible has recorded this specific prophecy through several different prophets and time periods. Hundreds of years later, God used Mary, who was from the family of David, to give birth to Jesus—the King. Prophecy fulfilled.

God's plans have worked out and will continue to work out as he intends. If you haven't done so already, take a minute to thank God for his unique plan related to your life and let him know you want to be a part of the eternal kingdom. He has room for you!

Related Texts: 1 Chronicles 17;
Psalms 2; 89; Jeremiah 33:14–26;
Romans 1:1–4

The LORD is my shepherd;
I have what I need.
He lets me lie down
    in green pastures;
he leads me beside quiet waters.
He renews my life;
he leads me along the right paths
for his name's sake.
Even when I go
    through the darkest valley,
I fear no danger,
for you are with me;
your rod and your staff —
    they comfort me.

You prepare a table before me
in the presence of my enemies;
you anoint my head with oil;
my cup overflows.
Only goodness and faithful love
    will pursue me
all the days of my life,
and I will dwell in the house
    of the LORD
as long as I live.

—Psalm 23:1–6

"I am the good shepherd. The
good shepherd lays down his life
for the sheep.

—John 10:11

TAKE A SHOT

Rewrite and paraphrase Psalm 23
in your own words. Personalize this
psalm by using specific examples of
how God is your Shepherd.

Related Texts: Isaiah 40:10–11;
Micah 5:2–5; Hebrews 13:20–21;
1 Peter 2:21–25; Revelation 7:15–17

In the spring when kings march out to war, David sent Joab with his officers and all Israel. They destroyed the Ammonites and besieged Rabbah, but David remained in Jerusalem.

One evening David got up from his bed and strolled around on the roof of the palace. From the roof he saw a woman bathing — a very beautiful woman. So David sent someone to inquire about her, and he said, "Isn't this Bathsheba, daughter of Eliam and wife of Uriah the Hethite?"

David sent messengers to get her, and when she came to him, he slept with her. Now she had just been purifying herself from her uncleanness. Afterward, she returned home. The woman conceived and sent word to inform David, "I am pregnant."

David sent orders to Joab: "Send me Uriah the Hethite." So Joab sent Uriah to David. When Uriah came to him, David asked how Joab and the troops were doing and how the war was going. Then he said to Uriah, "Go down to your house and wash your feet." So Uriah left the palace, and a gift from the king followed him. But Uriah slept at the door of the palace with all his master's servants; he did not go down to his house.

−2 Samuel 11:1−9

HERE'S THE DEAL

David was tempted when he saw Bathsheba taking a bath. Yikes! Most guys can understand this temptation. The sin in this event was not the temptation, rather it was acting upon the temptation. Then, David sinned again when he tried to cover up his first sin. He messed up big — and this was a guy who loved God!

It's not uncommon to be sexually tempted. Sex is everywhere, and it is tempting! But if you have trusted in Jesus, then the Holy Spirit dwells within you. Therefore, with the Holy Spirit's help, you can control your sexual urges. Even though David didn't control his, he could have. God knows you will be tempted, but with his help you can grow in self-control.

David was a great king, but he should have left the roof and ran from his temptation. He could have controlled this temptation, but he chose not to. God's enemy, the devil, uses temptation to take your eyes off God and put them on things that are pleasing to you. It's subtle and dangerous.

Today, be thinking of the tempting situations you may need to run from. And remember, God has given you the strength to have control over any temptation — it's your choice.

Related Texts: Deuteronomy 5:18; Job 31:1; Psalm 119:9−16; Proverbs 5−6; 1 Corinthians 6:9−11

The next morning David wrote a letter to Joab and sent it with Uriah. In the letter he wrote:

Put Uriah at the front of the fiercest fighting, then withdraw from him so that he is struck down and dies.

When Joab was besieging the city, he put Uriah in the place where he knew the best enemy soldiers were. Then the men of the city came out and attacked Joab, and some of the men from David's soldiers fell in battle; Uriah the Hethite also died. . . .

When Uriah's wife heard that her husband, Uriah, had died, she mourned for him. When the time of mourning ended, David had her brought to his house. She became his wife and bore him a son. However, the LORD considered what David had done to be evil.

−2 Samuel 11:14−17,26−27

David responded to Nathan, "I have sinned against the LORD."

Then Nathan replied to David, "And the LORD has taken away your sin; you will not die. However, because you treated the LORD with such contempt in this matter, the son born to you will die."

−2 Samuel 12:13−14

For the wages of sin is death, but the gift of God is eternal life in Christ Jesus our Lord.

−Romans 6:23

JUST A THOUGHT

Another way to consider sin is "the wrong use of a right thing."

Related Texts: Numbers 32:23; 2 Samuel 12:15−25; Proverbs 26:27; Matthew 1:1−6; Hebrews 13:4

Be gracious to me, God,
according to
your faithful love;
according to your abundant
compassion,
blot out my rebellion.
Completely wash away my guilt
and cleanse me from my sin.
For I am conscious of my rebellion,
and my sin is always before me.
Against you — you alone —
I have sinned
and done this evil in your sight.
So you are right
when you pass sentence;
you are blameless when you judge.
Indeed, I was guilty when I was born;
I was sinful when my mother
conceived me.

Surely you desire integrity
in the inner self,
and you teach me wisdom
deep within.
Purify me with hyssop,
and I will be clean;
wash me, and I will be
whiter than snow.
Let me hear joy and gladness;
let the bones you have crushed
rejoice.
Turn your face away from my sins
and blot out all my guilt.

God, create a clean heart for me
and renew a steadfast spirit
within me.
Do not banish me from your presence
or take your Holy Spirit from me.
Restore the joy of your salvation
to me,
and sustain me by giving me
a willing spirit.
Then I will teach the rebellious
your ways,
and sinners will return to you.
—*Psalm 51:1–13*

TAKE A SHOT

After reading David's prayer of forgiveness, write God a letter asking him to create in you a new and clean heart.

Related Texts: 2 Samuel 12; Psalm 32; Isaiah 40:28–31; Habakkuk 3:2; Titus 3:3–7

As the time approached for David to die, he ordered his son Solomon, "As for me, I am going the way of all of the earth. Be strong and be a man, and keep your obligation to the LORD your God to walk in his ways and to keep his statutes, commands, ordinances, and decrees. This is written in the law of Moses, so that you will have success in everything you do and wherever you turn, and so that the LORD will fulfill his promise that he made to me: 'If your sons take care to walk faithfully before me with all their heart and all their soul, you will never fail to have a man on the throne of Israel.'

—1 Kings 2:1–4

Solomon sat on the LORD's throne as king in place of his father David. He prospered, and all Israel obeyed him. All the leaders and the mighty men, and all of King David's sons as well, pledged their allegiance to King Solomon. The LORD highly exalted Solomon in the sight of all Israel and bestowed on him such royal majesty as had not been bestowed on any king over Israel before him.

—1 Chronicles 29:23–25

In all your ways know him, and he will make your paths straight.

—Proverbs 3:6

ONE MINUTE MEMORY

"In all your ways know him, and he will make your paths straight" (Pr 3:6).

Related Texts: 2 Samuel 7; 1 Kings 1; 1 Chronicles 17:23–29; Matthew 1:1–6; Luke 12:22–31

At Gibeon the LORD appeared to Solomon in a dream at night. God said, "Ask. What should I give you?"

And Solomon replied, "You have shown great and faithful love to your servant, my father David, because he walked before you in faithfulness, righteousness, and integrity. You have continued this great and faithful love for him by giving him a son to sit on his throne, as it is today.

"LORD my God, you have now made your servant king in my father David's place. Yet I am just a youth with no experience in leadership. Your servant is among your people you have chosen, a people too many to be numbered or counted. So give your servant a receptive heart to judge your people and to discern between good and evil. For who is able to judge this great people of yours?"

Now it pleased the Lord that Solomon had requested this. So God said to him, "Because you have requested this and did not ask for long life or riches for yourself, or the death of your enemies, but you asked discernment for yourself to administer justice, I will therefore do what you have asked. I will give you a wise and understanding heart, so that there has never been anyone like you before and never will be again. In addition, I will give you what you did not ask for: both riches and honor, so that no king will be your equal during your entire life. If you walk in my ways and keep my statutes and commands just as your father David did, I will give you a long life."

–1 Kings 3:5–14

BIG TIME WORD

Wisdom has nothing to do with your grade point average or your test scores. God told Solomon to ask for something, and Solomon asked for an obedient heart to judge and the ability to discern good from evil. He asked God for something that comes from God: wisdom. Another biblical word used for wisdom is *understanding*. Solomon needed an understanding mind in his role as king. Understanding is one of the essential elements of wisdom.

If you DON'T have wisdom, you'll . . .

- struggle between knowing right from wrong.
- follow the crowd rather than take the lead.
- be confused about what to do in and with your life.
- be unsure of God's plan for your life.
- conform to others' standards.

Ask God to give you his wisdom for the decisions you need to make today.

Related Texts: 1 Kings 3:16–28; 2 Chronicles 1:1–13; Proverbs 1–4; 8:10–21; James 1:5–8

Judah and Israel were as numerous as the sand by the sea; they were eating, drinking, and rejoicing. Solomon ruled all the kingdoms from the Euphrates River to the land of the Philistines and as far as the border of Egypt. They offered tribute and served Solomon all the days of his life. . . .

God gave Solomon wisdom, very great insight, and understanding as vast as the sand on the seashore. Solomon's wisdom was greater than the wisdom of all the people of the East, greater than all the wisdom of Egypt. He was wiser than anyone — wiser than Ethan the Ezrahite, and Heman, Calcol, and Darda, sons of Mahol. His reputation extended to all the surrounding nations.

Solomon spoke 3,000 proverbs, and his songs numbered 1,005. He spoke about trees, from the cedar in Lebanon to the hyssop growing out of the wall. He also spoke about animals, birds, reptiles, and fish. Emissaries of all peoples, sent by every king on earth who had heard of his wisdom, came to listen to Solomon's wisdom.

—1 Kings 4:20–21,29–34

WEIRD OR WHAT?

Did you know Solomon was a big-time multimillionaire? The Bible reveals that he received $250,000,000 worth of gold each year from the kings of Arabia. He also sold horses and exotic goods, as well as copper and bronze that were manufactured in his mines. He would be considered a very wealthy person in today's economy, so there's no question he was one of the richest men alive. But with all his wealth and fame, Solomon still asked God for wisdom. He knew money couldn't buy what God offered.

Try to live today without concern over your financial situation and ask God for the things that money can't buy—like wisdom.

Related Texts: 1 Kings 10:1–13; Psalm 72; Proverbs 13:10; 16:16; 23:23; Matthew 12:38–42

The proverbs of Solomon
    son of David, king of Israel:
For learning wisdom
    and discipline;
for understanding
    insightful sayings;
for receiving prudent instruction
in righteousness, justice,
    and integrity;
for teaching shrewdness
    to the inexperienced,
knowledge and discretion
    to a young man —
let a wise person listen
    and increase learning,
and let a discerning person
    obtain guidance —
for understanding a proverb
    or a parable,
the words of the wise,
    and their riddles.

The fear of the LORD
is the beginning of knowledge;
fools despise wisdom
    and discipline.

—Proverbs 1:1–7

As the crowds were increasing, he began saying, "This generation is an evil generation. It demands a sign, but no sign will be given to it except the sign of Jonah. For just as Jonah became a sign to the people of Nineveh, so also the Son of Man will be to this generation. The queen of the south will rise up at the judgment with the men of this generation and condemn them, because she came from the ends of the earth to hear the wisdom of Solomon, and look — something greater than Solomon is here.

—Luke 11:29–31

BIBLICAL BIO

Solomon was the son of David and Bathsheba. He followed his family line and became king of Israel. He had great wealth, wisdom, and respect. But he also had problems, as so many other biblical characters did. Though he appeared to have it all, he made some bad decisions by marrying ungodly women and allowing them to weaken his commitment to God.

Everyone lacks wisdom at times and must be ready to pay the consequences.

Try reading through the Proverbs and see if you can find any advice that could have helped Solomon with his relationships—there's a lot to find.

Related Texts: 2 Chronicles 9:1–12; Proverbs 10:1; 25:1; Song of Songs 1–8; Jonah 3; 1 Corinthians 12:1–11

A s a large crowd was gathering, and people were coming to Jesus from every town, he said in a parable, "A sower went out to sow his seed. As he sowed, some seed fell along the path; it was trampled on, and the birds of the sky devoured it. Other seed fell on the rock; when it grew up, it withered away, since it lacked moisture. Other seed fell among thorns; the thorns grew up with it and choked it. Still other seed fell on good ground; when it grew up, it produced fruit: a hundred times what was sown." As he said this, he called out, "Let anyone who has ears to hear listen."

Then his disciples asked him, "What does this parable mean?" So he said, "The secrets of the kingdom of God have been given for you to know, but to the rest it is in parables, so that

Looking they may not see, and hearing they may not understand.

—Luke 8:4–10

IN OTHER WORDS

A parable was usually a story or a verbal illustration. Jesus didn't have the technology of using a video presentation or media to make his message clearer. Instead, he told parables.

The parables are a great read! If you don't know any, you might read the parables of the good Samaritan (Lk 10:30–37), the lost coin (Lk 15:8–10), or the ten virgins (Mt 25:1–13). There are several more; check them out and allow the power of God's story to take root in your life so that you'll never forget his incredible message of love and salvation.

Related Texts: Psalm 126; Proverbs 11:18–21; Hosea 10:12–13; Matthew 13:1–17; Mark 4:1–12

This is the meaning of the parable: The seed is the word of God. The seed along the path are those who have heard and then the devil comes and takes away the word from their hearts, so that they may not believe and be saved. And the seed on the rock are those who, when they hear, receive the word with joy. Having no root, these believe for a while and fall away in a time of testing. As for the seed that fell among thorns, these are the ones who, when they have heard, go on their way and are choked with worries, riches, and pleasures of life, and produce no mature fruit. But the seed in the good ground — these are the ones who, having heard the word with an honest and good heart, hold on to it and by enduring, produce fruit.

"No one, after lighting a lamp, covers it with a basket or puts it under a bed, but puts it on a lampstand so that those who come in may see its light. For nothing is concealed that won't be revealed, and nothing hidden that won't be made known and brought to light. Therefore take care how you listen. For whoever has, more will be given to him; and whoever does not have, even what he thinks he has will be taken away from him."

—Luke 8:11–18

IN OTHER WORDS

The word *good* is easy to define. You've heard it a million times, and you know the meaning well. *News* is also a simple word that might be translated as "information." When these two words are put together, good news refers to the gospel — the good news of salvation in Jesus Christ, which we read about in the Bible.

The Bible is one of God's ways to communicate to you. It's his love letter written with you in mind. As you know, this book in your hands is filled with the good news, but it isn't the complete Bible. If you don't have a Bible, ask a friend, parent, or pastor to help get you one. It's one of the ways God chooses to speak to you. Open it, read it, and begin to see what God wants for your life. It's a lot like what you've been reading in this book, only more verses; and in this case, more is better.

Related Texts: Proverbs 11:30; Matthew 13:18–23; Mark 4:13–25; John 15:1–17; Galatians 6:7–10

He presented another parable to them: "The kingdom of heaven is like a mustard seed that a man took and sowed in his field. It's the smallest of all the seeds, but when grown, it's taller than the garden plants and becomes a tree, so that the birds of the sky come and nest in its branches."

He told them another parable: "The kingdom of heaven is like leaven that a woman took and mixed into fifty pounds of flour until all of it was leavened." . . .

"The kingdom of heaven is like treasure, buried in a field, that a man found and reburied. Then in his joy he goes and sells everything he has and buys that field.

"Again, the kingdom of heaven is like a merchant in search of fine pearls. When he found one priceless pearl, he went and sold everything he had and bought it.

"Again, the kingdom of heaven is like a large net thrown into the sea. It collected every kind of fish, and when it was full, they dragged it ashore, sat down, and gathered the good fish into containers, but threw out the worthless ones. So it will be at the end of the age. The angels will go out, separate the evil people from the righteous, and throw them into the blazing furnace, where there will be weeping and gnashing of teeth.

—Matthew 13:31–33,44–50

TAKE A SHOT

After reading today's selection, write what you believe heaven will be like.

Related Texts: Psalm 45:6; Mark 1:1– 15; 4:30–32; Luke 13:18–19

All the tax collectors and sinners were approaching to listen to him. And the Pharisees and scribes were complaining, "This man welcomes sinners and eats with them."

So he told them this parable: "What man among you, who has a hundred sheep and loses one of them, does not leave the ninety-nine in the open field and go after the lost one until he finds it? When he has found it, he joyfully puts it on his shoulders, and coming home, he calls his friends and neighbors together, saying to them, 'Rejoice with me, because I have found my lost sheep!' I tell you, in the same way, there will be more joy in heaven over one sinner who repents than over ninety-nine righteous people who don't need repentance.

"Or what woman who has ten silver coins, if she loses one coin, does not light a lamp, sweep the house, and search carefully until she finds it? When she finds it, she calls her friends and neighbors together, saying, 'Rejoice with me, because I have found the silver coin I lost!' I tell you, in the same way, there is joy in the presence of God's angels over one sinner who repents."

—Luke 15:1–10

JUST A THOUGHT

The sheep could return to the flock, the coin could be found, and you could return to the Father; and he would welcome you home with open arms.

Related Texts: Psalm 119:169–176; Matthew 18:12–14; Luke 9:22–26; 19:1–10

He also said, "A man had two sons. The younger of them said to his father, 'Father, give me the share of the estate I have coming to me.' So he distributed the assets to them. Not many days later, the younger son gathered together all he had and traveled to a distant country, where he squandered his estate in foolish living. After he had spent everything, a severe famine struck that country, and he had nothing. Then he went to work for one of the citizens of that country, who sent him into his fields to feed pigs. He longed to eat his fill from the pods that the pigs were eating, but no one would give him anything. When he came to his senses, he said, 'How many of my father's hired workers have more than enough food, and here I am dying of hunger! I'll get up, go to my father, and say to him, "Father, I have sinned against heaven and in your sight. I'm no longer worthy to be called your son. Make me like one of your hired workers."' So he got up and went to his father. But while the son was still a long way off, his father saw him and was filled with compassion. He ran, threw his arms around his neck, and kissed him. The son said to him, 'Father, I have sinned against heaven and in your sight. I'm no longer worthy to be called your son.'
—Luke 15:11–21

IN OTHER WORDS

The son goes his own way, blows all he was given, and then returns to his father's home with little hope of being hired for a job. But the story shifts when the father accepts him back, not as an employee but as his beloved son.

This parable is an incredible image of God's love for you. When you go your own way and turn your back on God, he is waiting to welcome you home. When you return home, God doesn't accept you as sinners—no! He forgives and brings you back as his son or daughter. Now that's an awesome God!

Right now, write in your notebook or on the palm of your hand something that will remind you of this truth all day—God loves you.

Related Texts: 2 Chronicles 7:13–14; Proverbs 17:6,21; Hosea 6:1–3; Acts 3:19–20

But the father told his servants, 'Quick! Bring out the best robe and put it on him; put a ring on his finger and sandals on his feet. Then bring the fattened calf and slaughter it, and let's celebrate with a feast, because this son of mine was dead and is alive again; he was lost and is found!' So they began to celebrate.

"Now his older son was in the field; as he came near the house, he heard music and dancing. So he summoned one of the servants, questioning what these things meant. 'Your brother is here,' he told him, 'and your father has slaughtered the fattened calf because he has him back safe and sound.'

"Then he became angry and didn't want to go in. So his father came out and pleaded with him. But he replied to his father, 'Look, I have been slaving many years for you, and I have never disobeyed your orders, yet you never gave me a goat so that I could celebrate with my friends. But when this son of yours came, who has devoured your assets with prostitutes, you slaughtered the fattened calf for him.'

" 'Son,' he said to him, 'you are always with me, and everything I have is yours. But we had to celebrate and rejoice, because this brother of yours was dead and is alive again; he was lost and is found.' "

—Luke 15:22–32

JUST A THOUGHT

If you're away from God and in need of a real party, return to him and he'll give you a celebration you'll never forget.

Related Texts: Isaiah 55:6–7; Matthew 18:12–14; Colossians 1:1–14; 1 Peter 2:24–25

King Hiram of Tyre sent his emissaries to Solomon when he heard that he had been anointed king in his father's place, for Hiram had always been friends with David.

Solomon sent this message to Hiram: "You know my father David was not able to build a temple for the name of the LORD his God. This was because of the warfare all around him until the LORD put his enemies under his feet. The LORD my God has now given me rest on every side; there is no enemy or misfortune. So I plan to build a temple for the name of the LORD my God, according to what the LORD promised my father David: 'I will put your son on your throne in your place, and he will build the temple for my name.'

"Therefore, command that cedars from Lebanon be cut down for me. My servants will be with your servants, and I will pay your servants' wages according to whatever you say, for you know that not a man among us knows how to cut timber like the Sidonians."

When Hiram heard Solomon's words, he rejoiced greatly and said, "Blessed be the LORD today! He has given David a wise son to be over this great people!"

—1 Kings 5:1–7

IN OTHER WORDS

Do you remember reading or hearing about the tabernacle? The tabernacle was a portable place of worship that traveled with the Israelites (prior to entering the promised land). The temple that Solomon built was like the tabernacle except it wasn't portable. The temple was a meeting place between God and his people where worship and sacrifice took place. The temple was not built to house or contain God. Solomon said: "But will God indeed live on earth? Even heaven, the highest heaven, cannot contain you, much less this temple I have built" (1 Kg 8:27).

Today, God is building a "holy temple" in the lives of his followers. What's the condition of your temple?

Related Texts: 1 Kings 5–9; 2 Chronicles 2–8; Psalm 127; Matthew 12:1–6; John 2:13–21; Ephesians 2:11–22

I, the Teacher, have been king over Israel in Jerusalem. I applied my mind to examine and explore through wisdom all that is done under heaven. God has given people this miserable task to keep them occupied. I have seen all the things that are done under the sun and have found everything to be futile, a pursuit of the wind.

—Ecclesiastes 1:12–14

There is an occasion
    for everything,
and a time for every activity
    under heaven:
a time to give birth and a time
    to die;
a time to plant and a time
    to uproot;
a time to kill and a time to heal;
a time to tear down and a time
    to build;
a time to weep and a time to laugh;
a time to mourn and a time
    to dance;
a time to throw stones and a time
    to gather stones;
a time to embrace and a time
    to avoid embracing;
a time to search and a time
    to count as lost;
a time to keep and a time
    to throw away;
a time to tear and a time to sew;
a time to be silent and a time
    to speak;
a time to love and a time to hate;
a time for war and a time
    for peace.

—Ecclesiastes 3:1–8

DIG DEEPER

Time has become a precious possession in today's world. We are a time-conscious society. Yet, we all have the same amount of time—twenty-four hours a day and God is in complete control of all time. He began the world in his timing, and he will return to take over the world in his timing. Because God is God, he knew exactly when to send Jesus to the world. Check out Gl 4:4–5: "When the time came to completion, God sent his Son, born of a woman, born under the law, to redeem those under the law, so that we might receive adoption as sons."

Take a minute to give God your time. Ask him to guide you on how you spend your time today.

Related Texts: Ecclesiastes 1:1–11; Galatians 4:4–5; 6:8–9; 1 Timothy 2:3–6; 1 Peter 5:5–6

Two are better than one because they have a good reward for their efforts. For if either falls, his companion can lift him up; but pity the one who falls without another to lift him up. Also, if two lie down together, they can keep warm; but how can one person alone keep warm? And if someone overpowers one person, two can resist him. A cord of three strands is not easily broken.

—Ecclesiastes 4:9–12

In addition to the Teacher being a wise man, he constantly taught the people knowledge; he weighed, explored, and arranged many proverbs. The Teacher sought to find delightful sayings and write words of truth accurately. The sayings of the wise are like cattle prods, and those from masters of collections are like firmly embedded nails. The sayings are given by one Shepherd.

But beyond these, my son, be warned: there is no end to the making of many books, and much study wearies the body. When all has been heard, the conclusion of the matter is this: fear God and keep his commands, because this is for all humanity. For God will bring every act to judgment, including every hidden thing, whether good or evil.

—Ecclesiastes 12:9–14

ONE-MINUTE MEMORY

"And if someone overpowers one person, two can resist him. A cord of three strands is not easily broken" (Ec 4:12).

Related Texts: 1 Samuel 20:24–42; Psalm 37; Proverbs 17:17; 27:6,10; 1 Corinthians 4:5; Revelation 20:11–15

King Solomon loved many foreign women in addition to Pharaoh's daughter: Moabite, Ammonite, Edomite, Sidonian, and Hittite women from the nations about which the LORD had told the Israelites, "You must not intermarry with them, and they must not intermarry with you, because they will turn your heart away to follow their gods." To these women Solomon was deeply attached in love . . . and they turned his heart away.

When Solomon was old, his wives turned his heart away to follow other gods. He was not wholeheartedly devoted to the LORD his God, as his father David had been. . . .

The LORD was angry with Solomon, because his heart had turned away from the LORD, the God of Israel, who had appeared to him twice. He had commanded him about this, so that he would not follow other gods, but Solomon did not do what the LORD had commanded.

Then the LORD said to Solomon, "Since you have done this and did not keep my covenant and my statutes, which I commanded you, I will tear the kingdom away from you and give it to your servant. However, I will not do it during your lifetime for the sake of your father David; I will tear it out of your son's hand. Yet I will not tear the entire kingdom away from him. I will give one tribe to your son for the sake of my servant David and for the sake of Jerusalem that I chose."

−1 Kings 11:1−2, 3−4, 9−13

WEIRD OR WHAT?

It seems weird that Solomon could be so wise and yet make such dumb mistakes. The law prohibited the king from acquiring many wives for himself (see Dt 17:17). But Solomon married many women from other nations in an attempt to gain the loyalty of those nations. These decisions turned out to be unwise and led Solomon to be disloyal to God.

Learn from Solomon's mistake. It's better to please God first and then others, rather than the other way around.

Take note and be wise today.

*Related Texts: Deuteronomy 7;
Ezra 9−10; Nehemiah 13:23−27;
1 Corinthians 7:39;
2 Corinthians 6:14−16*

The length of Solomon's reign in Jerusalem over all Israel totaled forty years. Solomon rested with his ancestors and was buried in the city of his father David. His son Rehoboam became king in his place. . . .

Then Rehoboam went to Shechem, for all Israel had gone to Shechem to make him king. When Jeroboam son of Nebat heard about it, he stayed in Egypt, where he had fled from King Solomon's presence. Jeroboam stayed in Egypt. But they summoned him, and Jeroboam and the whole assembly of Israel came and spoke to Rehoboam: "Your father made our yoke harsh. You, therefore, lighten your father's harsh service and the heavy yoke he put on us, and we will serve you."

So Jeroboam and all the people came to Rehoboam on the third day, as the king had ordered: "Return to me on the third day." Then the king answered the people harshly. He rejected the advice the elders had given him and spoke to them according to the young men's advice: "My father made your yoke heavy, but I will add to your yoke; my father disciplined you with whips, but I will discipline you with barbed whips." . . .

When all Israel saw that the king had not listened to them, the people answered him:

What portion do we have
    in David? . . .
No one followed the house of David except the tribe of Judah alone.

−1 Kings 11:42−12:4; 12−14,16,20

HERE'S THE DEAL

Rehoboam chose not to take the advice of the older men. Instead, he followed the advice of the younger men, and the results split the nation in half. Who knows how history might have been different if he had followed the older men.

An attractive quality in a person is their ability to take advice from others. When you are open to advice, you display humility and leadership.

If you have the opportunity to get advice, take it (especially if it's free). Always evaluate the advice against the Bible before you make your decisions—it's not good advice if it points you in a different direction than God.

If you can get advice from older people, take it quickly. Why? Because peers and friends may have a tendency to tell you what you want to hear. Actually, that's not even advice; it's confirmation of what you already know.

It's wise to realize that many people are quick to give advice but slow to take it. Try turning that around in your own life: Be slow to give advice and quick to receive it.

Related Texts: 1 Kings 11:26−40;
2 Chronicles 9:29−10:19; Proverbs 15:1

Jeroboam built Shechem in the hill country of Ephraim and lived there. From there he went out and built Penuel. Jeroboam said to himself, "The kingdom might now return to the house of David. If these people regularly go to offer sacrifices in the LORD's temple in Jerusalem, the heart of these people will return to their lord, King Rehoboam of Judah. They will kill me and go back to the king of Judah." So the king sought advice.

Then he made two golden calves, and he said to the people, "Going to Jerusalem is too difficult for you. Israel, here are your gods who brought you up from the land of Egypt." He set up one in Bethel, and put the other in Dan. This led to sin; the people walked in procession before one of the calves all the way to Dan.

Jeroboam also made shrines on the high places and made priests from the ranks of the people who were not Levites.

−1 Kings 12:25−31

This was the sin that caused the house of Jeroboam to be cut off and obliterated from the face of the earth.

−1 Kings 13:34

IN OTHER WORDS

For over one hundred years three kings ruled the Israelites: Saul, David, and Solomon. When Solomon died, his son, Rehoboam, became the next king. But his leadership created a rebellion because he promised to increase the Israelites' pain. His peers essentially told him: "This is what you should tell those complainers: 'If you think my father was hard on you, just wait and see what I'll be like!'" (see 1Kg 12:10). When the Israelites heard those words, ten of the twelve kingdoms revolted and formed a new nation. The new nation became the northern kingdom—called Israel. King Rehoboam maintained control of the southern kingdom—which was called Judah.

The northern kingdom had a new king named Jeroboam. He was even worse than Rehoboam because he tried to replace God with two golden calves.

As you read about how God patiently cared for the Israelites, even after they continually messed up, it should give you hope. Pray a prayer of thanksgiving today, thanking God that he has patience with you too.

Related Texts: Exodus 32;
2 Kings 10:16−31; 23:1−15;
2 Chronicles 11:14−16; Acts 17:15−31;
1 Corinthians 6:9−10

Ahab son of Omri became king over Israel in the thirty-eighth year of Judah's King Asa; Ahab son of Omri reigned over Israel in Samaria twenty-two years. But Ahab son of Omri did what was evil in the LORD's sight more than all who were before him. Then, as if following the sin of Jeroboam son of Nebat were not enough, he married Jezebel, the daughter of Ethbaal king of the Sidonians, and then proceeded to serve Baal and bow in worship to him. He set up an altar for Baal in the temple of Baal that he had built in Samaria. Ahab also made an Asherah pole. Ahab did more to anger the LORD God of Israel than all the kings of Israel who were before him.

−1 Kings 16:29−33

Now Elijah the Tishbite, from the Gilead settlers, said to Ahab, "As the LORD God of Israel lives, in whose presence I stand, there will be no dew or rain during these years except by my command!"

−1 Kings 17:1

If I shut the sky so there is no rain, or if I command the grasshopper to consume the land, or if I send pestilence on my people, and my people, who bear my name, humble themselves, pray and seek my face, and turn from their evil ways, then I will hear from heaven, forgive their sin, and heal their land.

−2 Chronicles 7:13−14

IN OTHER WORDS

God was slow to give the Israelites a king because he wanted to be the King of the Israelites. Only he could be a totally wise and just king. The Israelites wanted to be ruled by a king just as the surrounding nations were ruled by kings. Because of this, they rejected God as their true King. This period of time—the reign of kings—replaced Israel's period of judges.

It's not uncommon in today's world to find people who want to be like others so much that they will reject God's ways to follow the ways of others. Have you ever done this? Have you ever rejected God's ways (what you know is right) so that you can be or do something like someone else?

Today, ask God to show you his way and then try to honor him as King of your life.

Related Texts: Deuteronomy 11:16−17; Mark 6:14−15; Luke 1:11−17; 9:7−8; James 5:17−18

After a long time, the word of the LORD came to Elijah in the third year: "Go and present yourself to Ahab. I will send rain on the surface of the land." ...

When Ahab saw Elijah, Ahab said to him, "Is that you, the one ruining Israel?"

He replied, "I have not ruined Israel, but you and your father's family have, because you have abandoned the LORD's commands and followed the Baals. Now summon all Israel to meet me at Mount Carmel, along with the 450 prophets of Baal and the 400 prophets of Asherah who eat at Jezebel's table."

So Ahab summoned all the Israelites and gathered the prophets at Mount Carmel. Then Elijah approached all the people and said, "How long will you waver between two opinions? If the LORD is God, follow him. But if Baal, follow him." But the people didn't answer him a word.

Then Elijah said to the people, "I am the only remaining prophet of the LORD, but Baal's prophets are 450 men. Let two bulls be given to us. They are to choose one bull for themselves, cut it in pieces, and place it on the wood but not light the fire. I will prepare the other bull and place it on the wood but not light the fire. Then you call on the name of your god, and I will call on the name of the LORD. The God who answers with fire, he is God."

All the people answered, "That's fine."

−1 Kings 18:1,17−24

WEIRD OR WHAT?

It's not unusual that Elijah would call on God to respond with fire. God was known to be a God of fire. Consider these biblical examples: a cherub with a flaming sword guarded the garden of Eden; a burning bush spoke to Moses; the authors of Scripture refer to God as a "consuming fire" (see Dt 4:29; Heb 12:29).

Here's the connection to you—fire is a purifier. As a follower of Jesus, God is working in your life to make you more like him. He is purifying you towards holiness. Are you willing and ready to be tested by God's fire?

Related Texts: Deuteronomy 12:28−31; 32:36−39; Mark 8:27−29; Luke 9:28−36; James 5:14−18

Then Elijah said to the prophets of Baal, "Since you are so numerous, choose for yourselves one bull and prepare it first. Then call on the name of your god but don't light the fire."

So they took the bull that he gave them, prepared it, and called on the name of Baal from morning until noon, saying, "Baal, answer us!" But there was no sound; no one answered. Then they danced around the altar they had made....

All afternoon they kept on raving until the offering of the evening sacrifice, but there was no sound; no one answered, no one paid attention....

At the time for offering the evening sacrifice, the prophet Elijah approached the altar and said, "Lord, the God of Abraham, Isaac, and Israel, today let it be known that you are God in Israel and I am your servant, and that at your word I have done all these things. Answer me, Lord! Answer me so that this people will know that you, the Lord, are God and that you have turned their hearts back."

Then the Lord's fire fell and consumed the burnt offering, the wood, the stones, and the dust, and it licked up the water that was in the trench. When all the people saw it, they fell facedown and said, "The Lord, he is God! The Lord, he is God!"

Then Elijah ordered them, "Seize the prophets of Baal! Do not let even one of them escape." So they seized them, and Elijah brought them down to the Wadi Kishon and slaughtered them there.

—1 Kings 18:25–26,29,36–40

BIBLICAL BIO

Elijah was the most famous of all the prophets. God used him in mighty ways. As you read today, you learned that idols were no match for Elijah's faith in the power of God. He counted on God's power and presence.

Though Elijah was a great prophet, he wasn't perfect. He did get tired and frustrated while working for God. He became depressed because he didn't believe people were responding to his message. During this time, God reminded Elijah that he is God. He understood Elijah's discouragement and cared for his prophetic ministry.

Serving God and doing good can get tiring. Because of this, it's important to know that being God's person will help you survive doing God's work. Focus on being a follower of Jesus, and God will give you the strength to do his work.

Related Texts: Deuteronomy 13; 17:2–5; 18:18–22; 1 Kings 21–22; 2 Kings 9:30–10:28; Philippians 2:5–11

The word of the LORD came to Jonah son of Amittai: "Get up! Go to the great city of Nineveh and preach against it because their evil has come up before me." Jonah got up to flee to Tarshish from the LORD's presence. He went down to Joppa and found a ship going to Tarshish. He paid the fare and went down into it to go with them to Tarshish from the LORD's presence.

But the LORD threw a great wind onto the sea, and such a great storm arose on the sea that the ship threatened to break apart. The sailors were afraid, and each cried out to his god. They threw the ship's cargo into the sea to lighten the load....

Come on!" the sailors said to each other. "Let's cast lots. Then we'll know who is to blame for this trouble we're in." So they cast lots, and the lot singled out Jonah....

So they said to him, "What should we do to you so that the sea will calm down for us?" For the sea was getting worse and worse.

He answered them, "Pick me up and throw me into the sea so that it will calm down for you, for I know that I'm to blame for this great storm that is against you." ...

Then they picked up Jonah and threw him into the sea, and the sea stopped its raging. The men were seized by great fear of the LORD, and they offered a sacrifice to the LORD and made vows.

The LORD appointed a great fish to swallow Jonah, and Jonah was in the belly of the fish three days and three nights.

—Jonah 1:1–5,7,11–12,15–17

TAKE A SHOT

Below you will find three ways that you may be like Jonah:

- You may run from good things.
- You may think you can hide from God.
- You may try to keep truth from people.

Write a few thoughts about how one of these three statements most relates to your life.

Related Texts: 2 Kings 14:25;
Matthew 12:38–41; 16:1–4;
Luke 11:29–32

Jonah prayed to the LORD his
God from the belly of the fish:
I called to the LORD in my distress,
and he answered me.
I cried out for help
    from deep inside Sheol;
you heard my voice.
When you threw me
    into the depths,
into the heart of the seas,
the current overcame me.
All your breakers and your billows
    swept over me.
And I said, "I have been banished
from your sight,
yet I will look once more
toward your holy temple."
The water engulfed me up
    to the neck;
the watery depths overcame me;
seaweed was wrapped
    around my head.
I sank to the foundations
    of the mountains,
the earth's gates shut
    behind me forever!
Then you raised my life
    from the Pit, LORD my God!
As my life was fading away,
I remembered the LORD,
and my prayer came to you,
to your holy temple.
Those who cherish worthless idols
abandon their faithful love,
but as for me, I will sacrifice
    to you
with a voice of thanksgiving.
I will fulfill what I have vowed.
Salvation belongs to the LORD.

Then the LORD commanded the
fish, and it vomited Jonah onto
dry land.

—Jonah 2:1–10

ONE MINUTE MEMORY

"But as for me, I will sacrifice to you
with a voice of thanksgiving. I will
fulfill what I have vowed. Salvation
belongs to the LORD." (Jnh 2:9).

Related Texts: 2 Kings 17:13–15;
Psalms 42; 69; Isaiah 44:9–20; Acts 27

The word of the LORD came to Jonah a second time: "Get up! Go to the great city of Nineveh and preach the message that I tell you." Jonah got up and went to Nineveh according to the LORD's command.

Now Nineveh was an extremely great city, a three-day walk. Jonah set out on the first day of his walk in the city and proclaimed, "In forty days Nineveh will be demolished!" Then the people of Nineveh believed God. They proclaimed a fast and dressed in sackcloth — from the greatest of them to the least.

When word reached the king of Nineveh, he got up from his throne, took off his royal robe, covered himself with sackcloth, and sat in ashes. Then he issued a decree in Nineveh:

By order of the king and his nobles: No person or animal, herd or flock, is to taste anything at all. They must not eat or drink water. Furthermore, both people and animals must be covered with sackcloth, and everyone must call out earnestly to God. Each must turn from his evil ways and from his wrongdoing. Who knows? God may turn and relent; he may turn from his burning anger so that we will not perish.

God saw their actions — that they had turned from their evil ways — so God relented from the disaster he had threatened them with. And he did not do it.

—Jonah 3:1–10

HERE'S THE DEAL

God has proven himself to be a God of second chances, forgiveness, and favor that is undeserved (grace). The Ninevites learned to thank God for these qualities after they turned from their evil ways and God spared them from destruction.

As a follower of Jesus, you can rest in the good news that God has promised to extend the same favor to you that he showed to the Ninevites. This is just one of the many reasons that God is worthy of your praise and worship.

Today, thank God for his unconditional love for you and spend a little time identifying an area of your life or an action that you know needs to be changed. While God graciously gives second chances, he prefers obedience.

Related Texts: Exodus 32:1–14; Jeremiah 18:1–11; Joel 2:12–14; Luke 11:29–32

E ven now —
this is the LORD's declaration —
turn to me with all your heart,
with fasting, weeping,
      and mourning.
Tear your hearts,
not just your clothes,
and return to the LORD your God.
For he is gracious
      and compassionate,
slow to anger,
      abounding in faithful love,
and he relents from sending disaster.
Who knows? He may turn
      and relent
and leave a blessing behind him,
so you can offer a grain offering
      and a drink offering
to the LORD your God.

Blow the ram's horn in Zion!
Announce a sacred fast;
proclaim a solemn assembly.
Gather the people;
sanctify the congregation;
assemble the aged;
gather the infants,
even babies nursing at the breast.
Let the groom leave his bedroom,
and the bride
      her honeymoon chamber.
Let the priests, the LORD's ministers,
weep between the portico
      and the altar.
Let them say,
"Have pity on your people, LORD,
and do not make your inheritance
      a disgrace,
an object of scorn
      among the nations.
Why should it be said
      among the peoples,
'Where is their God?'"

Then the LORD became jealous for
his land and spared his people.
                              —Joel 2:12–18

CHECK THIS OUT

Today's reading describes Joel's calling for Judah to repent from her sinfulness. Prior to Joel's calling, God sent his judgment on the people of Judah in the form of locusts. Millions of locusts invaded them, darkened the skies, and devastated the land.

In Rv 9:3,7 there is a similar image used to turn people away from God: "Then locusts came out of the smoke on to the earth, and power was given to them like the power that scorpions have on the earth. . . . The appearance of the locusts was like horses prepared for battle. Something like golden crowns was on their heads; their faces were like human faces."

There's no reason to be scared if you are a follower of Jesus. The enemy can use locusts, anteaters, or wild boars; but the blood of Jesus will protect you from the enemy's tricks. Thank God for that truth today.

Related Texts: Exodus 34:1–7;
Deuteronomy 10:16; Jonah 3;
James 4:6–8

Look, the eyes of the Lord God
are on the sinful kingdom,
and I will obliterate it
from the face of the earth.
However, I will not totally destroy
the house of Jacob —
  this is the Lord's declaration —

All the sinners among my people
who say, "Disaster will never
  overtake
or confront us,"
will die by the sword.

Look, the days are coming —
  this is the Lord's declaration —
when the plowman will overtake
  the reaper
and the one who treads grapes,
the sower of seed.
The mountains will drip
  with sweet wine,
and all the hills will flow with it.
I will restore the fortunes
  of my people Israel.
They will rebuild and occupy
  ruined cities,
plant vineyards and drink
  their wine,
make gardens and eat
  their produce.
I will plant them on their land,
and they will never again
  be uprooted
from the land I have given them.
The Lord your God has spoken.
                    —Amos 9:8,10,13–15

IN OTHER WORDS

Amos finished his prophecy with the key words, "The Lord your God has spoken" (9:15). These words were used to guarantee that his spoken vision would be fulfilled by the God of creation, the God of Abraham, the God of Moses. He wanted the people to know that his prophetic words weren't his own; rather they were God's words and vision for his chosen people.

You hold in your hands the words of God. The Bible isn't filled merely with words of men—it's filled with God's words. These words are life-changing because they're inspired from God himself.

If you read these words, reflect on them, share them and apply them. You'll find yourself with a better life than you've ever dreamed of. Why? Because your God has spoken.

Related Texts: 2 Samuel 7; Isaiah 55; Acts 15:1–21; Romans 9–11

When Israel was a child,
I loved him,
and out of Egypt I called my son.
Israel called to the Egyptians
even as Israel was leaving them.
They kept sacrificing to the Baals
and burning offerings to idols.
It was I who taught Ephraim
to walk,
taking them by the hand,
but they never knew
that I healed them.
I led them with human cords,
with ropes of love.
To them I was like one
who eases the yoke
from their jaws;
I bent down to give them food.
Israel will not return to the land
of Egypt
and Assyria will be his king,
because they refused to repent.

How can I give you up, Ephraim?
How can I surrender you, Israel?
How can I make you like Admah?
How can I treat you like Zeboiim?
I have had a change of heart;
my compassion is stirred!
I will not vent the full fury
of my anger;
I will not turn back
to destroy Ephraim.
For I am God and not man,
the Holy One among you;
I will not come in rage.
—*Hosea 11:1–5,8–9*

JUST A THOUGHT

Today's reading in Hosea and Jesus's parable of the prodigal son (see Luke 15) are similar because they reveal the character of a loving God—the heart of a Father.

Related Texts: Genesis 19:1–29;
Deuteronomy 29:18–23;
Zechariah 10:6–12; 2 Peter 3:8–15

In the year that King Uzziah died, I saw the Lord seated on a high and lofty throne, and the hem of his robe filled the temple. Seraphim were standing above him; they each had six wings: with two they covered their faces, with two they covered their feet, and with two they flew. And one called to another:

Holy, holy, holy is the Lord of Armies;
his glory fills the whole earth.

Then I said:

Woe is me for I am ruined
because I am a man of unclean lips
and live among a people
of unclean lips,
and because my eyes have seen
the King,
the Lord of Armies.

Then one of the seraphim flew to me, and in his hand was a glowing coal that he had taken from the altar with tongs. He touched my mouth with it and said:

Now that this has touched your lips,
your iniquity is removed
and your sin is atoned for.

Then I heard the voice of the Lord asking:

Who will I send?
Who will go for us?

I said:

Here I am. Send me.

And he replied:

Go! Say to these people:
Keep listening,
but do not understand;
keep looking, but do not perceive.
Make the minds of these
people dull;
deafen their ears and blind
their eyes;
otherwise they might see
with their eyes
and hear with their ears,
understand with their minds,
turn back, and be healed.

–Isaiah 6:1–3,5–10

HERE'S THE DEAL

God spoke, and his people didn't hear. He repeated miracles, and the people didn't understand their meaning. God continually revealed himself to the Israelites, and yet they continued to worship idols instead of him. Hundreds of years later, people reacted in a similar way when Jesus spoke. Some people just didn't respond.

You may run into a similar reaction when you're trying to share your life and story as a follower of Jesus. You may display Christian love, invite them to church, help them with problems, and provide them specific examples of God's love—and yet they still may not respond. If that happens, realize you're in good company—it happened to God the Father and to God the Son.

You can't make decisions for your friends—they make their own decisions. A follower of Jesus is to be an example of God's love and remain faithful to God's ways. You do your part today (the possible) and leave it to God to do the rest (the impossible).

Related Texts: Exodus 3:1–6; 33:15–23; Job 19:25–27; Matthew 5:8; 13:10–17; Revelation 4

The word of the LORD that came to Micah the Moreshite — what he saw regarding Samaria and Jerusalem in the days of Jotham, Ahaz, and Hezekiah, kings of Judah.

Listen, all you peoples;
pay attention, earth and everyone
    in it!
The Lord GOD will be a witness
    against you,
the Lord, from his holy temple.
Look, the LORD is leaving his place
and coming down to trample
the heights of the earth.
The mountains will melt
    beneath him,
and the valleys will split apart,
like wax near a fire,
like water cascading down
    a mountainside.
All this will happen because of
    Jacob's rebellion
and the sins of the house of Israel.
What is the rebellion of Jacob?
Isn't it Samaria?
And what is the high place
    of Judah?
Isn't it Jerusalem?
Therefore, I will make Samaria
a heap of ruins in the countryside,
a planting area for a vineyard.
I will roll her stones
    into the valley
and expose her foundations.
All her carved images
    will be smashed to pieces;
all her wages will be burned
    in the fire,
and I will destroy all her idols.
Since she collected the wages
    of a prostitute,
they will be used again
    for a prostitute.
                              —Micah 1:1–7

IN OTHER WORDS

Samaria was the capital of the northern kingdom. The leaders within this kingdom were disobedient to God's ways and led people into idol worship. God sent Elijah, Elisha, and Amos in an attempt to get them to turn from their idols. But there was no change—and the people were going to pay for their leader's mistakes.

When Micah came, he prophesied about their future destruction as God's judgment for their unfaithfulness. Micah 6:8 reminds the Israelites what God wanted from them: "to act justly, to love faithfulness, and to walk humbly with your God." These words are a good reminder for us. Circle one of them and try to work on it in your life today.

Related Texts: Deuteronomy 5:6–10; Judges 10:11–16; Psalms 68:1–3; 97; Jeremiah 26; Acts 1:1–8

In the ninth year of Hoshea, the king of Assyria captured Samaria. He deported the Israelites to Assyria and settled them in Halah, along the Habor (Gozan's river), and in the cities of the Medes.

This disaster happened because the people of Israel sinned against the LORD their God who had brought them out of the land of Egypt from the power of Pharaoh king of Egypt and because they worshiped other gods. They lived according to the customs of the nations that the LORD had dispossessed before the Israelites and according to what the kings of Israel did. The Israelites secretly did things against the LORD their God that were not right. They built high places in all their towns from watchtower to fortified city. They set up for themselves sacred pillars and Asherah poles on every high hill and under every green tree. They burned incense there on all the high places just like the nations that the LORD had driven out before them had done. They did evil things, angering the LORD. They served idols, although the LORD had told them, "You must not do this." Still, the LORD warned Israel and Judah through every prophet and every seer, saying, "Turn from your evil ways and keep my commands and statutes according to the whole law I commanded your ancestors and sent to you through my servants the prophets."

But they would not listen. Instead they became obstinate like their ancestors who did not believe the LORD their God.

—2 Kings 17:6–14

BIG TIME WORD

Obstinate (see 2Kg 17:14) is simply another word that means "stubborn." What's your initial response when someone says, "Don't be so stubborn"? Do you get defensive? Angry? Being stubborn usually is a negative quality displayed by a selfish person who is unwilling to move from a strongly held position or belief. A stubborn person rarely wants to compromise or listen to the thoughts, opinions, and ideas of others.

Have you ever been called stubborn? Occasionally? Or are you called stubborn on a regular basis? If you like being stubborn, consider becoming "stubborn for God." Being stubborn for God means you don't bend your beliefs, and you won't compromise to the distractions that can turn your thoughts, actions, and focus from God.

Related Texts: Deuteronomy 28:14–68; 2 Kings 15:16–20; Acts 7:51–53

H e removed the high places, shattered the sacred pillars, and cut down the Asherah poles. He broke into pieces the bronze snake that Moses made, for until then the Israelites were burning incense to it. It was called Nehushtan.

Hezekiah relied on the LORD God of Israel; not one of the kings of Judah was like him, either before him or after him. He remained faithful to the LORD and did not turn from following him but kept the commands the LORD had commanded Moses.

The LORD was with him, and wherever he went he prospered. He rebelled against the king of Assyria and did not serve him. He defeated the Philistines as far as Gaza and its borders, from watchtower to fortified city.

In the fourth year of King Hezekiah, which was the seventh year of Israel's King Hoshea son of Elah, Assyria's King Shalmaneser marched against Samaria and besieged it. The Assyrians captured it at the end of three years. In the sixth year of Hezekiah, which was the ninth year of Israel's King Hoshea, Samaria was captured.

−2 Kings 18:4−10

HERE'S THE DEAL

King Hezekiah is a rare example of someone who followed God during a time of sin and rebellion. Today's reading reveals that God blessed King Hezekiah because of his obedience. God was with him, and he prospered in everything he did. Those are great results for following and obeying God's ways!

As a follower of God, you will stand out as unique. Following God doesn't mean you will prosper financially, but it does mean you will have a relationship with God that will cause you to live a different life.

Following God won't mean you'll have an easy or perfect life, but being obedient to God's ways will be rewarded both here on earth and into eternity. Whatever way you look at it, obedience wins!

Related Texts: Numbers 21:1−9; Deuteronomy 28:1−14; 2 Chronicles 29−31; Proverbs 25:1; Matthew 1:1−10

I n the fourteenth year of King Hezekiah, Assyria's King Sennacherib attacked all the fortified cities of Judah and captured them.

—2 Kings 18:13

Then Hezekiah prayed before the LORD:

LORD God of Israel, enthroned between the cherubim, you are God — you alone — of all the kingdoms of the earth. You made the heavens and the earth. Listen closely, LORD, and hear; open your eyes, LORD, and see. Hear the words that Sennacherib has sent to mock the living God. LORD, it is true that the kings of Assyria have devastated the nations and their lands. They have thrown their gods into the fire, for they were not gods but made by human hands — wood and stone. So they have destroyed them. Now, LORD our God, please save us from his power so that all the kingdoms of the earth may know that you, LORD, are God — you alone.

Then Isaiah son of Amoz sent a message to Hezekiah: "The LORD, the God of Israel says, 'I have heard your prayer to me about King Sennacherib of Assyria.' . . .

That night the angel of the LORD went out and struck down one hundred eighty-five thousand in the camp of the Assyrians. When the people got up the next morning — there were all the dead bodies! So King Sennacherib of Assyria broke camp and left. He returned home and lived in Nineveh.

—2 Kings 19:15–20,35–36

JUST A THOUGHT

Prayers of trouble need to be followed by prayers of praise.

Related Texts: 2 Kings 19–20; 2 Chronicles 32; Isaiah 36–39; Acts 12

The LORD is a jealous
and avenging God;
the LORD takes vengeance
and is fierce in wrath.
The LORD takes vengeance
against his foes;
he is furious with his enemies.
The LORD is slow to anger but great
in power;
the LORD will never leave
the guilty unpunished.
His path is in the whirlwind
and storm,
and clouds are the dust
beneath his feet....

Who can withstand
his indignation?
Who can endure
his burning anger?
His wrath is poured out like fire;
even rocks are shattered
before him.

The LORD is good,
a stronghold in a day of distress;
he cares for those who take refuge
in him.
But he will completely
destroy Nineveh
with an overwhelming flood,
and he will chase his enemies
into darkness.

Whatever you plot
against the LORD,
he will bring it
to complete destruction;
oppression will not rise up
a second time.

—Nahum 1:2–3,6–9

DIG DEEPER

God's anger is aimed at those who push away his truth. Check out Romans 1:18–20:

> For God's wrath is revealed from heaven against all godlessness and unrighteousness of people who by their unrighteousness suppress the truth, since what can be known about God is evident among them, because God has shown it to them. For his invisible attributes, that is, his eternal power and divine nature, have been clearly seen since the creation of the world, being understood through what he has made. As a result, people are without excuse.

You can avoid God's anger by following the truth he has revealed in his Word. If you know the truth, the truth will set you free from God's anger.

Related Texts: Exodus 34:1–7;
John 3:31–36; Romans 1:18–19;
Ephesians 5:5–6

W oe to the city
that is rebellious
and defiled,
the oppressive city!
She has not obeyed;
she has not accepted discipline.
She has not trusted in the LORD;
she has not drawn near
　　to her God.
The princes within her are
　　roaring lions;
her judges are wolves of the night,
which leave nothing
　　for the morning.
Her prophets are reckless —
treacherous men.
Her priests profane the sanctuary;
they do violence to instruction.
The righteous LORD is in her;
he does no wrong.
He applies his justice morning
　　by morning;
he does not fail at dawn,
yet the one who does wrong
　　knows no shame. . . .

Sing for joy, Daughter Zion;
shout loudly, Israel!
Be glad and celebrate with all
　　your heart,
Daughter Jerusalem!
The LORD has removed
　　your punishment;
he has turned back your enemy.
The King of Israel, the LORD,
　　is among you;
you need no longer fear harm.
On that day it will be said
　　to Jerusalem:
"Do not fear;
Zion, do not let your hands
　　grow weak.
The LORD your God is among you,
a warrior who saves.
He will rejoice over you
　　with gladness.
He will be quiet in his love.

He will delight in you
　　with singing."
　　　　　—*Zephaniah 3:1–5,14–17*

ONE MINUTE MEMORY

"The LORD your God is among you, a warrior who saves. He will rejoice over you with gladness. He will be quiet in his love. He will delight in you with singing" (Zph 3:17).

Related Texts: Psalm 25; 34:1–5; Isaiah 40; Romans 10:9–11

The words of Jeremiah, the son of Hilkiah, one of the priests living in Anathoth in the territory of Benjamin. The word of the LORD came to him in the thirteenth year of the reign of Josiah son of Amon, king of Judah. It also came throughout the days of Jehoiakim son of Josiah, king of Judah, until the fifth month of the eleventh year of Zedekiah son of Josiah, king of Judah, when the people of Jerusalem went into exile.

The word of the LORD came to me:

I chose you before I formed you
in the womb;
I set you apart
before you were born.
I appointed you a prophet
to the nations.

But I protested, "Oh no, Lord GOD! Look, I don't know how to speak since I am only a youth."

Then the LORD said to me:
Do not say, "I am only a youth,"
for you will go to everyone
I send you to
and speak whatever I tell you.
Do not be afraid of anyone,
for I will be with you
to rescue you.
This is the LORD's declaration.

Then the LORD reached out his hand, touched my mouth, and told me:
I have now filled your mouth
with my words.
See, I have appointed you today
over nations and kingdoms
to uproot and tear down,
to destroy and demolish,
to build and plant.
—*Jeremiah 1:1–10*

HERE'S THE DEAL

When God wants to use someone, he doesn't give in to lame excuses like Jeremiah used: "Oh no, Lord GOD! Look, I don't know how to speak since I am only a youth." (Jr 1:6).

Jeremiah may not have felt qualified because he lacked training and experience, but that didn't matter to God. God overruled his excuses and let him know that his authority and presence didn't depend on Jeremiah's training, experience, or age. God was present in the prophet's life, and with his presence came his power.

Excuses don't limit God when he wants to get hold of your life. Ditch the excuses and prepare yourself to be used by God. Preparing yourself means being open to God and faithful to live by his design and standards. If you have any excuses, write them down, share them with a close friend, and then throw them away. Remember it's not about you anyway—it's about God working in you.

Related Texts: Psalm 136; Isaiah 6; Luke 1:13–16; 1 Timothy 4:12

Again the word of the LORD came to me asking, "What do you see?"

And I replied, "I see a boiling pot, its lip tilted from the north to the south."

Then the LORD said to me, "Disaster will be poured out from the north on all who live in the land. Indeed, I am about to summon all the clans and kingdoms of the north."

This is the LORD's declaration.
They will come, and each king
will set up his throne
at the entrance
to Jerusalem's gates.
They will attack
all her surrounding walls
and all the other cities of Judah.
"I will pronounce my judgments against them for all the evil they did when they abandoned me to burn incense to other gods and to worship the works of their own hands.

"Now, get ready. Stand up and tell them everything that I command you. Do not be intimidated by them or I will cause you to cower before them. Today, I am the one who has made you a fortified city, an iron pillar, and bronze walls against the whole land — against the kings of Judah, its officials, its priests, and the population. They will fight against you but never prevail over you, since I am with you to rescue you."

This is the LORD's declaration.
—Jeremiah 1:13—19

JUST A THOUGHT

Where God leads, he will provide for your needs!

Related Texts: Deuteronomy 28; Joshua 1; Ezekiel 11; 24; 33:1—20; 1 John 5:3—4

At the beginning of the reign of Jehoiakim son of Josiah, king of Judah, this word came from the LORD: . . .

You are to say to them, 'This is what the LORD says: If you do not listen to me by living according to my instruction that I set before you and by listening to the words of my servants the prophets — whom I have been sending to you time and time again, though you did not listen — I will make this temple like Shiloh. I will make this city an example for cursing for all the nations of the earth.' "

When he finished the address the LORD had commanded him to deliver to all the people, immediately the priests, the prophets, and all the people took hold of him, yelling, "You must surely die! . . .

Some of the elders of the land stood up and said to all the assembled people, "Micah the Moreshite prophesied in the days of King Hezekiah of Judah and said to all the people of Judah, 'This is what the LORD of Armies says:

Zion will be plowed like a field,
Jerusalem will become ruins,
and the temple's mountain
will be a high thicket.'

Did King Hezekiah of Judah and all the people of Judah put him to death? Did not the king fear the LORD and plead for the LORD's favor, and did not the LORD relent concerning the disaster he had pronounced against them? We are about to bring a terrible disaster on ourselves! "

—Jeremiah 26:1,4–6,8,17–19

WEIRD OR WHAT?

Although being a prophet was a huge responsibility, holding that job had nothing to do with who one's parents were. Being a king or priest was a hereditary position, which parents passed down the ranks. Prophets were different because they had a special calling from God that wasn't limited to family line.

Over and over the Bible reveals ordinary people doing extraordinary things. Let that be an encouragement to you today. And be reminded that if you're a follower of Jesus, you're part of an incredible family line! Eternal life is passed on to you from Jesus.

Related Texts: Jeremiah 18:1–11; 19:1–20:2; 38:1–13; Lamentations 3:52–57; Micah 3:9–12; Matthew 16:13–14

Zedekiah was twenty-one years old when he became king, and he reigned eleven years in Jerusalem. He did what was evil in the sight of the LORD his God and did not humble himself before the prophet Jeremiah at the LORD's command. . . .

But the LORD, the God of their ancestors sent word against them by the hand of his messengers, sending them time and time again, for he had compassion on his people and on his dwelling place. But they kept ridiculing God's messengers, despising his words, and scoffing at his prophets, until the LORD's wrath was so stirred up against his people that there was no remedy. So he brought up against them the king of the Chaldeans, who killed their fit young men with the sword in the house of their sanctuary. He had no pity on young men or young women, elderly or aged; he handed them all over to him. He took everything to Babylon — all the articles of God's temple, large and small, the treasures of the LORD's temple, and the treasures of the king and his officials. Then the Chaldeans burned God's temple. They tore down Jerusalem's wall, burned all its palaces, and destroyed all its valuable articles.

He deported those who escaped from the sword to Babylon, and they became servants to him and his sons until the rise of the Persian kingdom. This fulfilled the word of the LORD through Jeremiah, and the land enjoyed its Sabbath rest all the days of the desolation until seventy years were fulfilled.

–2 Chronicles 36:11–12,15–21

IN OTHER WORDS

Jeremiah had warned the Israelites that their temple would be destroyed. This destruction was the result of their sin—for worshiping idols instead of the living and true God. God was compassionate to the Israelites and used the prophets to warn them. The Babylonians showed no compassion and even killed people in the temple. God's presence had left the temple, and the Babylonians burned the temple and plundered its treasures.

People love their church building and take great pride in it. That's fine, but God is bigger than any building. The Bible reveals that when God's presence lives in you, you are God's temple. His presence lives in people.

Are you doing anything to your body or life that might be destroying God's temple? If so, what can you do today to stop the destruction?

Related Texts: Leviticus 26:1–43; 2 Kings 20:12–18; 25; Isaiah 39; Jeremiah 25; 38; 52; Matthew 1:1–17

H ow she sits alone,
the city once crowded
    with people!
She who was great
    among the nations
has become like a widow.
The princess among the provinces
has been put to forced labor.
She weeps bitterly
    during the night,
with tears on her cheeks.
There is no one to offer
    her comfort,
not one from all her lovers.
All her friends have betrayed her;
they have become her enemies.
                    —Lamentations 1:1–2

Then I thought, "My future is lost,
as well as my hope from the LORD."
Remember my affliction
    and my homelessness,
the wormwood and the poison.
I continually remember them
and have become depressed.
Yet I call this to mind,
and therefore I have hope:
Because of the LORD's faithful love
we do not perish,
for his mercies never end.
They are new every morning;
great is your faithfulness!
I say, "The LORD is my portion,
therefore I will put my hope
    in him."
The LORD is good to those
    who wait for him,
to the person who seeks him.
It is good to wait quietly
for salvation from the LORD.
                    —Lamentations 3:18–26

ONE MINUTE MEMORY

"The LORD is good to those who wait for him, to the person who seeks him" (Lm 3:25).

Related Texts: Psalm 137; Ezekiel 19; 24; Matthew 23:33–39

Look, his ego is inflated;
he is without integrity.
But the righteous one will live
    by his faith.
Moreover, wine betrays;
an arrogant man is never at rest.
He enlarges his appetite like Sheol,
and like Death he is
    never satisfied.
He gathers all the nations
    to himself;
he collects all the peoples
    for himself.
        —*Habakkuk 2:4–5*

I heard, and I trembled within;
my lips quivered at the sound.
Rottenness entered my bones;
I trembled where I stood.
Now I must quietly wait
    for the day of distress
to come against the people
    invading us.
Though the fig tree does not bud
and there is no fruit on the vines,
though the olive crop fails
and the fields produce no food,
though the flocks disappear
    from the pen
and there are no herds
    in the stalls,
yet I will celebrate in the LORD;
I will rejoice in the God
    of my salvation!
The LORD my Lord is my strength;
he makes my feet like those
    of a deer
and enables me to walk
    on mountain heights!
        —*Habakkuk 3:16–19*

DIG DEEPER

Obadiah describes God's punishment on Edom for helping Babylon invade and conquer Israel. He prophesied that God would destroy the Edomites because of their actions.

In many places throughout the Bible, it has been prophesied that God will punish and destroy all those who have not repented of their sin. Check out Peter's description of what this future will look like: "But the day of the Lord will come like a thief; on that day the heavens will pass away with a loud noise, the elements will burn and be dissolved, and the earth and the works on it will be disclosed" (2Pt 3:10).

You want some good advice? Be on God's side! God is compassionate and slow to anger, but his final judgment against the godless will be severe. Read the rest of 2 Peter 3 and see how you are called to prepare yourself.

Related Texts: Genesis 9:5–6; 12:1–3; Romans 1:16–17; Galatians 3:8–14; Hebrews 10:32–39

In that day —
this is the LORD's declaration —
will I not eliminate the wise ones
    of Edom
and those who understand
from the hill country of Esau? . . .

You will be covered with shame
and destroyed forever
because of violence done
    to your brother Jacob.
On the day you stood aloof,
on the day strangers captured
    his wealth,
while foreigners entered
    his city gate
and cast lots for Jerusalem,
you were just like one of them.
Do not gloat over your brother
in the day of his calamity;
do not rejoice over the people
    of Judah
in the day of their destruction;
do not boastfully mock
in the day of distress. . . .

For the day of the LORD is near,
against all the nations.
As you have done, it will be done
    to you;
what you deserve will return
    on your own head.
As you have drunk
    on my holy mountain,
so all the nations will
    drink continually.
They will drink and gulp down
and be as though they had
    never been.
But there will be a deliverance
    on Mount Zion,
and it will be holy;
the house of Jacob will dispossess
those who dispossessed them.
    —Obadiah 8,10–12,15–17

WEIRD OR WHAT?

Obadiah is the shortest of the thirty-nine Old Testament books. In only twenty-one verses, the prophet Obadiah expressed nothing but bad news. His words were directed at the Edomites, who rejoiced at the destruction of Jerusalem. Edom was a neighboring nation that always opposed the Israelites.

God loved the Israelites, his chosen children, and promised to deal forcefully with the nations who went against them. As a follower of Jesus, God loves you too and you are considered one of his children. He will protect you—count on it.

Related Texts: Isaiah 13; Joel 3; 2 Peter 3

The hand of the LORD was on me, and he brought me out by his Spirit and set me down in the middle of the valley; it was full of bones. He led me all around them. . . .

He said to me, "Prophesy concerning these bones and say to them: Dry bones, hear the word of the LORD! This is what the Lord GOD says to these bones: I will cause breath to enter you, and you will live.

So I prophesied as I had been commanded. While I was prophesying, there was a noise, a rattling sound, and the bones came together, bone to bone. . . . He said to me, "Prophesy to the breath, prophesy, son of man. Say to it: This is what the Lord GOD says: Breath, come from the four winds and breathe into these slain so that they may live!" So I prophesied as he commanded me; the breath entered them, and they came to life and stood on their feet, a vast army.

Then he said to me, "Son of man, these bones are the whole house of Israel. Look how they say, 'Our bones are dried up, and our hope has perished; we are cut off.' Therefore, prophesy and say to them, 'This is what the Lord GOD says: I am going to open your graves and bring you up from them, my people, and lead you into the land of Israel. . . . I will put my Spirit in you, and you will live, and I will settle you in your own land. Then you will know that I am the LORD. I have spoken, and I will do it. This is the declaration of the LORD.'"

—*Ezekiel 37:1–2,4–5,7,9–12*

IN OTHER WORDS

Ezekiel's vision is an example of something that only God could accomplish. The scattered bones refer to the nation of Israel. They seemed to be spiritually dead and hopeless, and only God could restore the nation. It was God's promise!

Today there are nations, churches, and people who are like scattered bones—spiritually dead and hopeless. And, like the nation of Israel, only God can restore them. Pray for the graveyard of scattered bones that surrounds your church and your home. Beg for God to breathe life into your community and friends. It may appear hopeless, but it's not impossible for God. There are some "dead bones" that only God can raise up.

Related Texts: Deuteronomy 30:1–10; Psalm 80; Isaiah 40; Ezekiel 36; Acts 17:24–25; 2 Thessalonians 2:7–8

King Belshazzar held a great feast for a thousand of his nobles and drank wine in their presence. Under the influence of the wine, Belshazzar gave orders to bring in the gold and silver vessels that his predecessor Nebuchadnezzar had taken from the temple in Jerusalem, so that the king and his nobles, wives, and concubines could drink from them.... They drank the wine and praised their gods made of gold and silver, bronze, iron, wood, and stone.

At that moment the fingers of a man's hand appeared and began writing on the plaster of the king's palace wall next to the lampstand. As the king watched the hand that was writing, his face turned pale, and his thoughts so terrified him that he soiled himself and his knees knocked together....

Because of the outcry of the king and his nobles, the queen came to the banquet hall. "May the king live forever," she said. "Don't let your thoughts terrify you or your face be pale. There is a man in your kingdom who has a spirit of the holy gods in him. In the days of your predecessor he was found to have insight, intelligence, and wisdom like the wisdom of the gods. Your predecessor, King Nebuchadnezzar, appointed him chief of the magicians, mediums, Chaldeans, and diviners. Your own predecessor, the king, did this because Daniel, the one the king named Belteshazzar, was found to have an extraordinary spirit, knowledge and intelligence, and the ability to interpret dreams, explain riddles, and solve problems. Therefore, summon Daniel, and he will give the interpretation."

—Daniel 5:1–2,4–6,10–12

BIBLICAL BIO

Daniel was born in Israel and taken captive in 605 BC by the Babylonians. He became a servant of the Babylonian king Nebuchadnezzar. In an attempt to take away Daniel's identity, he was given the name Belteshazzar. But Daniel had an unwavering and deep-rooted faith in God. And, because of this faith, God granted Daniel the gifts of exceptional wisdom and understanding.

As you read about Daniel, you'll see his godliness expressed in his courage.

Related Texts: Genesis 41; Daniel 1–4; Joel 2:28–32; Acts 2:1–21

T hen Daniel was brought before the king. The king said to him, "Are you Daniel, one of the Judean exiles that my predecessor the king brought from Judah? . . . However, I have heard about you that you can give interpretations and solve problems. Therefore, if you can read this inscription and give me its interpretation, you will be clothed in purple, have a gold chain around your neck, and have the third highest position in the kingdom."

Then Daniel answered the king, "You may keep your gifts and give your rewards to someone else; however, I will read the inscription for the king and make the interpretation known to him. . . .

Instead, you have exalted yourself against the Lord of the heavens. The vessels from his house were brought to you, and as you and your nobles, wives, and concubines drank wine from them, you praised the gods made of silver and gold, bronze, iron, wood, and stone, which do not see or hear or understand. But you have not glorified the God who holds your life-breath in his hand and who controls the whole course of your life. Therefore, he sent the hand, and this writing was inscribed.

"This is the writing that was inscribed: MENE, MENE, TEKEL, and PARSIN. This is the interpretation of the message:

'Mene' means that God has numbered the days of your kingdom and brought it to an end.

'Tekel' means that you have been weighed on the balance and found deficient.

'Peres' means that your kingdom has been divided and given to the Medes and Persians.". . .

That very night Belshazzar the king of the Chaldeans was killed, and Darius the Mede received the kingdom at the age of sixty-two.
–Daniel 5:13,16–17,23–28,30–31

JUST A THOUGHT

It's much easier to keep your mouth closed and your hand open for gifts than it is to reject rewards and speak against the wickedness of the gift giver!

Related Texts: Isaiah 47; Daniel 4; Matthew 24:14–22; 1 Corinthians 12

In the first year of King Cyrus of Persia, in order to fulfill the word of the LORD spoken through Jeremiah, the LORD roused the spirit of King Cyrus to issue a proclamation throughout his entire kingdom and to put it in writing:

This is what King Cyrus of Persia says: "The LORD, the God of the heavens, has given me all the kingdoms of the earth and has appointed me to build him a house at Jerusalem in Judah. Any of his people among you, may his God be with him, and may he go to Jerusalem in Judah and build the house of the LORD, the God of Israel, the God who is in Jerusalem. Let every survivor, wherever he resides, be assisted by the men of that region with silver, gold, goods, and livestock, along with a freewill offering for the house of God in Jerusalem."

So the family heads of Judah and Benjamin, along with the priests and Levites — everyone whose spirit God had roused — prepared to go up and rebuild the LORD's house in Jerusalem. All their neighbors supported them with silver articles, gold, goods, livestock, and valuables, in addition to all that was given as a freewill offering. King Cyrus also brought out the articles of the LORD's house that Nebuchadnezzar had taken from Jerusalem and had placed in the house of his gods.

—Ezra 1:1–7

HERE'S THE DEAL

In the rebuilding of the temple, the Israelites needed to help out with the workload or contribute to the finances that would be needed for this incredible task.

When you think of contributing to a task it's easy to think of just donating money and letting the pros do the work. But you can contribute more than your money—God can use your skills and your time. Numerous ministries exist outside your church that need your contribution.

Make a contribution today! Your contribution may not seem like much to you, but it may be a treasure to another.

Related Texts: 2 Chronicles 36:22–23; Jeremiah 25:11–12; 29:10–14

The LORD of Armies says this: These people say: The time has not come for the house of the LORD to be rebuilt."

The word of the LORD came through the prophet Haggai: "Is it a time for you yourselves to live in your paneled houses, while this house lies in ruins?" ...

The LORD of Armies says this: "Think carefully about your ways. Go up into the hills, bring down lumber, and build the house; and I will be pleased with it and be glorified," says the LORD. "You expected much, but then it amounted to little. When you brought the harvest to your house, I ruined it. Why?" This is the declaration of the LORD of Armies. "Because my house still lies in ruins, while each of you is busy with his own house.

So on your account,
the skies have withheld the dew
and the land its crops.
I have summoned a drought
on the fields and the hills,
on the grain, new wine,
    fresh oil,
and whatever the ground yields,
on people and animals,
and on all that
    your hands produce."

Then Zerubbabel son of Shealtiel, the high priest Joshua son of Jehozadak, and the entire remnant of the people obeyed the LORD their God and the words of the prophet Haggai, because the LORD their God had sent him. So the people feared the LORD.
    —*Haggai 1:2–4,7–12*

TAKE A SHOT

God withheld his blessing from the people because of their selfish hearts. What are two things in your life that cause you to have a selfish heart?

1.

2.

Today, ask God to work on the selfish areas in your life.

Related Texts: Haggai 2; Zechariah 1–6; 1 Corinthians 3:9– 17; 2 Corinthians 6:14–16; Ephesians 2:11–22

On the twenty-fourth day of the eleventh month, which is the month of Shebat, in the second year of Darius, the word of the LORD came to the prophet Zechariah son of Berechiah, son of Iddo:

I looked out in the night and saw a man riding on a chestnut horse. He was standing among the myrtle trees in the valley. Behind him were chestnut, brown, and white horses. . . .

They reported to the angel of the LORD standing among the myrtle trees, "We have patrolled the earth, and right now the whole earth is calm and quiet."

Then the angel of the LORD responded, "How long, LORD of Armies, will you withhold mercy from Jerusalem and the cities of Judah that you have been angry with these seventy years?" The LORD replied with kind and comforting words to the angel who was speaking with me.

So the angel who was speaking with me said, "Proclaim: The LORD of Armies says: I am extremely jealous for Jerusalem and Zion. I am fiercely angry with the nations that are at ease, for I was a little angry, but they made the destruction worse. Therefore, this is what the LORD says: In mercy, I have returned to Jerusalem; my house will be rebuilt within it — this is the declaration of the LORD of Armies — and a measuring line will be stretched out over Jerusalem.

"Proclaim further: This is what the LORD of Armies says: My cities will again overflow with prosperity; the LORD will once more comfort Zion and again choose Jerusalem."

–Zechariah 1:7–8,11–17

DIG DEEPER

The Israelites suffered great pain and defeat. God responded by directing his anger toward the nations that wounded the Israelites, and he also expressed compassion toward the Israelites' pain.

In the New Testament, God expresses compassion for suffering Christians. Check out 2 Corinthians 1:3–4: "Blessed be the God and Father of our Lord Jesus Christ, the Father of mercies and the God of all comfort. He comforts us in all our affliction, so that we may be able to comfort those who are in any kind of affliction, through the comfort we ourselves receive from God."

Rest in the promise that God continues to give encouragement and support to those in need. Do you need to be comforted right now?

Related Texts: Isaiah 40:1–2; Zechariah 1–6; 1 Corinthians 14:3; 2 Corinthians 1:3–7

When the enemies of Judah and Benjamin heard that the returned exiles were building a temple for the LORD, the God of Israel, they approached Zerubbabel and the family heads and said to them, "Let us build with you, for we also worship your God and have been sacrificing to him since the time King Esar-haddon of Assyria brought us here."

But Zerubbabel, Jeshua, and the other heads of Israel's families answered them, "You may have no part with us in building a house for our God, since we alone will build it for the LORD, the God of Israel, as King Cyrus, the king of Persia has commanded us." Then the people who were already in the land discouraged the people of Judah and made them afraid to build. They also bribed officials to act against them to frustrate their plans throughout the reign of King Cyrus of Persia and until the reign of King Darius of Persia.

–Ezra 4:1–5

Then Tattenai governor of the region west of the Euphrates River, Shethar-bozenai, and their colleagues diligently carried out what King Darius had decreed. So the Jewish elders continued successfully with the building under the prophesying of Haggai the prophet and Zechariah son of Iddo. They finished the building according to the command of the God of Israel and the decrees of Cyrus, Darius, and King Artaxerxes of Persia. This house was completed on the third day of the month of Adar in the sixth year of the reign of King Darius.

–Ezra 6:13–15

JUST A THOUGHT

Discouragement and fear are two tactics the devil uses to stop God's work. Don't let them into your life and distract you from following God.

Related Texts: Ezra 3–6; Ezekiel 40–48; Haggai 1–2; John 2:13–21

The words of Nehemiah son of Hacaliah:

During the month of Chislev in the twentieth year, when I was in the fortress city of Susa, Hanani, one of my brothers, arrived with men from Judah, and I questioned them about Jerusalem and the Jewish remnant that had survived the exile. They said to me, "The remnant in the province, who survived the exile, are in great trouble and disgrace. Jerusalem's wall has been broken down, and its gates have been burned."

When I heard these words, I sat down and wept. I mourned for a number of days, fasting and praying before the God of the heavens. I said,

LORD, the God of the heavens, the great and awe-inspiring God who keeps his gracious covenant with those who love him and keep his commands, let your eyes be open and your ears be attentive to hear your servant's prayer that I now pray to you day and night for your servants, the Israelites. I confess the sins we have committed against you. Both I and my father's family have sinned. We have acted corruptly toward you and have not kept the commands, statutes, and ordinances you gave your servant Moses. Please remember what you commanded your servant Moses: "If you are unfaithful, I will scatter you among the peoples. But if you return to me and carefully observe my commands, even though your exiles were banished to the farthest horizon, I will gather them from there and bring them to the place where I chose to have my name dwell."

−Nehemiah 1:1−9

BIBLICAL BIO

Nehemiah is an example of a great leader. One of his jobs was to provide the necessary leadership to rebuild the wall of Jerusalem. This was no easy task! He faced one obstacle after another, but his vision, courage, and faith were much stronger than any of the problems that came his way.

Of Nehemiah's many leadership skills displayed, his prayer life is one leadership action worth studying. He understood that his strongest defense against the enemy was to be on his knees and in conversation with God. He is as well known for what he did behind the scenes (and on his knees) as he is for being an upfront leader.

Check out Nehemiah, copy his characteristics, begin praying and asking God to bless your leadership.

Related Texts: Leviticus 26:14−46; Deuteronomy 7:6−15; 28:15−68; Daniel 9:1−19; James 5:13−16

S o we rebuilt the wall until the entire wall was joined together up to half its height, for the people had the will to keep working.

When Sanballat, Tobiah, and the Arabs, Ammonites, and Ashdodites heard that the repair to the walls of Jerusalem was progressing and that the gaps were being closed, they became furious. They all plotted together to come and fight against Jerusalem and throw it into confusion. So we prayed to our God and stationed a guard because of them day and night....

From that day on, half of my men did the work while the other half held spears, shields, bows, and armor. The officers supported all the people of Judah, who were rebuilding the wall. The laborers who carried the loads worked with one hand and held a weapon with the other. Each of the builders had his sword strapped around his waist

—Nehemiah 4:6—9,16—18

The wall was completed in fifty-two days, on the twenty-fifth day of the month Elul. When all our enemies heard this, all the surrounding nations were intimidated and lost their confidence, for they realized that this task had been accomplished by our God.

—Nehemiah 6:15—16

DIG DEEPER

Being a follower of Jesus isn't easy. Trying to follow God and keeping his commandments will bring opposition, frustration, and trials. But in the midst of these, it's good to know that Jesus understands your struggles and he reminds his followers that problems are only temporary. Check out the good news in John 16:33: "I have told you these things so that in me you may have peace. You will have suffering in this world. Be courageous! I have conquered the world."

This is a great verse to recall when you're struggling. Realize that pain is temporary, trials will clear up, and problems will eventually pass away. As a follower of Jesus, you will have an eternity to rejoice and celebrate because Jesus has overcome the world.

Praise him today.

Related Texts: Nehemiah 2—6; Psalms 27; 51:18—19; 127:1; John 16:33; 1 John 4:4

I rejoiced with those who said
to me,
"Let's go to the house of the LORD."
Our feet were standing
within your gates, Jerusalem —

Jerusalem, built as a city
    should be,
solidly united,
where the tribes, the LORD's tribes,
    go up
to give thanks to the name
    of the LORD.
(This is an ordinance for Israel.)
There, thrones for judgment
    are placed,
thrones of the house of David.

Pray for the well-being
    of Jerusalem:
"May those who love you
    be secure;
may there be peace
    within your walls,
security within your fortresses."
Because of my brothers
    and friends,
I will say, "May peace be in you."
Because of the house of the LORD
    our God,
I will pursue your prosperity.
    —Psalm 122

BIG TIME WORD

Peace is an important word for Christians. Those without a relationship with God don't understand or experience the peace God offers. This peace comes from being in harmony with God and also with others. This peace provides a confidence that can replace worry. It's a peace that can't be quenched. God used Jesus to bring this type of peace into the world. Those who rejected Jesus rejected his peace.

If you're a follower of Jesus and don't feel peace, please talk to someone who can provide you wise counsel and help you experience this peace. It's worth the risk of asking someone for help!

Related Texts: Psalm 85;
Zechariah 9:9–17; Luke 13:34–35;
Ephesians 2:11–22

On the first day of the seventh month, the priest Ezra brought the law before the assembly of men, women, and all who could listen with understanding. While he was facing the square in front of the Water Gate, he read out of it from daybreak until noon before the men, the women, and those who could understand. All the people listened attentively to the book of the law.... Ezra opened the book in full view of all the people, since he was elevated above everyone. As he opened it, all the people stood up. Ezra blessed the LORD, the great God, and with their hands uplifted all the people said, "Amen, Amen!" Then they knelt low and worshiped the LORD with their faces to the ground....

They read out of the book of the law of God, translating and giving the meaning so that the people could understand what was read. Nehemiah the governor, Ezra the priest and scribe, and the Levites who were instructing the people said to all of them, "This day is holy to the LORD your God. Do not mourn or weep." For all the people were weeping as they heard the words of the law. Then he said to them, "Go and eat what is rich, drink what is sweet, and send portions to those who have nothing prepared, since today is holy to our Lord. Do not grieve, because the joy of the LORD is your strength."

—Nehemiah 8:2–3,5–6,8–10

BIBLICAL BIO

Ezra was a priest known for his diligent study of the Scriptures. While living in exile, he took advantage of a negative situation and made it positive for himself as well as for the Israelites. Ezra's work strengthened the Israelites' faith and helped them stay focused on God.

How much work would it take for you to become a man or woman of God who knows that the Scriptures can spiritually influence others? That would be something to be remembered for!

Try putting together an action plan on how you might become this type of person.

Related Texts: Deuteronomy 16:13–15; Ezra 6:19–22; Isaiah 58; Matthew 13:18–23; Acts 17:10–11

These events took place during the days of Ahasuerus, who ruled 127 provinces from India to Cush. In those days King Ahasuerus reigned from his royal throne in the fortress at Susa. He held a feast in the third year of his reign for all his officials and staff, the army of Persia and Media, the nobles, and the officials from the provinces....

On the seventh day, when the king was feeling good from the wine, Ahasuerus commanded Mehuman, Biztha, Harbona, Bigtha, Abagtha, Zethar, and Carkas — the seven eunuchs who personally served him — to bring Queen Vashti before him with her royal crown. He wanted to show off her beauty to the people and the officials, because she was very beautiful. But Queen Vashti refused to come at the king's command that was delivered by his eunuchs. The king became furious and his anger burned within him....

Memucan said in the presence of the king and his officials, "Queen Vashti has wronged not only the king, but all the officials and the peoples who are in every one of King Ahasuerus's provinces....

"If it meets the king's approval, he should personally issue a royal decree. Let it be recorded in the laws of the Persians and the Medes, so that it cannot be revoked: Vashti is not to enter King Ahasuerus's presence, and her royal position is to be given to another woman who is more worthy than she. The decree the king issues will be heard throughout his vast kingdom, so all women will honor their husbands, from the greatest to the least."

—*Esther 1:1–3,10–12,16,19–20*

WEIRD OR WHAT?

The name of God is not mentioned in the entire book of Esther. Nevertheless, the book's 167 verses definitely show the hand of God working in people's lives. Esther is a story of God's love for the Israelites and his protection for them.

God is always loving and protecting—even when you're not aware of it. Today, look for ways God might be working in your life that you typically wouldn't notice. His work doesn't stop, even when his name isn't mentioned.

Related Texts: Ezra 4:1–6;
Proverbs 31:1–9; Daniel 9:1–2;
1 Corinthians 6:9–10

In the fortress of Susa, there was a Jewish man named Mordecai son of Jair, son of Shimei, son of Kish, a Benjaminite. Kish had been taken into exile from Jerusalem with the other captives when King Nebuchadnezzar of Babylon took King Jeconiah of Judah into exile. Mordecai was the legal guardian of his cousin Hadassah (that is, Esther), because she had no father or mother. The young woman had a beautiful figure and was extremely good-looking. When her father and mother died, Mordecai had adopted her as his own daughter.

When the king's command and edict became public knowledge and when many young women were gathered at the fortress of Susa under Hegai's supervision, Esther was taken to the palace, into the supervision of Hegai, keeper of the women. The young woman pleased him and gained his favor so that he accelerated the process of the beauty treatments and the special diet that she received. He assigned seven hand-picked female servants to her from the palace and transferred her and her servants to the harem's best quarters.

Esther did not reveal her ethnicity or her family background, because Mordecai had ordered her not to make them known. Every day Mordecai took a walk in front of the harem's courtyard to learn how Esther was doing and to see what was happening to her. . . .

The king loved Esther more than all the other women. She won more favor and approval from him than did any of the other virgins. He placed the royal crown on her head and made her queen in place of Vashti.

–Esther 2:5–11,17

BIBLICAL BIO

Esther was a Jewish orphan raised in Persia by her uncle Mordecai. She became the queen of Persia when the previous queen refused to appear at a banquet hosted by her husband. Her absence offended the king, and he chose Esther to replace her.

As queen, Esther kept her Jewish identity a secret even though she remained faithful to the Jewish people by stopping a madman from destroying the Jewish race (see tomorrow's reading).

Over and over, the Bible reveals that God uses unlikely people like Esther to do great things. Sometimes God uses men; other times he uses women. You never know when he's going to use you. Prepare yourself to be used by God—it may be your turn today.

Related Texts: Genesis 39; 41; Nehemiah 1:1–11; 1 Peter 3:1–6

After all this took place, King Ahasuerus honored Haman, son of Hammedatha the Agagite. He promoted him in rank and gave him a higher position than all the other officials. The entire royal staff at the King's Gate bowed down and paid homage to Haman, because the king had commanded this to be done for him. But Mordecai would not bow down or pay homage....

When Haman saw that Mordecai was not bowing down or paying him homage, he was filled with rage. And when he learned of Mordecai's ethnic identity, it seemed repugnant to Haman to do away with Mordecai alone. He planned to destroy all of Mordecai's people, the Jews, throughout Ahasuerus's kingdom....

Then Haman informed King Ahasuerus, "There is one ethnic group, scattered throughout the peoples in every province of your kingdom, keeping themselves separate. Their laws are different from everyone else's and they do not obey the king's laws. It is not in the king's best interest to tolerate them. If the king approves, let an order be drawn up authorizing their destruction, and I will pay 375 tons of silver to the officials for deposit in the royal treasury."

The king removed his signet ring from his hand and gave it to Haman son of Hammedatha the Agagite, the enemy of the Jews. Then the king told Haman, "The money and people are given to you to do with as you see fit."

—*Esther 3:1–2,5–6,8–11*

IN OTHER WORDS

Haman was a madman full of pride who became outraged when Mordecai didn't bow to him. Rather than confronting Mordecai with his anger, he made an oath to kill the entire race of Jewish people. But God stopped his plans and used Esther to save them. Haman was then killed as a result of his evil plans.

Throughout the years, Haman has been followed by others like him who have expressed rage and hatred by committing crimes on innocent victims. These angry people are all around you. Today, ask God to give you a sensitive heart that mourns over the hatred expressed by others. Walk in love today and be a living example of someone who loves and follows God's ways.

Related Texts: Genesis 12:1–3; Deuteronomy 30:1–7; Esther 4–6; Psalm 44:1–8; Daniel 3; 6; Romans 9–11

The king and Haman came to feast with Esther the queen. Once again, on the second day while drinking wine, the king asked Esther, "Queen Esther, whatever you ask will be given to you. Whatever you seek, even to half the kingdom, will be done."

Queen Esther answered, "If I have found favor with you, Your Majesty, and if the king is pleased, spare my life; this is my request. And spare my people; this is my desire. For my people and I have been sold to destruction, death, and annihilation. If we had merely been sold as male and female slaves, I would have kept silent. Indeed, the trouble wouldn't be worth burdening the king."

King Ahasuerus spoke up and asked Queen Esther, "Who is this, and where is the one who would devise such a scheme?"

Esther answered, "The adversary and enemy is this evil Haman."

Haman stood terrified before the king and queen. . . .

Harbona, one of the king's eunuchs, said, "There is a gallows seventy-five feet tall at Haman's house that he made for Mordecai, who gave the report that saved the king."

The king said, "Hang him on it."

They hanged Haman on the gallows he had prepared for Mordecai. Then the king's anger subsided.

—Esther 7:1–6, 9–10

JUST A THOUGHT

When a situation seems hopeless, remind yourself of God's power and ask him to turn things around. He has done it before and can do it again.

Related Texts: Deuteronomy 23:3–5; Esther 8–10; Joel 3:1–8; Obadiah 15; Revelation 19:11–20:10

See, I am going to send my messenger, and he will clear the way before me. Then the Lord you seek will suddenly come to his temple, the Messenger of the covenant you delight in — see, he is coming," says the LORD of Armies. But who can endure the day of his coming? And who will be able to stand when he appears? For he will be like a refiner's fire and like launderer's bleach. He will be like a refiner and purifier of silver; he will purify the sons of Levi and refine them like gold and silver. Then they will present offerings to the LORD in righteousness. And the offerings of Judah and Jerusalem will please the LORD as in days of old and years gone by.

—Malachi 3:1–4

"For look, the day is coming, burning like a furnace, when all the arrogant and everyone who commits wickedness will become stubble. The coming day will consume them," says the LORD of Armies, "not leaving them root or branches. But for you who fear my name, the sun of righteousness will rise with healing in its wings, and you will go out and playfully jump like calves from the stall. You will trample the wicked, for they will be ashes under the soles of your feet on the day I am preparing," says the LORD of Armies. . . .

Look, I am going to send you the prophet Elijah before the great and terrible day of the LORD comes. And he will turn the hearts of fathers to their children and the hearts of children to their fathers. Otherwise, I will come and strike the land with a curse."

—Malachi 4:1–3,5–6

WEIRD OR WHAT?

Malachi is the last of the Old Testament prophets. But we know nothing about Malachi himself — all we have are his written words. Yet by these words, we can sense his dynamic love for God and faith in God's plan.

What would your words tell the world about your love and faith in God?

Related Texts: Isaiah 60; Matthew 3:1–12; 17:10–13; Luke 1:1–17

And now, says the LORD,
who formed me
from the womb to be
his servant,
to bring Jacob back to him
so that Israel might be gathered
to him;
for I am honored in the sight
of the LORD,
and my God is my strength —
he says,
"It is not enough for you to be
my servant
raising up the tribes of Jacob
and restoring the protected ones
of Israel.
I will also make you a light
for the nations,
to be my salvation to the ends
of the earth."
—Isaiah 49:5–6

Bethlehem Ephrathah,
you are small among the clans
of Judah;
one will come from you
to be ruler over Israel for me.
His origin is from antiquity,
from ancient times.
Therefore, Israel will be
abandoned until the time
when she who is in labor
has given birth;
then the rest of the ruler's
brothers will return
to the people of Israel.
He will stand and shepherd them
in the strength of the LORD,
in the majestic name of the LORD
his God.
They will live securely,
for then his greatness will extend
to the ends of the earth.
—Micah 5:2–4

DIG DEEPER

When God says, "I will appoint you,"(Isa 49:8) it means to "to receive the authority, permission, and support to be sent out." Today, churches often "appoint" or "commission" ministers and missionaries as they are sent out. They are appointed and supported with prayer and often with finances to serve God in different parts of the world.

In Matthew 28:19–20, Jesus appointed his followers by saying, "Go, therefore, and make disciples of all nations, baptizing them in the name of the Father and of the Son and of the Holy Spirit, teaching them to observe everything I have commanded you. And remember, I am with you always, to the end of the age."

Today, pray for a missionary you know and ask God to show you how you might be appointed to make disciples in your "nation" (school, neighborhood, church, etc.).

Related Texts: Genesis 35:14–19; Ruth 4:10–17; 1 Samuel 17:12; Matthew 2:1–6

I continued watching in the night visions,
and suddenly one like a son of man
was coming with the clouds of heaven.
He approached the Ancient of Days
and was escorted before him.
He was given dominion
and glory and a kingdom,
so that those of every people, nation, and language
should serve him.
His dominion is
an everlasting dominion
that will not pass away,
and his kingdom is one
that will not be destroyed.
—*Daniel 7:13–14*

Long ago God spoke to our ancestors by the prophets at different times and in different ways. In these last days, he has spoken to us by his Son. God has appointed him heir of all things and made the universe through him. The Son is the radiance of God's glory and the exact expression of his nature, sustaining all things by his powerful word. After making purification for sins, he sat down at the right hand of the Majesty on high. So he became superior to the angels, just as the name he inherited is more excellent than theirs.

For to which of the angels did he ever say,

You are my Son;
today I have become your Father,

or again,

I will be his Father,
and he will be my Son?
—*Hebrews 1:1–5*

ONE-MINUTE MEMORY

"The Son is the radiance of God's glory and the exact expression of his nature, sustaining all things by his powerful word" (Heb 1:3).

Related Texts: 2 Samuel 7:14;
1 Chronicles 17:13; Psalm 2:7;
Matthew 23:63–64; Mark 14:61–62;
Luke 22:67–70; John 1:32–34

The birth of Jesus Christ came about this way: After his mother Mary had been engaged to Joseph, it was discovered before they came together that she was pregnant from the Holy Spirit. So her husband, Joseph, being a righteous man, and not wanting to disgrace her publicly, decided to divorce her secretly.

But after he had considered these things, an angel of the Lord appeared to him in a dream, saying, "Joseph, son of David, don't be afraid to take Mary as your wife, because what has been conceived in her is from the Holy Spirit. She will give birth to a son, and you are to name him Jesus, because he will save his people from their sins."

Now all this took place to fulfill what was spoken by the Lord through the prophet:

**See, the virgin will
    become pregnant
and give birth to a son,
and they will
    name him Immanuel,**

which is translated "God is with us."

When Joseph woke up, he did as the Lord's angel had commanded him. He married her but did not have sexual relations with her until she gave birth to a son. And he named him Jesus.

—Matthew 1:18–25

IN OTHER WORDS

There is one God who exists in three persons: Father, Son, and Holy Spirit. God the Holy Spirit lives within followers of Jesus. When Jesus left the earth, God gave Christians the Holy Spirit to guide them. The Bible reveals that God the Holy Spirit is one with God the Father and God the Son. The Holy Spirit is also called our Helper, Counselor, and Comforter.

The Holy Spirit's role is to direct Christians, comfort them, convict them of sin, help them understand and obey God's will, and speak to God on their behalf.

Today, pray that the Holy Spirit would be evident in your life.

Related Texts: Isaiah 7:14; Matthew 2; Luke 1–2; John 4:1–42

Every year his parents traveled to Jerusalem for the Passover Festival. When he was twelve years old, they went up according to the custom of the festival. After those days were over, as they were returning, the boy Jesus stayed behind in Jerusalem, but his parents did not know it. Assuming he was in the traveling party, they went a day's journey. Then they began looking for him among their relatives and friends. When they did not find him, they returned to Jerusalem to search for him. After three days, they found him in the temple sitting among the teachers, listening to them and asking them questions. And all those who heard him were astounded at his understanding and his answers. When his parents saw him, they were astonished, and his mother said to him, "Son, why have you treated us like this? Your father and I have been anxiously searching for you."

"Why were you searching for me?" he asked them. "Didn't you know that it was necessary for me to be in my Father's house?" But they did not understand what he said to them.

Then he went down with them and came to Nazareth and was obedient to them. His mother kept all these things in her heart. And Jesus increased in wisdom and stature, and in favor with God and with people.

—Luke 2:41–52

WEIRD OR WHAT?

The Bible is God's complete instruction manual to the world. But it's interesting that God provides very little information about Jesus's teenage years. For some reason God didn't reveal much about what Jesus did from his birth until his public ministry (which began when Jesus was approximately thirty years old). It's assumed that Jesus grew up like most Jewish boys—except that Jesus was also fully God.

Related Texts: 1 Samuel 2:21,26; Psalms 26:8; 27:4; 65; Matthew 2:13–23; John 2:13–17; 2 Corinthians 4:18–5:4

The beginning of the gospel of Jesus Christ, the Son of God. As it is written in Isaiah the prophet:

**See, I am sending
my messenger ahead
of you;
he will prepare your way.
A voice of one crying out
in the wilderness:
Prepare the way for the Lord;
make his paths straight!**

John came baptizing in the wilderness and proclaiming a baptism of repentance for the forgiveness of sins. The whole Judean countryside and all the people of Jerusalem were going out to him, and they were baptized by him in the Jordan River, confessing their sins. John wore a camel-hair garment with a leather belt around his waist and ate locusts and wild honey.

He proclaimed, "One who is more powerful than I am is coming after me. I am not worthy to stoop down and untie the strap of his sandals. I baptize you with water, but he will baptize you with the Holy Spirit."

In those days Jesus came from Nazareth in Galilee and was baptized in the Jordan by John. As soon as he came up out of the water, he saw the heavens being torn open and the Spirit descending on him like a dove. And a voice came from heaven: "You are my beloved Son; with you I am well-pleased."

—Mark 1:1–11

IN OTHER WORDS

Baptism can be defined as an outward act that represents an inward decision. Baptism follows a faith decision and shouts to the world, "I'm a follower of Jesus!" Baptism without faith is nothing more than a bath taken in front of others.

During baptism, when the person is dunked under water, it is symbolic of the person dying to the world and being buried. Then the rising up from the water symbolizes a resurrection to a new beginning and a new life in Jesus. It's a picture of your old, sinful nature being buried in water, while the new person (in Jesus) is risen to a new life.

If you haven't been baptized, you might want to ask about it so you can follow Jesus's command to be baptized and express your commitment to follow him.

Related Texts: Isaiah 40:3; Malachi 3:1; Matthew 3; Luke 3; John 1:19–34

Then Jesus was led up by the Spirit into the wilderness to be tempted by the devil. After he had fasted forty days and forty nights, he was hungry. Then the tempter approached him and said, "If you are the Son of God, tell these stones to become bread."

He answered, "It is written: **Man must not live on bread alone but on every word that comes from the mouth of God."**

Then the devil took him to the holy city, had him stand on the pinnacle of the temple, and said to him, "If you are the Son of God, throw yourself down. For it is written:

He will give his angels orders concerning you,
and **they will support you with their hands**
so that you will not strike your foot against a stone."

Jesus told him, "It is also written: **Do not test the Lord your God."**

Again, the devil took him to a very high mountain and showed him all the kingdoms of the world and their splendor. And he said to him, "I will give you all these things if you will fall down and worship me."

Then Jesus told him, "Go away, Satan! For it is written: **Worship the Lord your God, and serve only him."**

Then the devil left him, and angels came and began to serve him.

—Matthew 4:1–11

HERE'S THE DEAL

Jesus experienced temptation so that God could reward his victory over Satan. But he was also tempted for your own good. Because he went through temptations as a human, he completely understands the temptations that you go through.

Jesus used the same weapons to fight temptation that are available to you today. He used the Scriptures, the power of the Holy Spirit, and prayer to defeat Satan's temptations. You have access to those same tools today.

Praise God that he understands everything you are going through. He cares about you! That should be enough good news to give you hope for another week.

Related Texts: Deuteronomy 6:13,16; 8:3; Psalm 91:11–12; Mark 1:12–13; Luke 4:1–13

On the third day a wedding took place in Cana of Galilee. Jesus's mother was there, and Jesus and his disciples were invited to the wedding as well. When the wine ran out, Jesus's mother told him, "They don't have any wine."

"What has this concern of yours to do with me, woman?" Jesus asked. "My hour has not yet come."

"Do whatever he tells you," his mother told the servants.

Now six stone water jars had been set there for Jewish purification. . . .

"Fill the jars with water," Jesus told them. So they filled them to the brim. Then he said to them, "Now draw some out and take it to the headwaiter." And they did.

When the headwaiter tasted the water (after it had become wine), he did not know where it came from — though the servants who had drawn the water knew. He called the groom and told him, "Everyone sets out the fine wine first, then, after people are drunk, the inferior. But you have kept the fine wine until now."

Jesus did this, the first of his signs, in Cana of Galilee. He revealed his glory, and his disciples believed in him.

—John 2:1–6,7–11

And there are also many other things that Jesus did, which, if every one of them were written down, I suppose not even the world itself could contain the books that would be written.

—John 21:25

JUST A THOUGHT

If you like to party, you can be assured that God is throwing a great one that will never end!

Related Texts: Isaiah 55; Joel 3:16–18; Amos 9:11–15; John 20:30–31

There was a man from the Pharisees named Nicodemus, a ruler of the Jews. This man came to him at night and said, "Rabbi, we know that you are a teacher who has come from God, for no one could perform these signs you do unless God were with him."

Jesus replied, "Truly I tell you, unless someone is born again, he cannot see the kingdom of God."

"How can anyone be born when he is old?" Nicodemus asked him. "Can he enter his mother's womb a second time and be born?"

Jesus answered, "Truly I tell you, unless someone is born of water and the Spirit, he cannot enter the kingdom of God. . . .

"How can these things be?" asked Nicodemus.

"Are you a teacher of Israel and don't know these things?" Jesus replied. . . . If I have told you about earthly things and you don't believe, how will you believe if I tell you about heavenly things? No one has ascended into heaven except the one who descended from heaven — the Son of Man.

"Just as Moses lifted up the snake in the wilderness, so the Son of Man must be lifted up, so that everyone who believes in him may have eternal life. For God loved the world in this way: He gave his one and only Son, so that everyone who believes in him will not perish but have eternal life.

—John 3:1–5,9–10,12–16

ONE MINUTE MEMORY

"Jesus replied, 'Truly I tell you, unless someone is born again, he cannot see the kingdom of God'" (Jn 3:3).

Related Texts: Numbers 21:1–9; John 1:1–13; 1 Peter 1; 1 John 2:28–29; 3:1–10; 4:7–8; 5

As the crowd was pressing in on Jesus to hear God's word, he was standing by Lake Gennesaret. He saw two boats at the edge of the lake; the fishermen had left them and were washing their nets. He got into one of the boats, which belonged to Simon, and asked him to put out a little from the land. Then he sat down and was teaching the crowds from the boat.

When he had finished speaking, he said to Simon, "Put out into deep water and let down your nets for a catch."

"Master," Simon replied, "we've worked hard all night long and caught nothing. But if you say so, I'll let down the nets."

When they did this, they caught a great number of fish, and their nets began to tear. So they signaled to their partners in the other boat to come and help them; they came and filled both boats so full that they began to sink.

When Simon Peter saw this, he fell at Jesus's knees and said, "Go away from me, because I'm a sinful man, Lord!" For he and all those with him were amazed at the catch of fish they had taken, and so were James and John, Zebedee's sons, who were Simon's partners.

"Don't be afraid," Jesus told Simon. "From now on you will be catching people." Then they brought the boats to land, left everything, and followed him.

—Luke 5:1–11

TAKE A SHOT

If Jesus came to you today and asked you to drop everything and leave everyone to follow him, how would you respond? Write your answer below.

Related Texts: Psalm 51:1–13; Matthew 4:18–22; Mark 1:16–20; John 1:35–51

O n one of those days while he was teaching, Pharisees and teachers of the law were sitting there who had come from every village of Galilee and Judea, and also from Jerusalem. And the Lord's power to heal was in him. Just then some men came, carrying on a stretcher a man who was paralyzed. They tried to bring him in and set him down before him. Since they could not find a way to bring him in because of the crowd, they went up on the roof and lowered him on the stretcher through the roof tiles into the middle of the crowd before Jesus.

Seeing their faith he said, "Friend, your sins are forgiven."

Then the scribes and the Pharisees began to think to themselves, "Who is this man who speaks blasphemies? Who can forgive sins but God alone?"

But perceiving their thoughts, Jesus replied to them, "Why are you thinking this in your hearts? Which is easier: to say, 'Your sins are forgiven,' or to say, 'Get up and walk'? But so that you may know that the Son of Man has authority on earth to forgive sins" — he told the paralyzed man, "I tell you: Get up, take your stretcher, and go home."

Immediately he got up before them, picked up what he had been lying on, and went home glorifying God. Then everyone was astounded, and they were giving glory to God. And they were filled with awe and said, "We have seen incredible things today."

–Luke 5:17–26

IN OTHER WORDS

The teachers of the law viewed this act of Jesus as blasphemous. They believed that only God could forgive sin and they didn't accept Jesus's claim to be God's Son. Because of their limited view of Jesus, his words and actions were unacceptable to these teachers.

Although the teachers didn't believe, they did observe Jesus heal a man they knew to be paralyzed. It's likely this experience left them confused and frustrated and fueled their feelings of hatred toward Jesus.

These leaders wouldn't admit they were wrong and their pride led to a lack of forgiveness. Do you have any areas of your life that you need to be forgiven for?

Ask God to forgive you and cleanse you from anything that is keeping you from following him.

Related Texts: Psalm 25:1–11; Micah 7:18; Matthew 9:1–8; Mark 2:1–12

As he got into the boat, his disciples followed him. Suddenly, a violent storm arose on the sea, so that the boat was being swamped by the waves — but Jesus kept sleeping. So the disciples came and woke him up, saying, "Lord, save us! We're going to die!"

He said to them, "Why are you afraid, you of little faith?" Then he got up and rebuked the winds and the sea, and there was a great calm.

The men were amazed and asked, "What kind of man is this? Even the winds and the sea obey him!"

When he had come to the other side, to the region of the Gadarenes, two demon-possessed men met him as they came out of the tombs. They were so violent that no one could pass that way. Suddenly they shouted, "What do you have to do with us, Son of God? Have you come here to torment us before the time?"

A long way off from them, a large herd of pigs was feeding. "If you drive us out," the demons begged him, "send us into the herd of pigs."

"Go!" he told them. So when they had come out, they entered the pigs, and the whole herd rushed down the steep bank into the sea and perished in the water.
—*Matthew 8:23–32*

TAKE A SHOT

What are some of the storms in your life that make you fearful?

1.

2.

3.

Spend a minute and talk to God about your fears.

Related Texts: Deuteronomy 14:8;
Isaiah 65:1–4; Mark 4:35–5:20
Luke 8:22–39

As he was telling them these things, suddenly one of the leaders came and knelt down before him, saying, "My daughter just died, but come and lay your hand on her, and she will live." So Jesus and his disciples got up and followed him.

Just then, a woman who had suffered from bleeding for twelve years approached from behind and touched the end of his robe, for she said to herself, "If I can just touch his robe, I'll be made well."

Jesus turned and saw her. "Have courage, daughter," he said. "Your faith has saved you." And the woman was made well from that moment.

When Jesus came to the leader's house, he saw the flute players and a crowd lamenting loudly. "Leave," he said, "because the girl is not dead but asleep." And they laughed at him. After the crowd had been put outside, he went in and took her by the hand, and the girl got up. Then news of this spread throughout that whole area.

—Matthew 9:18–26

The prayer of faith will save the sick person, and the Lord will raise him up; if he has committed sins, he will be forgiven. Therefore, confess your sins to one another and pray for one another, so that you may be healed. The prayer of a righteous person is very powerful in its effect.

—James 5:15–16

HERE'S THE DEAL

Jesus isn't walking the earth today performing miracles. But that doesn't mean miracles aren't happening on a daily basis. God's miraculous healing power hasn't stopped!

Today, healing happens in many different ways. One type of healing involves you if you're a Christian. A verse from today's reading states that healing can come from sharing with another person. Here it is again: "Therefore, confess your sins to one another and pray for one another, so that you may be healed" (Jms 5:16).

There's something powerful about confessing your faults or sins to another person. Confession, followed up by prayer, is one way in which God heals. If you are suffering with anger or hatred toward someone or something, try sharing your pain and confessing your feelings to a friend. Pray together and allow God to begin the healing in you. God wants you to live life to its fullest, and unconfessed pain doesn't allow you to live abundantly. Find someone today who will share in your pain.

Related Texts: Habakkuk 2:4; Matthew 9:27–30; Mark 5:21–43; Luke 7:1–10,36–50; 8:22–25,40–56; 17:11–19; 18:35–43

Jesus entered a house, and the crowd gathered again so that they were not even able to eat. When his family heard this, they set out to restrain him, because they said, "He's out of his mind."

The scribes who had come down from Jerusalem said, "He is possessed by Beelzebul," and, "He drives out demons by the ruler of the demons."

So he summoned them and spoke to them in parables: "How can Satan drive out Satan? If a kingdom is divided against itself, that kingdom cannot stand. If a house is divided against itself, that house cannot stand. And if Satan opposes himself and is divided, he cannot stand but is finished. But no one can enter a strong man's house and plunder his possessions unless he first ties up the strong man. Then he can plunder his house.

"Truly I tell you, people will be forgiven for all sins and whatever blasphemies they utter. But whoever blasphemes against the Holy Spirit never has forgiveness, but is guilty of an eternal sin" — because they were saying, "He has an unclean spirit."

—Mark 3:20–30

BIBLICAL BIO

Satan was once a glorious angel, whose glory and power were overshadowed only by God himself. Satan was big time before he messed up! His downfall came when he desired to have the same power as God. This act of pride got him thrown out of heaven.

Today, Satan is intent on demolishing God's kingdom and followers. Satan is effective in this plot because his methods are discreet. He destroys Christians with temptation, guilt, fear, and doubt. He'd love to see you live a life that doesn't reflect godliness. Watch out for the subtle ways he will try to take your eyes off God. He's not a fairytale character; he's for real! Don't let him have any part of you!

Related Texts: Exodus 22:28; Psalm 106:1–37; Matthew 12:22–37; 13:53–58; Mark 6:1–6; Luke 11:14–23; 12:10

So when Jesus looked up and noticed a huge crowd coming toward him, he asked Philip, "Where will we buy bread so that these people can eat?" He asked this to test him, for he himself knew what he was going to do.

Philip answered him, "Two hundred denarii worth of bread wouldn't be enough for each of them to have a little."

One of his disciples, Andrew, Simon Peter's brother, said to him, "There's a boy here who has five barley loaves and two fish — but what are they for so many?"

Jesus said, "Have the people sit down."

There was plenty of grass in that place; so they sat down. The men numbered about five thousand. Then Jesus took the loaves, and after giving thanks he distributed them to those who were seated — so also with the fish, as much as they wanted.

When they were full, he told his disciples, "Collect the leftovers so that nothing is wasted." So they collected them and filled twelve baskets with the pieces from the five barley loaves that were left over by those who had eaten.

When the people saw the sign he had done, they said, "This truly is the Prophet who is to come into the world."

—John 6:5–14

JUST A THOUGHT

A little faith left in the hands of God can turn into big results.

Related Texts: Deuteronomy 8:2–3; Matthew 14:13–21; Mark 6:32–44; Luke 9:10–17

When Jesus came to the region of Caesarea Philippi, he asked his disciples, "Who do people say that the Son of Man is?"

They replied, "Some say John the Baptist; others, Elijah; still others, Jeremiah or one of the prophets."

"But you," he asked them, "who do you say that I am?"

Simon Peter answered, "You are the Messiah, the Son of the living God."

Jesus responded, "Blessed are you, Simon son of Jonah, because flesh and blood did not reveal this to you, but my Father in heaven. And I also say to you that you are Peter, and on this rock I will build my church, and the gates of Hades will not overpower it. I will give you the keys of the kingdom of heaven, and whatever you bind on earth will have been bound in heaven, and whatever you loose on earth will have been loosed in heaven." Then he gave the disciples orders to tell no one that he was the Messiah.

From then on Jesus began to point out to his disciples that it was necessary for him to go to Jerusalem and suffer many things from the elders, chief priests, and scribes, be killed, and be raised the third day.

—*Matthew 16:13–21*

TAKE A SHOT

How would you answer Jesus's question? "Who do you say that I am?" (Mt 16:15). Write a brief description of what you know about Jesus.

Related Texts: Isaiah 52:14–15; Mark 8:27–33; Luke 9:18–22; John 6:67–71

A fter six days Jesus took Peter, James, and John and led them up a high mountain by themselves to be alone. He was transfigured in front of them, and his clothes became dazzling — extremely white as no launderer on earth could whiten them. Elijah appeared to them with Moses, and they were talking with Jesus. Peter said to Jesus, "Rabbi, it's good for us to be here. Let's set up three shelters: one for you, one for Moses, and one for Elijah" — because he did not know what to say, since they were terrified.

A cloud appeared, over-shadowing them, and a voice came from the cloud: "This is my beloved Son; listen to him!"

Suddenly, looking around, they no longer saw anyone with them except Jesus.

As they were coming down the mountain, he ordered them to tell no one what they had seen until the Son of Man had risen from the dead. They kept this word to themselves, questioning what "rising from the dead" meant.

—Mark 9:2–10

The Word became flesh and dwelt among us. We observed his glory, the glory as the one and only Son from the Father, full of grace and truth.

—John 1:14

ONE MINUTE MEMORY

"The Word became flesh and dwelt among us. We observed his glory, the glory as the one and only Son from the Father, full of grace and truth" (Jn 1:14).

Related Texts: Exodus 40:33–35; Matthew 17:1–9; Luke 9:28–36; Romans 16:25–27; 1 Timothy 1:17; Jude 24–25

When they reached the crowd, a man approached and knelt down before him. "Lord," he said, "have mercy on my son, because he has seizures and suffers terribly. He often falls into the fire and often into the water. I brought him to your disciples, but they couldn't heal him."

Jesus replied, "You unbelieving and perverse generation, how long will I be with you? How long must I put up with you? Bring him here to me." Then Jesus rebuked the demon, and it came out of him, and from that moment the boy was healed.

Then the disciples approached Jesus privately and said, "Why couldn't we drive it out?"

"Because of your little faith," he told them. "For truly I tell you, if you have faith the size of a mustard seed, you will tell this mountain, 'Move from here to there,' and it will move. Nothing will be impossible for you."

—Matthew 17:14–20

"Truly I tell you, the one who believes in me will also do the works that I do. And he will do even greater works than these, because I am going to the Father. Whatever you ask in my name, I will do it so that the Father may be glorified in the Son.

—John 14:12–13

HERE'S THE DEAL

You probably won't ever need the opportunity to physically move a mountain—but keep reading. When Jesus used this illustration, he wasn't referring to the finer points of landscaping. Instead, he was teaching a vital truth about faith. Jesus wanted his followers to know that all things are possible with faith. By using the example of the mustard seed, Jesus was emphasizing littleness. He wanted you to know that you don't need a lot of faith to see God do incredible things. With just a little faith, you can move the mountains of difficulty facing you.

Faith is believing that God is God and that he's totally in control.

If you believe this to be true, ask God to help you move a mountain in your life and perform the impossible. Remember, it doesn't take a lot of faith—just a little.

Related Texts: 1 Samuel 16:14–23; Mark 9:14–32; Luke 9:37–45; Romans 4:18–21; 11:1–23; Hebrews 3:16–19

He was praying in a certain place, and when he finished, one of his disciples said to him, "Lord, teach us to pray, just as John also taught his disciples."

He said to them, "Whenever you pray, say,

Father,
your name be honored as holy.
Your kingdom come.
Give us each day
  our daily bread.
And forgive us our sins,
for we ourselves also
  forgive everyone
in debt to us.
And do not bring us
  into temptation."

He also said to them, "Suppose one of you has a friend and goes to him at midnight and says to him, 'Friend, lend me three loaves of bread, because a friend of mine on a journey has come to me, and I don't have anything to offer him.' Then he will answer from inside and say, 'Don't bother me! The door is already locked, and my children and I have gone to bed. I can't get up to give you anything.' I tell you, even though he won't get up and give him anything because he is his friend, yet because of his friend's shameless boldness, he will get up and give him as much as he needs.

"So I say to you, ask, and it will be given to you. Seek, and you will find. Knock, and the door will be opened to you. For everyone who asks receives, and the one who seeks finds, and to the one who knocks, the door will be opened.
—Luke 11:1–10

ONE-MINUTE MEMORY

"He said to them, 'Whenever you pray, say, Father, your name be honored as holy. Your kingdom come. Give us each day our daily bread. And forgive us our sins, for we ourselves also forgive everyone in debt to us. And do not bring us into temptation'" (Lk 11:2–4).

Related Texts: Psalm 89:19–29; Isaiah 9:6–7; Matthew 6:6–13; 7:7–11; Revelation 3:14–22

An argument started among them about who was the greatest of them. But Jesus, knowing their inner thoughts, took a little child and had him stand next to him. He told them, "Whoever welcomes this little child in my name welcomes me. And whoever welcomes me welcomes him who sent me. For whoever is least among you — this one is great."

—Luke 9:46–48

People were bringing little children to him in order that he might touch them, but the disciples rebuked them. When Jesus saw it, he was indignant and said to them, "Let the little children come to me. Don't stop them, because the kingdom of God belongs to such as these. Truly I tell you, whoever does not receive the kingdom of God like a little child will never enter it." After taking them in his arms, he laid his hands on them and blessed them.

—Mark 10:13–16

At that time he rejoiced in the Holy Spirit and said, "I praise you, Father, Lord of heaven and earth, because you have hidden these things from the wise and intelligent and revealed them to infants. Yes, Father, because this was your good pleasure. All things have been entrusted to me by my Father. No one knows who the Son is except the Father, and who the Father is except the Son, and anyone to whom the Son desires to reveal him."

—Luke 10:21–22

BIG TIME WORD

You can learn a lot from a child. Jesus knew this and referred to them as examples to follow.

Look at the following four words that begin with the letters *LIFE* and try to think of ways you can be more childlike (not childish) in your faith.

- Laughter
- Imagination
- Faith
- Enthusiasm

Ask God to help you possess these childlike qualities today!

Related Texts: Psalm 127:3–5; Matthew 18:1–14; 19:13–15; Mark 9:33–37; Luke 18:15–17

A s he was teaching in one of the synagogues on the Sabbath, a woman was there who had been disabled by a spirit for over eighteen years. She was bent over and could not straighten up at all. When Jesus saw her, he called out to her, "Woman, you are free of your disability." Then he laid his hands on her, and instantly she was restored and began to glorify God.

But the leader of the synagogue, indignant because Jesus had healed on the Sabbath, responded by telling the crowd, "There are six days when work should be done; therefore come on those days and be healed and not on the Sabbath day."

But the Lord answered him and said, "Hypocrites! Doesn't each one of you untie his ox or donkey from the feeding trough on the Sabbath and lead it to water? Satan has bound this woman, a daughter of Abraham, for eighteen years — shouldn't she be untied from this bondage on the Sabbath day?"

When he had said these things, all his adversaries were humiliated, but the whole crowd was rejoicing over all the glorious things he was doing.

—Luke 13:10–17

IN OTHER WORDS

The leader accusing Jesus of healing on the Sabbath cared more about the law being broken than he did about the woman who had a broken life. Jesus scolded this man by calling him a hypocrite for not seeing beyond the Sabbath rules and into the needs of a hurting woman. This religious leader would rather the woman suffer than break the rules. He put statutes before personal well-being, and Jesus corrected him.

Don't wait for good timing to ask for a miracle. Right now God is waiting for your words. He's equipped to heal if it's in his plan. It sure can't hurt to ask!

Related Texts: Exodus 20:8–11; Matthew 12:1–14; Mark 2:23–3:6; Luke 6:1–11; 14:1–6; John 5:1–18

Some Pharisees approached him to test him. They asked, "Is it lawful for a man to divorce his wife on any grounds?"

"Haven't you read," he replied, "that he who created them in the beginning **made them male and female**, and he also said, '**For this reason a man will leave his father and mother and be joined to his wife, and the two will become one flesh**'? So they are no longer two, but one flesh. Therefore, what God has joined together, let no one separate."

"Why then," they asked him, "did Moses command us to give divorce papers and to send her away?"

He told them, "Moses permitted you to divorce your wives because of the hardness of your hearts, but it was not like that from the beginning. I tell you, whoever divorces his wife, except for sexual immorality, and marries another commits adultery."

His disciples said to him, "If the relationship of a man with his wife is like this, it's better not to marry."

He responded, "Not everyone can accept this saying, but only those to whom it has been given. For there are eunuchs who were born that way from their mother's womb, there are eunuchs who were made by men, and there are eunuchs who have made themselves that way because of the kingdom of heaven. The one who is able to accept it should accept it."

–Matthew 19:3–12

BIG TIME WORD

Divorce is devastating! If your parents aren't divorced, that's good news. Most likely you know a friend who has or is experiencing the pain of divorce. It isn't easy to live with the pain, loss, guilt, and frustration that goes along with being separated from two people you love the most.

God hates divorce and understands the deep pain associated with it. If you have been affected by divorce, ask God to comfort you. Your pain won't quickly disappear, but be assured that you aren't alone, and you don't have to go through it by yourself. If your parents aren't divorced, pray for the strength of their marriage and ask God to provide you an opportunity to care for a friend who has been hurt by divorce.

Related Texts: Deuteronomy 24:1–4; Mark 10:2–12; 1 Corinthians 7:10–13

A ruler asked him, "Good teacher, what must I do to inherit eternal life?"

"Why do you call me good?" Jesus asked him. "No one is good except God alone. You know the commandments: **Do not commit adultery; do not murder; do not steal; do not bear false witness; honor your father and mother.**"

"I have kept all these from my youth," he said.

When Jesus heard this, he told him, "You still lack one thing: Sell all you have and distribute it to the poor, and you will have treasure in heaven. Then come, follow me."

After he heard this, he became extremely sad, because he was very rich.

Seeing that he became sad, Jesus said, "How hard it is for those who have wealth to enter the kingdom of God! For it is easier for a camel to go through the eye of a needle than for a rich person to enter the kingdom of God."

Those who heard this asked, "Then who can be saved?"

He replied, "What is impossible with man is possible with God."

Then Peter said, "Look, we have left what we had and followed you."

So he said to them, "Truly I tell you, there is no one who has left a house, wife or brothers or sisters, parents or children because of the kingdom of God, who will not receive many times more at this time, and eternal life in the age to come."

–Luke 18:18–30

JUST A THOUGHT

Wealth and happiness don't always go together. Wealthy people who don't know God are spiritually bankrupt. Don't allow yourself to love money more than you love the Creator of money.

Related Texts: Exodus 20:12–16; Deuteronomy 5:16–20; Matthew 19:16–30; Mark 10:17–31; 1 Corinthians 13:3

He entered Jericho and was passing through. There was a man named Zacchaeus who was a chief tax collector, and he was rich. He was trying to see who Jesus was, but he was not able because of the crowd, since he was a short man. So running ahead, he climbed up a sycamore tree to see Jesus, since he was about to pass that way. When Jesus came to the place, he looked up and said to him, "Zacchaeus, hurry and come down because today it is necessary for me to stay at your house."

So he quickly came down and welcomed him joyfully. All who saw it began to complain, "He's gone to stay with a sinful man."

But Zacchaeus stood there and said to the Lord, "Look, I'll give half of my possessions to the poor, Lord. And if I have extorted anything from anyone, I'll pay back four times as much."

"Today salvation has come to this house," Jesus told him, "because he too is a son of Abraham. For the Son of Man has come to seek and to save the lost."

–Luke 19:1–10

And just as it is appointed for people to die once — and after this, judgment — so also Christ, having been offered once to bear the sins of many, will appear a second time, not to bear sin, but to bring salvation to those who are waiting for him.

–Hebrews 9:27–28

HERE'S THE DEAL

Today's society has established an unwritten and often unspoken standard by which many people measure their self-worth. This standard often includes money, popularity, possessions, and career positions. Many people spend their life trying to be noticed for what they have and what they do. And, if they reach a certain standard, they feel better about themselves. This isn't a universal standard, and it's definitely not a biblical standard for being important or influential.

The Bible's standard for being influential is in complete opposition to those who are working to acquire and achieve status. Jesus told his closest followers that influential people in God's eyes are those who serve. Think about that for a minute. If you want to be great—if you want status in God's eyes—if you want to be an influencer in today's world—you need to learn to serve others.

Try living by God's standards and discover ways you can influence someone today by serving them.

Related Texts: Ezekiel 34:7–16; Mark 2:14–17; Luke 7:36–47

Six days before the Passover, Jesus came to Bethany where Lazarus was, the one Jesus had raised from the dead. So they gave a dinner for him there; Martha was serving them, and Lazarus was one of those reclining at the table with him. Then Mary took a pound of perfume, pure and expensive nard, anointed Jesus's feet, and wiped his feet with her hair. So the house was filled with the fragrance of the perfume.

Then one of his disciples, Judas Iscariot (who was about to betray him), said, "Why wasn't this perfume sold for three hundred denarii and given to the poor?" He didn't say this because he cared about the poor but because he was a thief. He was in charge of the money-bag and would steal part of what was put in it.

Jesus answered, "Leave her alone; she has kept it for the day of my burial. For you always have the poor with you, but you do not always have me."

Then a large crowd of the Jews learned he was there. They came not only because of Jesus but also to see Lazarus, the one he had raised from the dead. But the chief priests had decided to kill Lazarus also, because he was the reason many of the Jews were deserting them and believing in Jesus.

—John 12:1–11

IN OTHER WORDS

The twelve men Jesus chose to be with him on a regular basis were called "disciples." The word *disciple* is related to a verb that means "to learn." A disciple was someone who developed a special relationship with a rabbi and learned from his teachings.

Today, "disciple" refers to someone who is committed to learn from another follower of Jesus. Do you know a leader or teacher who is more knowledgeable than you? Can you become that person's disciple and learn more about God's ways? This relationship can be a great investment of your time as long as you remember to put your faith in Jesus and not in the other person.

Related Texts: Psalm 16:9–11;
Matthew 26:6–13; Mark 14:3–9;
Luke 7:36–50; John 11

As he approached Bethphage and Bethany, at the place called the Mount of Olives, he sent two of the disciples and said, "Go into the village ahead of you. As you enter it, you will find a colt tied there, on which no one has ever sat. Untie it and bring it. If anyone asks you, 'Why are you untying it?' say this: 'The Lord needs it.'"

So those who were sent left and found it just as he had told them. As they were untying the colt, its owners said to them, "Why are you untying the colt?"

"The Lord needs it," they said. Then they brought it to Jesus, and after throwing their clothes on the colt, they helped Jesus get on it. As he was going along, they were spreading their clothes on the road. Now he came near the path down the Mount of Olives, and the whole crowd of the disciples began to praise God joyfully with a loud voice for all the miracles they had seen:

Blessed is the King who comes in the name of the Lord.
Peace in heaven
and glory in the highest heaven!

Some of the Pharisees from the crowd told him, "Teacher, rebuke your disciples."

He answered, "I tell you, if they were to keep silent, the stones would cry out."

–Luke 19:29–40

DIG DEEPER

Jesus entered Jerusalem as the Messiah. His arrival had been prophesied for hundreds of years, but the Jewish people did not recognize him as their Messiah and Savior (and most don't even to this day). Check out the prophecy in Psalm 118:22–26:

The stone that the builders rejected has become the cornerstone. This came from the LORD; it is wondrous in our sight. This is the day the LORD has made; let's rejoice and be glad in it. LORD, save us! LORD, please grant us success! He who comes in the name of the LORD is blessed. From the house of the LORD we bless you.

It has also been foretold in the Bible that Jesus will return to earth again someday. This is called the second coming. And, as before, some will reject this truth. Don't allow yourself to miss the signs of Jesus's return.

Related Texts: Psalm 118;
Matthew 21:1–9; Mark 11:1–10;
John 12:12–19

Now he began to tell the people this parable: "A man planted a vineyard, leased it to tenant farmers, and went away for a long time. At harvest time he sent a servant to the farmers so that they might give him some fruit from the vineyard. But the farmers beat him and sent him away empty-handed. He sent yet another servant, but they beat that one too, treated him shamefully, and sent him away empty-handed. And he sent yet a third, but they wounded this one too and threw him out.

"Then the owner of the vineyard said, 'What should I do? I will send my beloved son. Perhaps they will respect him.'

"But when the tenant farmers saw him, they discussed it among themselves and said, 'This is the heir. Let's kill him, so that the inheritance will be ours.' So they threw him out of the vineyard and killed him.

"What then will the owner of the vineyard do to them? He will come and kill those farmers and give the vineyard to others."

But when they heard this they said, "That must never happen!"

But he looked at them and said, "Then what is the meaning of this Scripture:

The stone that the builders
rejected
has become the cornerstone?
Everyone who falls on that stone will be broken to pieces, but on whomever it falls, it will shatter him."

–Luke 20:9–18

IN OTHER WORDS

Jesus didn't answer the question that he was asked. Instead, he responded by telling them the parable you just read.

This parable illustrates the fact that some people will reject Jesus as God's Son. This rejection will result in their destruction. The message of this parable leaves no room for a compromising position with one's faith. Jesus will either save you or judge you. Those are the two options given.

Take a minute to let God know you have no compromise in your faith and are spiritually prepared for his return.

Related Texts: Psalm 118;
Matthew 21:33–46; Mark 12:1–12

Then one of the Twelve, the man called Judas Iscariot, went to the chief priests and said, "What are you willing to give me if I hand him over to you?" So they weighed out thirty pieces of silver for him. And from that time he started looking for a good opportunity to betray him.

On the first day of Unleavened Bread the disciples came to Jesus and asked, "Where do you want us to make preparations for you to eat the Passover?"

"Go into the city to a certain man," he said, "and tell him, 'The Teacher says: My time is near; I am celebrating the Passover at your place with my disciples.'" So the disciples did as Jesus had directed them and prepared the Passover. When evening came, he was reclining at the table with the Twelve. While they were eating, he said, "Truly I tell you, one of you will betray me."

Deeply distressed, each one began to say to him, "Surely not I, Lord?"

He replied, "The one who dipped his hand with me in the bowl — he will betray me. The Son of Man will go just as it is written about him, but woe to that man by whom the Son of Man is betrayed! It would have been better for him if he had not been born."

Judas, his betrayer, replied, "Surely not I, Rabbi?"

"You have said it," he told him.
—*Matthew 26:14–25*

BIG TIME WORD

One common factor of healthy relationships is that they are built on trust. Betrayal breaks this trust and makes the relationship difficult to repair. Restoration isn't impossible, but it's always difficult to forget when someone has wounded you through an act of betrayal.

Even though humans are known to betray others and even betray God, he has promised not to betray his people. For thousands of years God has kept this promise, and his faithfulness to his promises means he's not about to change his ways. This is good news!

Thank God for this truth and think about how you can keep betrayal out of your life.

Related Texts: Psalm 41:9;
Proverbs 11:13; Mark 14:10–25;
Luke 22:3–23; John 13–17

Then Jesus said to them, "All of you will fall away, because it is written:

I will strike the shepherd,
and the sheep will be
    scattered.

But after I have risen, I will go ahead of you to Galilee."

Peter told him, "Even if everyone falls away, I will not."

"Truly I tell you," Jesus said to him, "today, this very night, before the rooster crows twice, you will deny me three times."

But he kept insisting, "If I have to die with you, I will never deny you." And they all said the same thing.

Then they came to a place named Gethsemane, and he told his disciples, "Sit here while I pray." He took Peter, James, and John with him, and he began to be deeply distressed and troubled. He said to them, "I am deeply grieved to the point of death. Remain here and stay awake." He went a little farther, fell to the ground, and prayed that if it were possible, the hour might pass from him. And he said, "*Abba*, Father! All things are possible for you. Take this cup away from me. Nevertheless, not what I will, but what you will." Then he came and found them sleeping. He said to Peter, "Simon, are you sleeping? Couldn't you stay awake one hour? Stay awake and pray so that you won't enter into temptation. The spirit is willing, but the flesh is weak."

—Mark 14:27–38

HERE'S THE DEAL

Peter swore that he would never deny or desert Jesus—no matter what the others did. Since that day, thousands of well-intending followers of Jesus have spoken those same words at church, youth retreats, or evangelistic revivals. They say it with the same boldness as Peter. They intend to get their act together and follow Jesus. Inside, they desire to do whatever it takes and change their ways in order to follow Jesus with excitement and intensity. Commonly, however, after the retreat is over and the warm feelings fade, it's easy to return to inconsistent living. Does this sound familiar to you?

Maintaining a vibrant commitment to God requires faith, focus, and discipline. Actually, it's a lot like a marriage. Imagine being married to someone you didn't talk to or spend time with. That marriage would dry up. The same is true in your relationship with God—it needs time. Also ask for help and accountability so that you can stay faithful to your commitment.

_____

_____

_____

_____

_____

_____

_____

_____

_____

_____

Related Texts: Zechariah 13:7;
Mark 14:26–42; Luke 22:31–46;
John 13:36–38

While he was still speaking, suddenly a mob came, and one of the Twelve named Judas was leading them. He came near Jesus to kiss him, but Jesus said to him, "Judas, are you betraying the Son of Man with a kiss?" ...

They seized him, led him away, and brought him into the high priest's house. Meanwhile Peter was following at a distance. They lit a fire in the middle of the courtyard and sat down together, and Peter sat among them. When a servant saw him sitting in the light, and looked closely at him, she said, "This man was with him too."

But he denied it: "Woman, I don't know him."

After a little while, someone else saw him and said, "You're one of them too."

"Man, I am not!" Peter said.

About an hour later, another kept insisting, "This man was certainly with him, since he's also a Galilean."

But Peter said, "Man, I don't know what you're talking about!" Immediately, while he was still speaking, a rooster crowed. Then the Lord turned and looked at Peter. So Peter remembered the word of the Lord, how he had said to him, "Before the rooster crows today, you will deny me three times." And he went outside and wept bitterly.

—Luke 22:47–48,54–62

BIBLICAL BIO

Peter was one of Jesus's most enthusiastic and committed followers. He was the first disciple and one of the closest to Jesus.

Although Peter denied Jesus when he was arrested, he later turned around and became very outspoken about Jesus's death, resurrection, and power to change a life. In the book of Acts, Peter is seen as an instrumental figure in the beginning of the early church—the same church that you are a part of today. Jesus referred to Peter as a "rock" (Mt 16:18). Jesus knew Peter's faults, but he viewed him as a solid rock and a person who played a key role in the foundation of the church.

Is there anything about your life and your current faith in Jesus that would give you rock-like status? Can you build faithfulness on the foundation of your faith?

Related Texts: Psalm 42;
Matthew 26:47–56,69–75;
Mark 14:43–53,66–72;
John 18:2–12,25–27

The chief priests and the whole Sanhedrin were looking for testimony against Jesus to put him to death, but they could not find any. For many were giving false testimony against him, and the testimonies did not agree. Some stood up and gave false testimony against him, stating, "We heard him say, 'I will destroy this temple made with human hands, and in three days I will build another not made by hands.'" Yet their testimony did not agree even on this.

Then the high priest stood up before them all and questioned Jesus, "Don't you have an answer to what these men are testifying against you?" But he kept silent and did not answer. Again the high priest questioned him, "Are you the Messiah, the Son of the Blessed One?"

"I am," said Jesus, "and you will see **the Son of Man seated at the right hand** of Power and **coming with the clouds of heaven.**"

Then the high priest tore his robes and said, "Why do we still need witnesses? You have heard the blasphemy. What is your decision?" They all condemned him as deserving death.

Then some began to spit on him, to blindfold him, and to beat him, saying, "Prophesy!" The temple servants also took him and slapped him.

—Mark 14:55–65

JUST A THOUGHT

Jesus could withstand the abuses of others because he had already surrendered to the will of God. He knew God was with him no matter what people said or did. What about you? Does that sound like you?

Related Texts: Exodus 20:16; Daniel 7:13–14; Matthew 26:59–67; Mark 14:55–65; Luke 23:63–71; John 18:19–24

Two others — criminals — were also led away to be executed with him. When they arrived at the place called The Skull, they crucified him there, along with the criminals, one on the right and one on the left. Then Jesus said, "Father, forgive them, because they do not know what they are doing." And they divided his clothes and cast lots.

The people stood watching, and even the leaders were scoffing: "He saved others; let him save himself if this is God's Messiah, the Chosen One!"...

Then one of the criminals hanging there began to yell insults at him: "Aren't you the Messiah? Save yourself and us!"

But the other answered, rebuking him: "Don't you even fear God, since you are undergoing the same punishment? We are punished justly, because we're getting back what we deserve for the things we did, but this man has done nothing wrong." Then he said, "Jesus, remember me when you come into your kingdom."

And he said to him, "Truly I tell you, today you will be with me in paradise."

It was now about noon, and darkness came over the whole land until three, because the sun's light failed. The curtain of the sanctuary was split down the middle. And Jesus called out with a loud voice, "Father, **into your hands I entrust my spirit.**" Saying this, he breathed his last.

When the centurion saw what happened, he began to glorify God, saying, "This man really was righteous!"

−Luke 23:32−35,39−47

IN OTHER WORDS

Grace is defined as "undeserved favor." God expresses grace to you even though you don't deserve it. You are shown God's grace not for anything you have done. Actually, there's nothing you can do to earn God's grace. It's a free gift from God . . . just because he's God.

Jesus expressed grace to one of the criminals hanging on a cross beside him. Imagine the scene: The crucifixion crowd was chaotic; people were yelling at Jesus; he was in unbelievable physical pain. And, in the midst of this moment, he still had compassion to extend grace to a criminal who didn't deserve God's favor.

Imagine yourself as a criminal being charged with the penalty of sin. Then imagine yourself receiving God's love that wipes away the sin. You didn't earn it and certainly don't deserve it. That's quite a gift. It's an unbelievable act of love.

Today, tell someone about God's grace and try to explain how they can receive his love and forgiveness that they don't deserve.

Related Texts: Psalm 22; Matthew 27; Mark 15; Luke 23; John 18:28−19:42

On the first day of the week Mary Magdalene came to the tomb early, while it was still dark. She saw that the stone had been removed from the tomb. So she went running to Simon Peter and to the other disciple, the one Jesus loved, and said to them, "They've taken the Lord out of the tomb, and we don't know where they've put him!"

At that, Peter and the other disciple went out, heading for the tomb. The two were running together, but the other disciple outran Peter and got to the tomb first. Stooping down, he saw the linen cloths lying there, but he did not go in. Then, following him, Simon Peter also came. He entered the tomb and saw the linen cloths lying there. The wrapping that had been on his head was not lying with the linen cloths but was folded up in a separate place by itself. The other disciple, who had reached the tomb first, then also went in, saw, and believed. For they did not yet understand the Scripture that he must rise from the dead....

When it was evening on that first day of the week, the disciples were gathered together with the doors locked because they feared the Jews. Jesus came, stood among them, and said to them, "Peace be with you."

Having said this, he showed them his hands and his side. So the disciples rejoiced when they saw the Lord.

—John 20:1–9,19–20

JUST A THOUGHT

If you don't believe in the resurrection of Jesus, your faith is worth nothing. If Jesus didn't rise from the grave, he's still dead, and so is your faith. Any questions? (See 1Co 15:17.)

Related Texts: Psalm 16:9–11; Isaiah 53:9–12; Matthew 28; Mark 16; Luke 24; John 20–21

Be careful that no one takes you captive through philosophy and empty deceit based on human tradition, based on the elements of the world, rather than Christ. For the entire fullness of God's nature dwells bodily in Christ, and you have been filled by him, who is the head over every ruler and authority. You were also circumcised in him with a circumcision not done with hands, by putting off the body of flesh, in the circumcision of Christ, when you were buried with him in baptism, in which you were also raised with him through faith in the working of God, who raised him from the dead. And when you were dead in trespasses and in the uncircumcision of your flesh, he made you alive with him and forgave us all our trespasses. He erased the certificate of debt, with its obligations, that was against us and opposed to us, and has taken it away by nailing it to the cross. He disarmed the rulers and authorities and disgraced them publicly; he triumphed over them in him.

—Colossians 2:8–15

IN OTHER WORDS

If you are a believer and follower of Jesus you can rejoice over the fact that your "old nature" passed away when Jesus forgave you and entered your life. The Bible teaches that the old nature represents your sinful life before coming to Jesus. Imagine the word *old* having negative images: "dusty," "bad," "smelly," "rotten," and "ragged."

The new nature represents "light," "life," and "eternity." These are great words! Jesus's death conquered the old and put it to death so that you could experience the new. Wow! What's that mean to you today?

You don't have to live life plagued by your past—the old. You're now new! Congratulations! Live it up!

Related Texts: Isaiah 1:11–14; Acts 2:22–36; Romans 6:1–11; 1 Corinthians 15:12–58

I wrote the first narrative, Theophilus, about all that Jesus began to do and teach until the day he was taken up, after he had given instructions through the Holy Spirit to the apostles he had chosen. After he had suffered, he also presented himself alive to them by many convincing proofs, appearing to them over a period of forty days and speaking about the kingdom of God.

While he was with them, he commanded them not to leave Jerusalem, but to wait for the Father's promise. "Which," he said, "you have heard me speak about; for John baptized with water, but you will be baptized with the Holy Spirit in a few days."

So when they had come together, they asked him, "Lord, are you restoring the kingdom to Israel at this time?"

He said to them, "It is not for you to know times or periods that the Father has set by his own authority. But you will receive power when the Holy Spirit has come on you, and you will be my witnesses in Jerusalem, in all Judea and Samaria, and to the ends of the earth."

After he had said this, he was taken up as they were watching, and a cloud took him out of their sight. While he was going, they were gazing into heaven, and suddenly two men in white clothes stood by them. They said, "Men of Galilee, why do you stand looking up into heaven? This same Jesus, who has been taken from you into heaven, will come in the same way that you have seen him going into heaven."

—Acts 1:1–11

ONE MINUTE MEMORY

"But you will receive power when the Holy Spirit has come on you, and you will be my witnesses in Jerusalem, in all Judea and Samaria, and to the ends of the earth" (Ac 1:8).

Related Texts: 1 Chronicles 16:8,23–31; Psalms 67; 72; Isaiah 45:22–23; 49:6; Luke 24:50–53

When the day of Pentecost had arrived, they were all together in one place. Suddenly a sound like that of a violent rushing wind came from heaven, and it filled the whole house where they were staying. They saw tongues like flames of fire that separated and rested on each one of them. Then they were all filled with the Holy Spirit and began to speak in different tongues, as the Spirit enabled them.

Now there were Jews staying in Jerusalem, devout people from every nation under heaven. When this sound occurred, a crowd came together and was confused because each one heard them speaking in his own language. They were astounded and amazed, saying, "Look, aren't all these who are speaking Galileans? How is it that each of us can hear them in our own native language? Parthians, Medes, Elamites; those who live in Mesopotamia, in Judea and Cappadocia, Pontus and Asia, Phrygia and Pamphylia, Egypt and the parts of Libya near Cyrene; visitors from Rome (both Jews and converts), Cretans and Arabs — we hear them declaring the magnificent acts of God in our own tongues." They were all astounded and perplexed, saying to one another, "What does this mean?" But some sneered and said, "They're drunk on new wine."

−Acts 2:1−13

IN OTHER WORDS

Traditionally, the Jewish people celebrated three major festivals every year and one of them was called the "Festival of Weeks," or Pentecost. It was a festival on the fiftieth day following the Passover celebration. The purpose of this event was for God's people to gather in Jerusalem and give thanks for his faithfulness and renew their commitment to him. It would have been a very common activity for Jesus's disciples to gather and celebrate Pentecost. But this particular Pentecost (described in Acts 2) was extraordinary because several amazing things happened including a diverse crowd hearing about the message of Jesus in their native language—which was quite a miracle! About three thousand people heard Peter's message that day, responded, and were baptized.

Related Texts: Leviticus 23:4−16; Matthew 3:1−12; John 14:15−26; 15:26−27; 16:12−15

Peter stood up with the Eleven, raised his voice, and proclaimed to them, "Fellow Jews and all you residents of Jerusalem, let this be known to you, and pay attention to my words. For these people are not drunk, as you suppose, since it's only nine in the morning. On the contrary, this is what was spoken through the prophet Joel:

And it will be in the last days,
    says God,
that **I will pour out my Spirit**
    on all people;
then your sons
    and your daughters
    will prophesy,
your young men will
    see visions,
and your old men will
    dream dreams.
I will even pour out my Spirit
on my servants in those days,
    both men and women
and they will prophesy. . . .

Then everyone who calls
on the name of the Lord
    will be saved.

"Fellow Israelites, listen to these words: This Jesus of Nazareth was a man attested to you by God with miracles, wonders, and signs that God did among you through him, just as you yourselves know. Though he was delivered up according to God's determined plan and foreknowledge, you used lawless people to nail him to a cross and kill him. God raised him up, ending the pains of death, because it was not possible for him to be held by death . . . .

Peter replied, "Repent and be baptized, each of you, in the name of Jesus Christ for the forgiveness of your sins, and you will receive the gift of the Holy Spirit.
    —Acts 2:14–18,21–24,38

JUST A THOUGHT

God knew the code word to break the lock of Satan's death grip—it was spelled "J E S U S."

Related Texts: Ezekiel 36:16–28;
39:21–29; Joel 2:28–32;
Romans 10:1–13

Now Peter and John were going up to the temple for the time of prayer at three in the afternoon. A man who was lame from birth was being carried there. He was placed each day at the temple gate called Beautiful, so that he could beg from those entering the temple. When he saw Peter and John about to enter the temple, he asked for money. Peter, along with John, looked straight at him and said, "Look at us." So he turned to them, expecting to get something from them. But Peter said, "I don't have silver or gold, but what I do have, I give you: In the name of Jesus Christ of Nazareth, get up and walk!" Then, taking him by the right hand he raised him up, and at once his feet and ankles became strong. So he jumped up and started to walk, and he entered the temple with them — walking, leaping, and praising God. All the people saw him walking and praising God, and they recognized that he was the one who used to sit and beg at the Beautiful Gate of the temple. So they were filled with awe and astonishment at what had happened to him.

—Acts 3:1–10

While they were speaking to the people, the priests, the captain of the temple police, and the Sadducees confronted them, because they were annoyed that they were teaching the people and proclaiming in Jesus the resurrection of the dead. So they seized them and took them into custody until the next day since it was already evening. But many of those who heard the message believed, and the number of the men came to about five thousand.

—Acts 4:1–4

IN OTHER WORDS

Peter and John preached the message that Jesus was alive and had risen from the dead. Jesus's resurrection made it possible for them to have power to heal the beggar.

The people who were mad at the preaching of Peter and John were the same people who forced the crucifixion of Jesus. They saw the five thousand new followers of Jesus responding to the good news, and they became afraid that word of the healing and salvation would spread throughout the country.

The first chapters in Acts record the beginning days of the early church. Two thousand years ago, people were being added to the kingdom of God on a daily basis—just like today!

Can you think of anything you can do to help spread the message of the resurrected Jesus?

_____

_____

_____

_____

_____

_____

Related Texts: Jeremiah 37:15; 38:6; Matthew 15:29–31; 21:1–16; John 5; 14:12–14

When they observed the boldness of Peter and John and realized that they were uneducated and untrained men, they were amazed and recognized that they had been with Jesus. And since they saw the man who had been healed standing with them, they had nothing to say in opposition. After they ordered them to leave the Sanhedrin, they conferred among themselves, saying, "What should we do with these men? For an obvious sign has been done through them, clear to everyone living in Jerusalem, and we cannot deny it. But so that this does not spread any further among the people, let's threaten them against speaking to anyone in this name again." So they called for them and ordered them not to speak or teach at all in the name of Jesus.

Peter and John answered them, "Whether it's right in the sight of God for us to listen to you rather than to God, you decide; for we are unable to stop speaking about what we have seen and heard."

After threatening them further, they released them. They found no way to punish them because the people were all giving glory to God over what had been done. For this sign of healing had been performed on a man over forty years old.

After they were released, they went to their own people and reported everything the chief priests and the elders had said to them.

—Acts 4:13–23

HERE'S THE DEAL

The Jewish council knew that Peter and John had no formal training, and yet they were amazed at their teaching and actions. Years earlier Jesus had also surprised the Jewish leaders by his teaching and actions. He handed down this wisdom to his disciples, and they continued by proclaiming the good news to others.

Ask God to give you godly wisdom so you too can amaze others at the power of God's good news.

Related Texts: Jeremiah 20:9; Matthew 5:10–12; Acts 5:17–42

So the word of God spread, the disciples in Jerusalem increased greatly in number, and a large group of priests became obedient to the faith.

Now Stephen, full of grace and power, was performing great wonders and signs among the people. Opposition arose, however, from some members of the Freedmen's Synagogue, composed of both Cyrenians and Alexandrians, and some from Cilicia and Asia, and they began to argue with Stephen. But they were unable to stand up against his wisdom and the Spirit by whom he was speaking.

Then they secretly persuaded some men to say, "We heard him speaking blasphemous words against Moses and God." They stirred up the people, the elders, and the scribes; so they came, seized him, and took him to the Sanhedrin.

—Acts 6:7–12

Stephen, full of the Holy Spirit, gazed into heaven. He saw the glory of God, and Jesus standing at the right hand of God. He said, "Look, I see the heavens opened and the Son of Man standing at the right hand of God!"

They yelled at the top of their voices, covered their ears, and together rushed against him. They dragged him out of the city and began to stone him. And the witnesses laid their garments at the feet of a young man named Saul. While they were stoning Stephen, he called out, "Lord Jesus, receive my spirit!" He knelt down and cried out with a loud voice, "Lord, do not hold this sin against them!" And after saying this, he fell asleep.

—Acts 7:55–60

TAKE A SHOT

Stephen was wrongly accused. Has this ever happened to you? After reading Stephen's response, is there anything you can learn from him if you're ever wrongly accused of something? Write out a blueprint for how you would handle it.

Related Texts: Leviticus 24:10–16; Mark 13:9–13; John 16:1–4; Acts 7:1–54; 8:1–4

O n that day a severe persecution broke out against the church in Jerusalem, and all except the apostles were scattered throughout the land of Judea and Samaria. Devout men buried Stephen and mourned deeply over him. Saul, however, was ravaging the church. He would enter house after house, drag off men and women, and put them in prison.

So those who were scattered went on their way preaching the word.

–Acts 8:1–4

Now Saul was still breathing threats and murder against the disciples of the Lord. He went to the high priest and requested letters from him to the synagogues in Damascus, so that if he found any men or women who belonged to the Way, he might bring them as prisoners to Jerusalem. As he traveled and was nearing Damascus, a light from heaven suddenly flashed around him. Falling to the ground, he heard a voice saying to him, "Saul, Saul, why are you persecuting me?"

"Who are you, Lord?" Saul said.

"I am Jesus, the one you are persecuting," he replied. "But get up and go into the city, and you will be told what you must do."

The men who were traveling with him stood speechless, hearing the sound but seeing no one. Saul got up from the ground, and though his eyes were open, he could see nothing. So they took him by the hand and led him into Damascus. He was unable to see for three days and did not eat or drink.

–Acts 9:1–9

JUST A THOUGHT

Will God have to knock you to the ground and blind you to fulfill his plan for your life? It seems much easier to give him your heart now and save yourself the unnecessary pain.

Related Texts: Daniel 8:26–27; Luke 1:18–20; Acts 22:1–2; 26:1–29

There was a disciple in Damascus named Ananias, and the Lord said to him in a vision, "Ananias."

"Here I am, Lord," he replied.

"Get up and go to the street called Straight," the Lord said to him, "to the house of Judas, and ask for a man from Tarsus named Saul, since he is praying there. In a vision he has seen a man named Ananias coming in and placing his hands on him so that he may regain his sight."

"Lord," Ananias answered, "I have heard from many people about this man, how much harm he has done to your saints in Jerusalem. And he has authority here from the chief priests to arrest all who call on your name."

But the Lord said to him, "Go, for this man is my chosen instrument to take my name to Gentiles, kings, and Israelites. . . .

Ananias went and entered the house. He placed his hands on him and said, "Brother Saul, the Lord Jesus, who appeared to you on the road you were traveling, has sent me so that you may regain your sight and be filled with the Holy Spirit."

At once something like scales fell from his eyes, and he regained his sight. Then he got up and was baptized. And after taking some food, he regained his strength.

Saul was with the disciples in Damascus for some time. Immediately he began proclaiming Jesus in the synagogues: "He is the Son of God."

—Acts 9:10–15,17–20

BIBLICAL BIO

In today's passage, Saul—who would later become known as Paul—was about to have his life changed. He started off with a zealous, anti-Jesus crusade and ended his life as one of the true heroes of the Christian faith.

After Paul's miraculous conversion, he helped grow the early church by announcing the good news about salvation through Jesus. Through his many years of traveling and preaching, Paul started several churches. He then wrote letters to those churches to instruct them on Christian living. Those letters eventually became included in the New Testament.

One of Paul's more interesting instructions was when he directed others to follow him just like he followed Jesus. Paul was worthy of following because he was totally committed to God's ways. Make it a goal to read Paul's letters and follow his teaching. The result will be that you'll become someone worth following too.

Related Texts: Genesis 20;
Numbers 12; 1 Corinthians 15:1–11;
Galatians 1:11–24

As they were worshiping the Lord and fasting, the Holy Spirit said, "Set apart for me Barnabas and Saul for the work to which I have called them." Then after they had fasted, prayed, and laid hands on them, they sent them off.

So being sent out by the Holy Spirit, they went down to Seleucia, and from there they sailed to Cyprus. Arriving in Salamis, they proclaimed the word of God in the Jewish synagogues.... When they had traveled the whole island as far as Paphos, they came across a sorcerer, a Jewish false prophet named Bar-Jesus. He was with the proconsul, Sergius Paulus, an intelligent man. This man summoned Barnabas and Saul and wanted to hear the word of God. But Elymas the sorcerer (that is the meaning of his name) opposed them and tried to turn the proconsul away from the faith.

But Saul — also called Paul — filled with the Holy Spirit, stared straight at Elymas and said, "You are full of all kinds of deceit and trickery, you son of the devil and enemy of all that is right. Won't you ever stop perverting the straight paths of the Lord? Now, look, the Lord's hand is against you. You are going to be blind, and will not see the sun for a time." Immediately a mist and darkness fell on him, and he went around seeking someone to lead him by the hand.

Then, when he saw what happened, the proconsul believed, because he was astonished at the teaching of the Lord.

—Acts 13:2–12

BIBLICAL BIO

Though Barnabas never wrote a book in the Bible, he was known for his tremendous encouragement to Paul and John—who, together, wrote over half of the New Testament. Barnabas was an important figure in the development of the early church because he empowered others through his encouraging words and actions. The name *Barnabas* means "son of encouragement." He lived up to his name!

It's tough to encourage others. Being an encourager requires that you be confident in yourself and in God's ability to use you. It's much easier to be critical than encouraging! Criticism doesn't take much time, thought, or intelligence. However, encouragement requires wisdom and can result in life-change. You'll be able to see great results in others if you replace criticism with encouragement. Try to live up to the name: "son or daughter of encouragement."

Related Texts: Numbers 27:22–23; Deuteronomy 34:9; Matthew 19:13–15; Luke 4:40; Acts 6:1–6; 8:5–25; 1 Timothy 4:11–14

In Lystra a man was sitting who was without strength in his feet, had never walked, and had been lame from birth. He listened as Paul spoke. After looking directly at him and seeing that he had faith to be healed, Paul said in a loud voice, "Stand up on your feet!" And he jumped up and began to walk around. . . .

Some Jews came from Antioch and Iconium, and when they won over the crowds, they stoned Paul and dragged him out of the city, thinking he was dead. After the disciples gathered around him, he got up and went into the town. The next day he left with Barnabas for Derbe.

After they had preached the gospel in that town and made many disciples, they returned to Lystra, to Iconium, and to Antioch, strengthening the disciples by encouraging them to continue in the faith and by telling them, "It is necessary to go through many hardships to enter the kingdom of God." When they had appointed elders for them in every church and prayed with fasting, they committed them to the Lord in whom they had believed. . . .

From there they sailed back to Antioch where they had been commended to the grace of God for the work they had now completed. After they arrived and gathered the church together, they reported everything God had done with them and that he had opened the door of faith to the Gentiles. And they spent a considerable time with the disciples.

—*Acts 14:8–10,19–23,26–28*

BIG TIME WORD

Continue is an important word to understand as a follower of Jesus because the act of growing spiritually is an important goal for a Christian. Your spiritual growth will slow down and eventually stop if you don't continue pursuing God and deepening your faith. Every follower of Christ needs to continue and grow spiritually. Spiritual growth is a reflection of what's taking place in your relationship with God. If you're growing in this relationship, it will be evident in your life and seen by your actions. Your actions and lifestyle will reflect that you are continuing in your faith development.

Are you growing spiritually? Are you continuing in the faith? If not, what actions might you need to take to ensure you're moving ahead and growing spiritually? Continuing in the faith is like learning to drive a car—no one can do it for you.

Related Texts: Exodus 17:1–4; Numbers 14:1–10; 1 Samuel 30:6; John 8:31–59; Acts 7:52–60; 14:1–7; Romans 1:1–17; Ephesians 2:11–22

Give thanks to the LORD; call on
his name;
proclaim his deeds among
the peoples.
Sing to him; sing praise to him;
tell about all his wondrous works!
—1 Chronicles 16:8–9

Come, let's shout joyfully
to the LORD,
shout triumphantly to the rock
of our salvation!
Let's enter his presence
with thanksgiving;
let's shout triumphantly to him
in song.

For the LORD is a great God,
a great King above all gods.
The depths of the earth are
in his hand,
and the mountain peaks are his.
The sea is his; he made it.
His hands formed the dry land.

Come, let's worship
and bow down;
let's kneel before the LORD
our Maker.
For he is our God,
and we are the people
of his pasture,
the sheep under his care.
—Psalm 95:1–7

Rejoice always, pray constantly,
give thanks in everything; for
this is God's will for you in Christ
Jesus.
—1 Thessalonians 5:16–18

ONE-MINUTE MEMORY

"Rejoice always, pray constantly,
give thanks in everything; for this is
God's will for you in Christ Jesus"
(1 Th 5:16–18).

*Related Texts: Nehemiah 12:27–43;
Psalms 77; 135:1–7; 148; Luke 22:14–19*

G ive thanks to the LORD,
  for he is good;
his faithful love endures forever.
Let the redeemed
    of the LORD proclaim
that he has redeemed them
    from the power of the foe
and has gathered them
    from the lands —
from the east and the west,
from the north and the south.

Some wandered
    in the desolate wilderness,
finding no way to a city
    where they could live.
They were hungry and thirsty;
their spirits failed within them.
Then they cried out to the LORD
    in their trouble;
he rescued them
    from their distress.
He led them by the right path
to go to a city where
    they could live.
Let them give thanks to the LORD
for his faithful love
and his wondrous works for
    all humanity.
For he has satisfied the thirsty
and filled the hungry
    with good things. . . .

Let them give thanks to the LORD
for his faithful love
and his wondrous works for
    all humanity.
Let them offer thanksgiving
    sacrifices
and announce his works
    with shouts of joy.
                    —Psalm 107:1−9,21−22

TAKE A SHOT

List five things you're thankful for today:

1.

2.

3.

4.

5.

If you did this exercise every day, your attitude and life would change dramatically. It's hard to be depressed then you're continually thankful.

Related Texts: 2 Chronicles 20:14−26; Psalms 104; 118; 145; Matthew 6:25−34

Let the whole earth shout
triumphantly to the LORD!
Serve the LORD with gladness;
come before him
   with joyful songs.
Acknowledge that the LORD is God.
He made us, and we are his—
his people, the sheep
   of his pasture.
Enter his gates with thanksgiving
and his courts with praise.
Give thanks to him and bless
   his name.
For the LORD is good, and his
   faithful love endures forever;
his faithfulness,
   through all generations.
—Psalm 100

And let the peace of Christ, to
which you were also called
in one body, rule your hearts.
And be thankful. Let the word
of Christ dwell richly among
you, in all wisdom teaching
and admonishing one another
through psalms, hymns, and
spiritual songs, singing to God
with gratitude in your hearts. And
whatever you do, in word or in
deed, do everything in the name
of the Lord Jesus, giving thanks to
God the Father through him.
—Colossians 3:15–17

IN OTHER WORDS

The "body of Christ" refers to the millions of followers of Jesus that make up Christianity. Jesus is the head of this body, and Christians who make up the body receive their life support from him. There are millions of Christians whom you have never met who are part of the same body as you.

As a part of Jesus's body, you represent him and his work to the world. For you to maintain a healthy role in the body you need to be connected to the head. Today, find someone who is part of the body of Christ and see how you might work together to serve others.

Related Texts: 2 Chronicles 6:41; Psalms 65; 84; 96; Ephesians 5:18–20; 3 John 11

G ive thanks to the LORD,
for he is good.
His faithful love endures forever.
Give thanks to the God of gods.
His faithful love endures forever.
Give thanks to the Lord of lords.
His faithful love endures forever.
—Psalm 136:1–3

We always thank God, the Father
of our Lord Jesus Christ, when we
pray for you, for we have heard of
your faith in Christ Jesus and of
the love you have for all the saints
because of the hope reserved for
you in heaven. You have already
heard about this hope in the word
of truth, the gospel that has come
to you. It is bearing fruit and
growing all over the world, just
as it has among you since the day
you heard it and came to truly
appreciate God's grace.
—Colossians 1:3–6

I always thank my God when
I mention you in my prayers,
because I hear of your love for
all the saints and the faith that
you have in the Lord Jesus. I
pray that your participation in
the faith may become effective
through knowing every good
thing that is in us for the glory of
Christ. For I have great joy and
encouragement from your love,
because the hearts of the saints
have been refreshed through
you, brother.
—Philemon 4–7

WEIRD OR WHAT?

In some of Paul's writings he
expresses a deep, heartfelt
thankfulness. At times, the Greek
word that he uses for "heart" or
"affection" literally means "bowels"
(e.g., Php 2:1; Phm 1:12). You
can understand why many biblical
translators have changed the word
from "bowels" to "heart." In Greek
thought (the language of Paul's
writings) the bowels were referred
to as the center of affection. Odd
right? But it wouldn't sound very
good today if "bowels" was used
instead of "heart." Imagine this:
"The Thanksgiving dinner was great,
Mom. I mean that compliment from
the bottom of my bowels!"

No matter what word you choose
to use, express your thankfulness
to God today for creating hearts,
bowels, and everything else that
keeps you alive.

*Related Texts: 1 Chronicles 16:34–36;
2 Chronicles 5–7; Psalms 118:1–4;
136:4–26; 2 Corinthians 9:10–15*

Now the Spirit explicitly says that in later times some will depart from the faith, paying attention to deceitful spirits and the teachings of demons, through the hypocrisy of liars whose consciences are seared. They forbid marriage and demand abstinence from foods that God created to be received with gratitude by those who believe and know the truth. For everything created by God is good, and nothing is to be rejected if it is received with thanksgiving, since it is sanctified by the word of God and by prayer.

If you point these things out to the brothers and sisters, you will be a good servant of Christ Jesus, nourished by the words of the faith and the good teaching that you have followed. But have nothing to do with pointless and silly myths. Rather, train yourself in godliness. For the training of the body has limited benefit, but godliness is beneficial in every way, since it holds promise for the present life and also for the life to come. This saying is trustworthy and deserves full acceptance. For this reason we labor and strive, because we have put our hope in the living God, who is the Savior of all people, especially of those who believe.

Command and teach these things.

−1 Timothy 4:1−11

HERE'S THE DEAL

Today's society values physical fitness and looking good. Billions of dollars are spent yearly by those in desperate search of getting into shape.

Unfortunately, exercise equipment sits unused in garages and gyms around the world. The money to buy the equipment was available, but the discipline to use it wasn't. You know what happens—discouragement sets in, and people give up. It's tough to get back into shape when you've lost your shape (you'll find this out as you get older).

The Bible teaches that spiritual fitness is a much more important goal than physical fitness. Your human body will eventually decay and rot away, but your spiritual body will last forever. Spiritual fitness requires discipline and hard work. If you're not in spiritual shape, get started on a training program that works for you. If you're spiritually fit, stay motivated so your faith doesn't get flabby.

Related Texts: 1 Chronicles 16:4−14; Romans 8:18−28; 1 Corinthians 10

Immediately I was in the Spirit, and there was a throne in heaven and someone was seated on it. The one seated there had the appearance of jasper and carnelian stone. A rainbow that had the appearance of an emerald surrounded the throne.

Around the throne were twenty-four thrones, and on the thrones sat twenty-four elders dressed in white clothes, with golden crowns on their heads.

Flashes of lightning and rumblings and peals of thunder came from the throne. Seven fiery torches were burning before the throne, which are the seven spirits of God. Something like a sea of glass, similar to crystal, was also before the throne.

Four living creatures covered with eyes in front and in back were around the throne on each side. . . . Each of the four living creatures had six wings; they were covered with eyes around and inside. Day and night they never stop, saying,

Holy, holy, holy,
Lord God, the Almighty,
who was, who is,
    and who is to come.

Whenever the living creatures give glory, honor, and thanks to the one seated on the throne, the one who lives forever and ever, the twenty-four elders fall down before the one seated on the throne and worship the one who lives forever and ever. They cast their crowns before the throne and say,

Our Lord and God,
you are worthy to receive
glory and honor and power,

because you have created
    all things,
and by your will
they exist and were created.
    –Revelation 4:2–6,8–11

IN OTHER WORDS

The book of Revelation is John's vision describing what the end of times will be like. The visions and scenes described in this book have been interpreted many different ways by many scholars over hundreds of years. If you struggle to understand the book, you're not alone.

The big picture of Revelation is that Jesus is King and wins the final battle over Satan. That's definitely worth reading about and trying to better understand.

You'll have eternity to praise and thank God for this victory, but why don't you get a head start and praise him today.

Related Texts: Exodus 24:1–11; Isaiah 6; Psalms 103:20–22; 148; Mark 10:17–18

Hallelujah!
Praise God in his sanctuary.
Praise him in his mighty expanse.
Praise him for his powerful acts;
praise him
    for his abundant greatness.

Praise him with the blast of
    a ram's horn;
praise him with harp and lyre.
Praise him with tambourine
    and dance;
praise him with strings and flute.
Praise him
    with resounding cymbals;
praise him with clashing cymbals.

Let everything that breathes
    praise the LORD.
Hallelujah!
                    —Psalm 150

And don't get drunk with wine,
which leads to reckless living, but
be filled by the Spirit: speaking
to one another in psalms, hymns,
and spiritual songs, singing and
making music with your heart to
the Lord, giving thanks always for
everything to God the Father in
the name of our Lord Jesus Christ,
                —Ephesians 5:18–20

ONE-MINUTE MEMORY

"And don't get drunk with wine, which leads to reckless living, but be filled by the Spirit" (Eph 5:18).

Related Texts: Exodus 15:1–21; 1 Chronicles 15–16; Colossians 3:16–17

This was not made known to people in other generations as it is now revealed to his holy apostles and prophets by the Spirit: The Gentiles are coheirs, members of the same body, and partners in the promise in Christ Jesus through the gospel. I was made a servant of this gospel by the gift of God's grace that was given to me by the working of his power.

This grace was given to me —the least of all the saints— to proclaim to the Gentiles the incalculable riches of Christ, and to shed light for all about the administration of the mystery hidden for ages in God who created all things. This is so that God's multi-faceted wisdom may now be made known through the church to the rulers and authorities in the heavens. This is according to his eternal purpose accomplished in Christ Jesus our Lord. In him we have boldness and confident access through faith in him.

—Ephesians 3:5–12

DIG DEEPER

Today's reading provides an important message that you may need to hear. Differences should never separate you from other Christians. We are one in Jesus regardless of gender, race, ethnicity, age, or socioeconomic status—it doesn't matter. We are all one in Jesus!

Paul explains this truth in Galatians 3:28–29: "There is no Jew or Greek, slave or free, male or female; since you are all one in Christ Jesus. And if you belong to Christ, then you are Abraham's seed, heirs according to the promise."

Celebrate this truth today with another follower of Jesus who is different from you by telling him or her you're related.

Related texts: Isaiah 49:1–6; Acts 15; Galatians 3:25–29; Ephesians 2:11–22

Now concerning spiritual gifts: brothers and sisters, I do not want you to be unaware....

Now there are different gifts, but the same Spirit. There are different ministries, but the same Lord. And there are different activities, but the same God works all of them in each person. A manifestation of the Spirit is given to each person for the common good: to one is given a message of wisdom through the Spirit, to another, a message of knowledge by the same Spirit, to another, faith by the same Spirit, to another, gifts of healing by the one Spirit, to another, the performing of miracles, to another, prophecy, to another, distinguishing between spirits, to another, different kinds of tongues, to another, interpretation of tongues. One and the same Spirit is active in all these, distributing to each person as he wills.

—1 Corinthians 12:1,4–11

WEIRD OR WHAT?

In the New Testament there are four different passages that reveal and describe spiritual gifts. It's interesting that none of these passages have the exact same list of gifts. Some believe that the lists weren't intended to be all-inclusive, and others debate that the ones listed are the only spiritual gifts available. Regardless of whether there are nine spiritual gifts or more, God has assigned every believer and follower of Jesus with specific gifts that can be used to strengthen the church. Read through the spiritual gift passages and begin to discover how God has specially gifted you.

(*Also read Rm 12:3–8; 1Co 12:28–30; Eph 4:7–12; 1Pt 4:10–11.)

Related Texts: Exodus 31:1–6; 35:30–36:2; Romans 12:1–8; 1 Corinthians 13–14; Ephesians 4:1–16; Hebrews 2:1–4; 1 Peter 4:7–11

For we know that if our earthly tent we live in is destroyed, we have a building from God, an eternal dwelling in the heavens, not made with hands. Indeed, we groan in this tent, desiring to put on our heavenly dwelling, since, when we are clothed, we will not be found naked. Indeed, we groan while we are in this tent, burdened as we are, because we do not want to be unclothed but clothed, so that mortality may be swallowed up by life. Now the one who prepared us for this very purpose is God, who gave us the Spirit as a down payment.

So we are always confident and know that while we are at home in the body we are away from the Lord. For we walk by faith, not by sight. In fact, we are confident, and we would prefer to be away from the body and at home with the Lord. Therefore, whether we are at home or away, we make it our aim to be pleasing to him. For we must all appear before the judgment seat of Christ, so that each may be repaid for what he has done in the body, whether good or evil.

—2 Corinthians 5:1–10

DIG DEEPER

For a follower of Jesus, a future in heaven and living with God is good news. Christians can view death as victory. Paul expressed this idea by describing the tension between living in pain on earth while spreading the gospel and his desire to depart to be with God. Check out Philippians 1:21: "For me, to live is Christ and to die is gain."

On your worst day, there is still hope for you! What God has planned for his children can't be matched by your greatest day on earth. But while you are on this earth, it works best to live with celebration in your heart and a joyful eye toward your future in God's presence.

Related Texts: Ecclesiastes 12; John 11:20–27; Romans 14:1–13; 1 Corinthians 15:35–54; Philippians 1:20–26

For he chose us in him, before the foundation of the world, to be holy and blameless in love before him. He predestined us to be adopted as sons through Jesus Christ for himself, according to the good pleasure of his will, to the praise of his glorious grace that he lavished on us in the Beloved One.

In him we have redemption through his blood, the forgiveness of our trespasses, according to the riches of his grace that he richly poured out on us with all wisdom and understanding. He made known to us the mystery of his will, according to his good pleasure that he purposed in Christ as a plan for the right time — to bring everything together in Christ, both things in heaven and things on earth in him.

In him we have also received an inheritance, because we were predestined according to the plan of the one who works out everything in agreement with the purpose of his will, so that we who had already put our hope in Christ might bring praise to his glory.

In him you also were sealed with the promised Holy Spirit when you heard the word of truth, the gospel of your salvation, and when you believed. The Holy Spirit is the down payment of our inheritance, until the redemption of the possession, to the praise of his glory.

—Ephesians 1:4–14

TAKE A SHOT

As a follower of Jesus you have been sealed for salvation with God through the Holy Spirit. How does that make you feel right now?

Related Texts: Psalm 113; Romans 8:29–39; Ephesians 2:4–10; Revelation 3:5; 13:8; 17:8; 20:15

If, then, there is any encouragement in Christ, if any consolation of love, if any fellowship with the Spirit, if any affection and mercy, make my joy complete by thinking the same way, having the same love, united in spirit, intent on one purpose. Do nothing out of selfish ambition or conceit, but in humility consider others as more important than yourselves. Everyone should look not to his own interests, but rather to the interests of others.

Adopt the same attitude as that of Christ Jesus,

who, existing in the form
of God,
did not consider equality
with God
as something to be exploited.
Instead he emptied himself
by assuming the form
of a servant,
taking on the likeness
of humanity.
And when he had come
as a man,
he humbled himself
by becoming obedient
to the point of death —
even to death on a cross.
For this reason God
highly exalted him
and gave him the name
that is above every name,
so that at the name of Jesus
every knee will bow —
in heaven and on earth
and under the earth —
and every tongue will confess
that Jesus Christ is Lord,
to the glory of God the Father.

—Philippians 2:1–11

BIG TIME WORD

Having a positive attitude in today's world can really make a difference in your life. People are attracted to those who have good attitudes. Most Christians are known for having good attitudes because of the power and presence of the Holy Spirit residing in them. The Spirit's indwelling allows you to live with confidence that God is in control of your life.

When your attitude is positive, people notice the difference. They can sense the security you have as a follower of Jesus. Peace and joy become reflections of your life. Does that describe you? Is your attitude one that people notice? If not, what may need to change in you to improve your attitude?

Related Texts: Is 45:22–25;
John 13:1–15; Romans 14:11–12;
1 Corinthians 15:20–28;
Philippians 2:19–21; 1 Peter 5:5–6

A lthough I have reasons for confidence in the flesh. If anyone else thinks he has grounds for confidence in the flesh, I have more: circumcised the eighth day; of the nation of Israel, of the tribe of Benjamin, a Hebrew born of Hebrews; regarding the law, a Pharisee; . . .

But everything that was a gain to me, I have considered to be a loss because of Christ. More than that, I also consider everything to be a loss in view of the surpassing value of knowing Christ Jesus my Lord. Because of him I have suffered the loss of all things and consider them as dung, so that I may gain Christ and be found in him, not having a righteousness of my own from the law, but one that is through faith in Christ — the righteousness from God based on faith. . . .

Brothers and sisters, I do not consider myself to have taken hold of it. But one thing I do: Forgetting what is behind and reaching forward to what is ahead, I pursue as my goal the prize promised by God's heavenly call in Christ Jesus.

—Philippians 3:4–5,7–9,13–14

ONE MINUTE MEMORY

"But one thing I do: Forgetting what is behind and reaching forward to what is ahead, I pursue as my goal the prize promised by God's heavenly call in Christ Jesus" (Php 3:13–14).

Related Texts: Psalm 18:30–33; Matthew 5:43–48; Mark 8:34–37; Acts 22:1–21; Colossians 1:24; Hebrews 12:1–3

He is the image
of the invisible God,
the firstborn over all creation.
For everything was created
   by him,
in heaven and on earth,
the visible and the invisible,
whether thrones or dominions
or rulers or authorities —
all things have been created
   through him and for him.
He is before all things,
and by him all things
   hold together.
He is also the head of the body,
   the church;
he is the beginning,
the firstborn from the dead,
so that he might come to have
first place in everything.
For God was pleased to have
all his fullness dwell in him,
and through him to reconcile
everything to himself,
whether things on earth or things
   in heaven,
by making peace
through his blood, shed
   on the cross.

Once you were alienated
and hostile in your minds as
expressed in your evil actions. But
now he has reconciled you by his
physical body through his death,
to present you holy, faultless,
and blameless before him — if
indeed you remain grounded and
steadfast in the faith and are not
shifted away from the hope of
the gospel that you heard. This
gospel has been proclaimed in
all creation under heaven, and I,
Paul, have become a servant of it.
   —Colossians 1:15–23

JUST A THOUGHT

If anyone asks you what God is like, open your Bible and point to Jesus — he's the exact likeness of God. When you know Jesus, you know God.

Related Texts: Genesis 1:26;
John 1:1–18; Romans 5:9–11;
2 Corinthians 5:17–21;
Colossians 2:9–10; Hebrews 1:1–3

We do not want you to be uninformed, brothers and sisters, concerning those who are asleep, so that you will not grieve like the rest, who have no hope. For if we believe that Jesus died and rose again, in the same way, through Jesus, God will bring with him those who have fallen asleep. For we say this to you by a word from the Lord: We who are still alive at the Lord's coming will certainly not precede those who have fallen asleep. For the Lord himself will descend from heaven with a shout, with the archangel's voice, and with the trumpet of God, and the dead in Christ will rise first. Then we who are still alive, who are left, will be caught up together with them in the clouds to meet the Lord in the air, and so we will always be with the Lord. Therefore encourage one another with these words.

−1 Thessalonians 4:13–18

About the times and the seasons: Brothers and sisters, you do not need anything to be written to you. For you yourselves know very well that the day of the Lord will come just like a thief in the night. When they say, "Peace and security," then sudden destruction will come upon them, like labor pains on a pregnant woman, and they will not escape. But you, brothers and sisters, are not in the dark, for this day to surprise you like a thief.

−1 Thessalonians 5:1–4

BIG TIME WORD

Grief is an appropriate emotion to express at the death of a loved one. It's a good thing to be able to grieve when necessary. God created you with the ability to cry and show compassion. If your grief is over the death of a Christian, the good news is that your tears can reflect hope. You can rest in the truth that a Christian's death is entrance into an eternal home in God's presence.

As a follower of Jesus, you have nothing to fear about your future. If you live by faith that your future is sealed with God, you can live with assurance. That's a great way to live! Try it today.

Related Texts: Daniel 12:1–3; Matthew 24; 2 Peter 3; Revelation 3:1–6

Now we command you, brothers and sisters, in the name of our Lord Jesus Christ, to keep away from every brother or sister who is idle and does not live according to the tradition received from us. For you yourselves know how you should imitate us: We were not idle among you; we did not eat anyone's food free of charge; instead, we labored and toiled, working night and day, so that we would not be a burden to any of you. It is not that we don't have the right to support, but we did it to make ourselves an example to you so that you would imitate us. In fact, when we were with you, this is what we commanded you: "If anyone isn't willing to work, he should not eat." For we hear that there are some among you who are idle. They are not busy but busybodies. Now we command and exhort such people by the Lord Jesus Christ to work quietly and provide for themselves. But as for you, brothers and sisters, do not grow weary in doing good.

If anyone does not obey our instruction in this letter, take note of that person; don't associate with him, so that he may be ashamed. Yet don't consider him as an enemy, but warn him as a brother.

—2 Thessalonians 3:6–15

IN OTHER WORDS

Today's passage is an example of biblical church discipline. Paul taught that Jesus would return, but some followers used this truth as an excuse to stop working. Some even began to sponge food and money from others. They wasted their time by gossiping and getting involved in other people's business. As a teacher and pastor, the apostle Paul told them to get busy and begin working.

Work is an important part of your life development. No matter what type of job you currently have, try to do your best to honor God with your positive attitude and hard work. Your work will provide you opportunities to tell coworkers about your love for God. Earn their respect first by living right and working hard.

Related Texts: Genesis 1:26–30; 2:15; 1 Corinthians 9; 2 Corinthians 12:12–18; 1 Thessalonians 2:1–12

If anyone teaches false doctrine and does not agree with the sound teaching of our Lord Jesus Christ and with the teaching that promotes godliness, he is conceited and understands nothing, but has an unhealthy interest in disputes and arguments over words. From these come envy, quarreling, slander, evil suspicions, and constant disagreement among people whose minds are depraved and deprived of the truth, who imagine that godliness is a way to material gain. But godliness with contentment is great gain. For we brought nothing into the world, and we can take nothing out. If we have food and clothing, we will be content with these. . . .

Instruct those who are rich in the present age not to be arrogant or to set their hope on the uncertainty of wealth, but on God, who richly provides us with all things to enjoy. Instruct them to do what is good, to be rich in good works, to be generous and willing to share, storing up treasure for themselves as a good foundation for the coming age, so that they may take hold of what is truly life.

–1 Timothy 6:3–8,17–19

HERE'S THE DEAL

Do you know someone who loves to argue? Some people actually enjoy creating, maintaining, and fueling tension. But arguing for the sake of an argument usually results in wasted chatter. No real purpose is ever served with empty arguments.

Some Christians love to argue about the Bible. They know a lot of biblical answers and enjoy debating non-Christians with their knowledge. Unfortunately, very few people enter into a relationship with God during an argument. Most are defensive and closed-minded while arguing—even if they hear the truth.

Learn as much as you can about the Bible so you can talk rationally, but reserve arguing for another topic. If you replace your arguments with love, you'll find people more responsive to the truth. Love works—even if you don't have all the right Bible answers. Keep learning and replace arguing with love.

Related Texts: Psalm 112:4; Proverbs 11:24–26; 14:31; 19:17; 22:9; 28:8; Luke 12:13–34; 16:1–15; Philippians 4:10–14

But you have followed my teaching, conduct, purpose, faith, patience, love, and endurance, along with the persecutions and sufferings that came to me in Antioch, Iconium, and Lystra. What persecutions I endured — and yet the Lord rescued me from them all. In fact, all who want to live a godly life in Christ Jesus will be persecuted. Evil people and impostors will become worse, deceiving and being deceived. But as for you, continue in what you have learned and firmly believed. You know those who taught you, and you know that from infancy you have known the sacred Scriptures, which are able to give you wisdom for salvation through faith in Christ Jesus. All Scripture is inspired by God and is profitable for teaching, for rebuking, for correcting, for training in righteousness, so that the man of God may be complete, equipped for every good work.

—2 Timothy 3:10–17

ONE-MINUTE MEMORY

"All Scripture is inspired by God and is profitable for teaching, for rebuking, for correcting, for training in righteousness" (2Tm 3:16).

Related Texts: Is 40:6–8;
Matthew 5:10–12; Acts 14;
2 Corinthians 4; 12:1–10;
1 Peter 1:23–2:3

Therefore, since we have a great high priest who has passed through the heavens — Jesus the Son of God — let us hold fast to our confession. For we do not have a high priest who is unable to sympathize with our weaknesses, but one who has been tempted in every way as we are, yet without sin. Therefore, let us approach the throne of grace with boldness, so that we may receive mercy and find grace to help us in time of need.

—Hebrews 4:14–16

During his earthly life, he offered prayers and appeals with loud cries and tears to the one who was able to save him from death, and he was heard because of his reverence. Although he was the Son, he learned obedience from what he suffered. After he was perfected, he became the source of eternal salvation for all who obey him, and he was declared by God a high priest according to the order of Melchizedek.

—Hebrews 5:7–10

Therefore, he had to be like his brothers and sisters in every way, so that he could become a merciful and faithful high priest in matters pertaining to God, to make atonement for the sins of the people. For since he himself has suffered when he was tempted, he is able to help those who are tempted.

—Hebrews 2:17–18

WEIRD OR WHAT?

During Old Testament times the high priest would present sacrifices to pay for—or atone for—people's sins. In the New Testament Jesus is called our "great high priest." His one sacrifice on the cross was totally sufficient for all to be forgiven.

As a follower of Jesus, you have direct access to God and don't need a high priest other than Jesus. Take advantage of that direct access and thank God for Jesus's ultimate sacrifice.

Related Texts: Genesis 14:18–20; Psalm 110; Matthew 4:1–11

Now faith is the reality of what is hoped for, the proof of what is not seen. For by this our ancestors were approved.

By faith we understand that the universe was created by the word of God, so that what is seen was made from things that are not visible.

By faith Abel offered to God a better sacrifice than Cain did. By faith he was approved as a righteous man, because God approved his gifts, and even though he is dead, he still speaks through his faith.

By faith Enoch was taken away, and so he did not experience death. **He was not to be found because God took him away.** For before he was taken away, he was approved as one who pleased God. Now without faith it is impossible to please God, since the one who draws near to him must believe that he exists and that he rewards those who seek him.

By faith Noah, after he was warned about what was not yet seen and motivated by godly fear, built an ark to deliver his family. By faith he condemned the world and became an heir of the righteousness that comes by faith.

By faith Abraham, when he was called, obeyed and set out for a place that he was going to receive as an inheritance. He went out, even though he did not know where he was going.

—Hebrews 11:1–8

TAKE A SHOT

Write your definition of faith:

Now, make it a goal to have a discussion with someone who is more knowledgeable than you regarding Christianity. Discuss your definition with this person.

Related Texts: Genesis 1; 4:1–16; 5:23–24; 6–8; 12; Jude 14–15

By faith even Sarah herself, when she was unable to have children, received power to conceive offspring, even though she was past the age, since she considered that the one who had promised was faithful. Therefore, from one man — in fact, from one as good as dead — came offspring as numerous as the stars of the sky and as innumerable as the grains of sand along the seashore. . . .

By faith Abraham, when he was tested, offered up Isaac. He received the promises and yet he was offering his one and only son, the one to whom it had been said, **Your offspring will be traced through Isaac.** He considered God to be able even to raise someone from the dead; therefore, he received him back, figuratively speaking. . . .

By faith Moses, when he had grown up, refused to be called the son of Pharaoh's daughter and chose to suffer with the people of God rather than to enjoy the fleeting pleasure of sin. For he considered reproach for the sake of Christ to be greater wealth than the treasures of Egypt, since he was looking ahead to the reward.

By faith he left Egypt behind, not being afraid of the king's anger, for Moses persevered as one who sees him who is invisible. . . .

All these were approved through their faith, but they did not receive what was promised, since God had provided something better for us, so that they would not be made perfect without us.

—Hebrews 11:11–12,17–19, 24–27,39–40

DIG DEEPER

Yesterday you wrote your own definition of faith. Today, look at how Jesus responded to his followers' questions about the amount of faith they needed. Check out Matthew 17:20: "If you have faith the size of a mustard seed, you will tell this mountain, 'Move from here to there,' and it will move. Nothing will be impossible for you."

Jesus didn't emphasize the amount of faith needed, instead he stressed that true faith, even in its smallest form, can do great things.

Ask God to help you strengthen your faith today.

Related Texts: Genesis 21–22; Exodus 2–3; Hebrews 10:36–39

C onsider it a great joy,
my brothers and sisters,
whenever you experience various
trials, because you know that the
testing of your faith produces
endurance. And let endurance
have its full effect, so that you
may be mature and complete,
lacking nothing.

Now if any of you lacks
wisdom, he should ask God —
who gives to all generously and
ungrudgingly — and it will be
given to him. But let him ask in
faith without doubting. For the
doubter is like the surging sea,
driven and tossed by the wind.
That person should not expect
to receive anything from the
Lord, being double-minded and
unstable in all his ways. . . .

Blessed is the one who endures
trials, because when he has stood
the test he will receive the crown
of life that God has promised to
those who love him.

No one undergoing a trial
should say, "I am being tempted
by God," since God is not tempted
by evil, and he himself doesn't
tempt anyone. But each person is
tempted when he is drawn away
and enticed by his own evil desire.
Then after desire has conceived,
it gives birth to sin, and when
sin is fully grown, it gives birth
to death.

—James 1:2–8,12–15

HERE'S THE DEAL

When you're tempted to sin, realize
it's not God doing the tempting.
He doesn't want you to sin, but he
does provide a way for you to escape
temptation. Good, biblical advice is
to run from temptation and not allow
temptation to know where you're
going. Think through tempting
situations before they happen to
you and plan your escape route so
that you'll know exactly how to run
and avoid falling into temptation's
trap. With an escape plan, the
temptations become an opportunity
to run to God for needed courage
and strength.

*Related Texts: Job 1–42; Matthew 6:9–
13; 21:18–22; 1 Corinthians 10:12–13*

If anyone does not stumble in what he says, he is mature, able also to control the whole body. Now if we put bits into the mouths of horses so that they obey us, we direct their whole bodies. And consider ships: Though very large and driven by fierce winds, they are guided by a very small rudder wherever the will of the pilot directs. So too, though the tongue is a small part of the body, it boasts great things. Consider how a small fire sets ablaze a large forest. And the tongue is a fire. The tongue, a world of unrighteousness, is placed among our members. It stains the whole body, sets the course of life on fire, and is itself set on fire by hell. Every kind of animal, bird, reptile, and fish is tamed and has been tamed by humankind, but no one can tame the tongue. It is a restless evil, full of deadly poison. With the tongue we bless our Lord and Father, and with it we curse people who are made in God's likeness. Blessing and cursing come out of the same mouth. My brothers and sisters, these things should not be this way. Does a spring pour out sweet and bitter water from the same opening? Can a fig tree produce olives, my brothers and sisters, or a grapevine produce figs? Neither can a saltwater spring yield fresh water.

—James 3:2–12

DIG DEEPER

Words can hurt! Everyone has been the victim of damaging words. If you don't have painful memories of hurtful words, consider yourself lucky and expect it to happen sooner or later (sorry!).

Jesus taught that our words are a reflection of our heart. Check out Matthew 12:35: "A good person produces good things from his storeroom of good, and an evil person produces evil things from his storeroom of evil."

Try using good words today and think about the power behind the words you use. Your words can either heal or hurt. Choose healing words today.

Related Texts: Psalm 12; Proverbs 6:16–19; 10:18–21,31–32; 12:17–19,22

Blessed be the God and Father of our Lord Jesus Christ. Because of his great mercy he has given us new birth into a living hope through the resurrection of Jesus Christ from the dead and into an inheritance that is imperishable, undefiled, and unfading, kept in heaven for you. You are being guarded by God's power through faith for a salvation that is ready to be revealed in the last time. You rejoice in this, even though now for a short time, if necessary, you suffer grief in various trials . . . Though you have not seen him, you love him; though not seeing him now, you believe in him, and you rejoice with inexpressible and glorious joy, because you are receiving the goal of your faith, the salvation of your souls.

Concerning this salvation, the prophets, who prophesied about the grace that would come to you, searched and carefully investigated. . . . It was revealed to them that they were not serving themselves but you. These things have now been announced to you through those who preached the gospel to you by the Holy Spirit sent from heaven — angels long to catch a glimpse of these things.

–1 Peter 1:3–6,8–10,12

JUST A THOUGHT

When you put your faith in Jesus, you not only receive a heavenly birth but also the promise of eternity and the presence of God's strength until then.

Related Texts: Isaiah 52:13–53:12; Zechariah 13:7–9; Hebrews 1–2; James 1

Therefore, rid yourselves of all malice, all deceit, hypocrisy, envy, and all slander. Like newborn infants, desire the pure milk of the word, so that by it you may grow up into your salvation, if **you have tasted that the Lord is good.** As you come to him, a living stone — rejected by people but chosen and honored by God — you yourselves, as living stones, a spiritual house, are being built to be a holy priesthood to offer spiritual sacrifices acceptable to God through Jesus Christ. For it stands in Scripture:

See, I lay a stone in Zion,
a chosen
   and honored cornerstone,
and the one who believes
   in him
will never be put to shame. . . .

But you are **a chosen race, a royal priesthood, a holy nation, a people for his possession, so that you may proclaim the praises** of the one who called you out of darkness into his marvelous light. Once you were not a people, but now you are God's people; you had not received mercy, but now you have received mercy.

—1 Peter 2:1–6,9–10

BIG TIME WORD

Unfortunately, today's world has a lot of hatred displayed in the words and actions of others. Hatred displays itself in many different ways and is often triggered by anger. When anger isn't processed in a godly manner, it can lead to resentment and then to hatred. This hatred usually reveals itself in some form of rebellion or rage.

Hatred is the opposite of peace. If you choose hatred, you'll slowly destroy yourself and will eventually fall to pieces. But if you refuse hatred, you'll experience God's peace.

What's your choice? Peace or pieces?

Related Texts: Psalms 34; 118:22–29; Isaiah 28:16–17; Matthew 16:13–19; Luke 20:9–19; Hebrews 5:11–14

F or we did not follow cleverly contrived myths when we made known to you the power and coming of our Lord Jesus Christ; instead, we were eyewitnesses of his majesty. For he received honor and glory from God the Father when the voice came to him from the Majestic Glory, saying "This is my beloved Son, with whom I am well-pleased!" We ourselves heard this voice when it came from heaven while we were with him on the holy mountain. We also have the prophetic word strongly confirmed, and you will do well to pay attention to it, as to a lamp shining in a dark place, until the day dawns and the morning star rises in your hearts. Above all, you know this: No prophecy of Scripture comes from the prophet's own interpretation, because no prophecy ever came by the will of man; instead, men spoke from God as they were carried along by the Holy Spirit.

−2 Peter 1:16−21

Your word is a lamp for my feet and a light on my path.

−Psalm 119:105

"I, Jesus, have sent my angel to attest these things to you for the churches. I am the Root and descendant of David, the bright morning star."

−Revelation 22:16

IN OTHER WORDS

Peter had an incredible experience at the Mount of Transfiguration. But he didn't allow his experience to replace his love and convictions for Scripture. Peter instructs Christians to trust Scripture (God's ways) more than experience.

Living by God's Word provides light and guides through the darkness. Although the Bible is filled with human words, it was God who inspired the writers with the right words. God "spoke" or "breathed" his words into life. The Scriptures are God's words and are as reliable as God himself.

When God's words are hidden in your heart, you will be different—it's guaranteed!

Related Texts: Isaiah 61; Jeremiah 26; Amos 3:1−8; Mark 9:2−9; Luke 1:1−4

My little children, I am writing you these things so that you may not sin. But if anyone does sin, we have an advocate with the Father — Jesus Christ the righteous one. He himself is the atoning sacrifice for our sins, and not only for ours, but also for those of the whole world.

This is how we know that we know him: if we keep his commands. The one who says, "I have come to know him," and yet doesn't keep his commands, is a liar, and the truth is not in him. But whoever keeps his word, truly in him the love of God is made complete. This is how we know we are in him: The one who says he remains in him should walk just as he walked.

Dear friends, I am not writing you a new command but an old command that you have had from the beginning. The old command is the word you have heard. Yet I am writing you a new command, which is true in him and in you, because the darkness is passing away and the true light is already shining.

−1 John 2:1−8

"I give you a new command: Love one another. Just as I have loved you, you are also to love one another. By this everyone will know that you are my disciples, if you love one another."

−John 13:34−35

HERE'S THE DEAL

The greatest gift of all is God's love expressed by Jesus's dying in your place. That's real love! The Bible is another example of God's love.

Jesus expressed this when he summarized all the commandments and used "love" three times. He took 513 Old Testament laws and put them into simple words when he said to love God with all of your heart, soul, and mind and to love your neighbors as you love yourself.

This love will not only change your life but will also show others you are a follower of Jesus. This is a biggie; try loving regardless of how others act or treat you — it's not easy. Soak in God's love and you'll find yourself loving just as God loves you.

Related Texts: 1 Kings 8:46−51; Psalm 119:9−11; John 14:15; Hebrews 2:17−18; 4:14−16; 7−9; 1 John 3:11−24

Do not love the world or the things in the world. If anyone loves the world, the love of the Father is not in him. For everything in the world — the lust of the flesh, the lust of the eyes, and the pride in one's possessions — is not from the Father, but is from the world. And the world with its lust is passing away, but the one who does the will of God remains forever.

—1 John 2:15–17

See what great love the Father has given us that we should be called God's children — and we are! The reason the world does not know us is that it didn't know him.

—1 John 3:1

Everyone who believes that Jesus is the Christ has been born of God, and everyone who loves the Father also loves the one born of him. This is how we know that we love God's children: when we love God and obey his commands. For this is what love for God is: to keep his commands. And his commands are not a burden, because everyone who has been born of God conquers the world. This is the victory that has conquered the world: our faith.

Who is the one who conquers the world but the one who believes that Jesus is the Son of God?

—1 John 5:1–5

ONE MINUTE MEMORY

"Everyone who believes that Jesus is the Christ has been born of God, and everyone who loves the Father also loves the one born of him" (1Jn 5:1)

Related Texts: Deuteronomy 30:11–16; John 15:17–25; 1 John 4:7–21

C hildren, it is the last hour. And as you have heard that antichrist is coming, even now many antichrists have come. By this we know that it is the last hour. They went out from us, but they did not belong to us; for if they had belonged to us, they would have remained with us. However, they went out so that it might be made clear that none of them belongs to us. . . .

Who is the liar, if not the one who denies that Jesus is the Christ? This one is the antichrist: the one who denies the Father and the Son. No one who denies the Son has the Father; he who confesses the Son has the Father as well.

—1 John 2:18–19,22–23

Many deceivers have gone out into the world; they do not confess the coming of Jesus Christ in the flesh. This is the deceiver and the antichrist. Watch yourselves so that you don't lose what we have worked for, but that you may receive a full reward. Anyone who does not remain in Christ's teaching but goes beyond it does not have God. The one who remains in that teaching, this one has both the Father and the Son. If anyone comes to you and does not bring this teaching, do not receive him into your home, and do not greet him; for the one who greets him shares in his evil works.

—2 John 7–11

BIBLICAL BIO

The word *antichrist* appears only five times in the New Testament, but the theme of an antichrist person is woven throughout the Old Testament prophecies. The word *anti* means "in place of" or "against." The Bible describes the antichrist as someone who will try to exalt himself and be worshiped. The antichrist will be given power or directed by Satan and try to lead people against God during the end times.

One of God's many responsibilities is to take care of history. During that time a responsibility of a follower of Jesus is to remain faithful to God's ways. A strong faith in God will replace your fears with the confident security that the antichrist will have no power over you.

Related Texts: Proverbs 13:5; Isaiah 44:24–25; Jeremiah 14:14–15; 2 Timothy 3; 2 Peter 2–3

I found it necessary to write, appealing to you to contend for the faith that was delivered to the saints once for all. For some people, who were designated for this judgment long ago, have come in by stealth; they are ungodly, turning the grace of our God into sensuality and denying Jesus Christ, our only Master and Lord....

But you, dear friends, remember what was predicted by the apostles of our Lord Jesus Christ. They told you, "In the end time there will be scoffers living according to their own ungodly desires." These people create divisions and are worldly, not having the Spirit....

Keep yourselves in the love of God, waiting expectantly for the mercy of our Lord Jesus Christ for eternal life. Have mercy on those who waver; save others by snatching them from the fire; have mercy on others but with fear, hating even the garment defiled by the flesh.

Now to him who is able to protect you from stumbling and to make you stand in the presence of his glory, without blemish and with great joy, to the only God our Savior, through Jesus Christ our Lord, be glory, majesty, power, and authority before all time, now and forever. Amen.

—Jude 3–4,17–19,21–25

IN OTHER WORDS

The problem addressed in Jude remains a problem today. There are still godless teachers trying to pervert or add to the Bible. Followers of Jesus need to watch out for them because their teaching can be seductive and subtle. False teachers can creep into the church and lead good people in the wrong direction.

One way to identify these teachers is to observe how they live their lives. If you are following someone's teachings, you need to ask yourself, "Does he practice what he teaches? Does he hate what is evil?"

Do what it takes to remain in God's love, and you'll be protected from the ungodly.

Related Texts: Amos 4:11; Zechariah 3; Acts 20:28–31; 1 Timothy 4:1–6; 2 Peter 3

Why do the nations rage
and the peoples plot
in vain?
The kings of the earth take
their stand,
and the rulers conspire together
against the LORD
and his Anointed One:
"Let's tear off their chains
and throw their ropes off of us."

The one enthroned in heaven
laughs;
the Lord ridicules them.
Then he speaks to them
in his anger
and terrifies them in his wrath:
"I have installed my king
on Zion, my holy mountain."

I will declare the LORD's decree.
He said to me, "You are my Son;
today I have become your Father.
Ask of me,
and I will make the nations
your inheritance
and the ends of the earth
your possession.
You will break them
with an iron scepter;
you will shatter them like pottery."

So now, kings, be wise;
receive instruction, you judges
of the earth.
Serve the LORD
with reverential awe
and rejoice with trembling.
Pay homage to the Son or he
will be angry
and you will perish
in your rebellion,
for his anger may ignite
at any moment.
All who take refuge in him
are happy.

—Psalm 2:1–12

IN OTHER WORDS

This psalm is a great example of how useless it is to try to rebel against God. God laughs at plans that go against his plans.

If you are searching for true freedom you will never find it in rebellion. Ironically, freedom is found in submission—which is the opposite of rebellion. Submission to God is giving everything you are into everything God is. Submission leads to freedom.

Don't you think that if God is capable of planning the coming of Jesus, he can also plan your life?

Trust in his wisdom and be a part of his eternal plan.

*Related Texts: 2 Samuel 7;
1 Chronicles 17; Mark 1:1–11;
Revelation 2:18–29*

This is the declaration of the LORD to my Lord:

"Sit at my right hand
until I make your enemies
    your footstool."
The LORD will extend
    your mighty scepter from Zion.
Rule over
    your surrounding enemies.
Your people will volunteer
on your day of battle.
In holy splendor, from the womb
    of the dawn,
the dew of your youth
    belongs to you.
The LORD has sworn an oath
    and will not take it back:
"You are a priest forever
according to the pattern
    of Melchizedek."

The Lord is at your right hand;
he will crush kings on the day
    of his anger.
He will judge the nations,
    heaping up corpses;
he will crush leaders
    over the entire world.
He will drink from the brook
    by the road;
therefore, he will lift up his head.
–Psalm 110

Now many have become Levitical priests, since they are prevented by death from remaining in office. But because he remains forever, he holds his priesthood permanently. Therefore, he is able to save completely those who come to God through him, since he always lives to intercede for them.

For this is the kind of high priest we need: holy, innocent, undefiled, separated from sinners, and exalted above the heavens.
–Hebrews 7:23–26

JUST A THOUGHT

If you have a personal relationship with Jesus, you have all you need—forever. He has taken care of all your needs!

Related Texts: Genesis 14:18–20;
Matthew 22:41–46; Hebrews 5:1–10; 7

Joseph also went up from the town of Nazareth in Galilee, to Judea, to the city of David, which is called Bethlehem, because he was of the house and family line of David, to be registered along with Mary, who was engaged to him and was pregnant. While they were there, the time came for her to give birth. Then she gave birth to her firstborn son, and she wrapped him tightly in cloth and laid him in a manger, because there was no guest room available for them.

In the same region, shepherds were staying out in the fields and keeping watch at night over their flock. Then an angel of the Lord stood before them, and the glory of the Lord shone around them, and they were terrified. But the angel said to them, "Don't be afraid, for look, I proclaim to you good news of great joy that will be for all the people: Today in the city of David a Savior was born for you, who is the Messiah, the Lord. This will be the sign for you: You will find a baby wrapped tightly in cloth and lying in a manger."

Suddenly there was a multitude of the heavenly host with the angel, praising God and saying:

Glory to God
in the highest heaven,
and peace on earth to people
he favors!

−Luke 2:4−14

TAKE A SHOT

Tomorrow you celebrate the birth of Jesus. Take a minute to write Jesus a birthday card that expresses your thankfulness.

_____

_____

_____

_____

_____

_____

_____

_____

_____

_____

_____

_____

_____

_____

_____

_____

_____

_____

_____

_____

_____

_____

_____

_____

_____

Related Texts: 2 Samuel 7:8−17;
Psalm 89:20−37; Isaiah 9:6−7;
Matthew 1:18−25; Luke 1−2

After Jesus was born in Bethlehem of Judea in the days of King Herod, wise men from the east arrived in Jerusalem, saying, "Where is he who has been born king of the Jews? For we saw his star at its rising and have come to worship him."

When King Herod heard this, he was deeply disturbed, and all Jerusalem with him. So he assembled all the chief priests and scribes of the people and asked them where the Messiah would be born.

"In Bethlehem of Judea," they told him, "because this is what was written by the prophet:

And you, Bethlehem,
in the land of Judah,
are by no means **least**
among the rulers of Judah:
Because out of you will come
a ruler
who will shepherd my people
Israel."

Then Herod secretly summoned the wise men and asked them the exact time the star appeared. He sent them to Bethlehem and said, "Go and search carefully for the child. When you find him, report back to me so that I too can go and worship him."

After hearing the king, they went on their way. And there it was — the star they had seen at its rising. It led them until it came and stopped above the place where the child was. When they saw the star, they were overwhelmed with joy. Entering the house, they saw the child with Mary his mother, and falling to their knees, they worshiped him.

Then they opened their treasures and presented him with gifts: gold, frankincense, and myrrh. And being warned in a dream not to go back to Herod, they returned to their own country by another route.

–Matthew 2:1–12

BIBLICAL BIO

Jesus is the key figure in the New Testament and the prophesied Messiah of the Old Testament. Although, in the Bible there is little about Jesus's life prior to his public ministry, it's clear from Scripture that Jesus is God's Son—the incarnation of the invisible God. He lived a perfect life; he is fully human and fully God; he died for your sins; he rose from the dead three days later; and he promised to return to earth someday. It may not seem like a lot of information, but it's enough to make it possible for anyone to live forever.

Not everyone celebrates Jesus's birth today, but someday, the entire world will bow and be judged according to their faith—or lack of faith—in Jesus. Today is a special day and it's more than a holiday if Jesus is a part of your life. Merry Christmas!

Related Texts: Exodus 30:22–33;
Micah 5:2–5; Mark 15:16–24;
Luke 1–2; John 12:1–7;
Hebrews 13:15–21

For I will create new heavens
and a new earth;
the past events will not
be remembered or come
to mind.
Then be glad and rejoice forever
in what I am creating;
for I will create Jerusalem to be
a joy
and its people to be a delight.
I will rejoice in Jerusalem
and be glad in my people.
The sound of weeping and crying
will no longer be heard in her.
In her, a nursing infant
will no longer live
only a few days,
or an old man not live out his days.
Indeed, the one who dies
at a hundred years old
will be mourned as a young man,
and the one who misses
a hundred years
will be considered cursed.

They will not labor
without success
or bear children destined
for disaster,
for they will be a people blessed
by the LORD
along with their descendants.
Even before they call,
I will answer;
while they are still speaking,
I will hear.
The wolf and the lamb
will feed together,
and the lion will eat straw
like cattle,
but the serpent's food will be dust!
They will not do what is evil
or destroy
on my entire holy mountain,"
says the LORD.
       —Isaiah 65:17–20,23–25

WEIRD OR WHAT?

No one knows the exact time of Jesus's eventual return and the establishment of a new heaven and new earth. But there are several prophecies regarding the last days, some of which include the following: widespread violence, the rejection of God's Word, the rise of false prophets and antichrists, abnormal sexual activity, intense demonic activity, extreme materialism, increase of wars, and political and religious uproar.

There are other signs, but these examples are enough to get you thinking. Would you agree that many of these signs are already present in today's world?

Take a risk and find someone who can help you better understand what the Bible teaches regarding the end times.

Related Texts: Genesis 3:1–14;
Isaiah 66:22–24; 2 Peter 3:1–14;
Revelation 21:1–5

He led me to the gate, the one that faces east, and I saw the glory of the God of Israel coming from the east. His voice sounded like the roar of a huge torrent, and the earth shone with his glory. The vision I saw was like the one I had seen when he came to destroy the city, and like the ones I had seen by the Chebar Canal. I fell facedown. The glory of the LORD entered the temple by way of the gate that faced east. Then the Spirit lifted me up and brought me to the inner court, and the glory of the LORD filled the temple.

While the man was standing beside me, I heard someone speaking to me from the temple. He said to me, "Son of man, this is the place of my throne and the place for the soles of my feet, where I will dwell among the Israelites forever. The house of Israel and their kings will no longer defile my holy name by their religious prostitution and by the corpses of their kings at their high places. Whenever they placed their threshold next to my threshold and their doorposts beside my doorposts, with only a wall between me and them, they were defiling my holy name by the detestable acts they committed. So I destroyed them in my anger. Now let them remove their prostitution and the corpses of their kings far from me, and I will dwell among them forever.

—Ezekiel 43:1–9

IN OTHER WORDS

Jerusalem is a city mentioned in both the Old and New Testaments. During biblical times this popular place was the capital of Israel as well as the center for worship. The temple was built in Jerusalem, and each succeeding temple that was destroyed was always rebuilt on its original site. Also, the majority of Jesus's ministry took place in Jerusalem, as did many events surrounding the beginning of the church. Much of the prophetic literature in the Bible (including today's reading) uses the city of Jerusalem or a Jerusalem-like setting as the place of Jesus's return and rule.

If you're ready for his return, it won't matter when or where—so be ready!

Related Texts: Ezekiel 1; 3; 8–11; Zechariah 14; Revelation 21:1–4

I, John, your brother and partner in the affliction, kingdom, and endurance that are in Jesus, was on the island called Patmos because of the word of God and the testimony of Jesus. I was in the Spirit on the Lord's day, and I heard a loud voice behind me like a trumpet saying, "Write on a scroll what you see and send it to the seven churches: Ephesus, Smyrna, Pergamum, Thyatira, Sardis, Philadelphia, and Laodicea."

Then I turned to see whose voice it was that spoke to me. When I turned I saw seven golden lampstands, and among the lampstands was one like the Son of Man, dressed in a robe and with a golden sash wrapped around his chest. The hair of his head was white as wool — white as snow — and his eyes like a fiery flame. His feet were like fine bronze as it is fired in a furnace, and his voice like the sound of cascading waters. He had seven stars in his right hand; a sharp double-edged sword came from his mouth, and his face was shining like the sun at full strength.

When I saw him, I fell at his feet like a dead man. He laid his right hand on me and said, "Don't be afraid. I am the First and the Last, and the Living One. I was dead, but look — I am alive forever and ever, and I hold the keys of death and Hades. Therefore write what you have seen, what is, and what will take place after this.

—Revelation 1:9–19

BIBLICAL BIO

John was one of Jesus's first disciples and was part of Jesus's inner group along with Peter and James. He was more than a fisherman who turned author; he was an intelligent man who educated himself with Jewish teachings.

John received the nickname "son of thunder" and is often described as being scrappy and ambitious. His claim to fame is that he's known as the disciple whom Jesus loved. John's life is really a snapshot of what Jesus's presence was able to do with others. Jesus took a self-centered fisherman and turned him into the man of love — that is clear from his writings.

Related Texts: Psalm 149; Daniel 7; 2 Timothy 3; Hebrews 4:12–13; Revelation 2–11; 19:11–21

Then I saw an angel coming down from heaven holding the key to the abyss and a great chain in his hand. He seized the dragon, that ancient serpent who is the devil and Satan, and bound him for a thousand years. He threw him into the abyss, closed it, and put a seal on it so that he would no longer deceive the nations until the thousand years were completed. After that, he must be released for a short time.

Then I saw thrones, and people seated on them who were given authority to judge. I also saw the souls of those who had been beheaded because of their testimony about Jesus and because of the word of God, who had not worshiped the beast or his image, and who had not accepted the mark on their foreheads or their hands. They came to life and reigned with Christ for a thousand years. The rest of the dead did not come to life until the thousand years were completed.

This is the first resurrection. Blessed and holy is the one who shares in the first resurrection! The second death has no power over them, but they will be priests of God and of Christ, and they will reign with him for a thousand years.

When the thousand years are completed, Satan will be released from his prison and will go out to deceive the nations at the four corners of the earth, Gog and Magog, to gather them for battle. Their number is like the sand of the sea. They came up across the breadth of the earth and surrounded the encampment of the saints, the beloved city. Then fire came down from heaven and consumed them. The devil who deceived them was thrown into the lake of fire and sulfur where the beast and the false prophet are, and they will be tormented day and night forever and ever.

–Revelation 20:1–10

JUST A THOUGHT

The book of Revelation is no fairy tale! It's difficult to understand everything written and requires faith to believe, but it's good to know that God wins in the end.

Related Texts: Genesis 3:1–15; Ezekiel 38–39; 1 Corinthians 6:1–3; Revelation 12–13; 17–19

Then I saw a great white throne and one seated on it. Earth and heaven fled from his presence, and no place was found for them. I also saw the dead, the great and the small, standing before the throne, and books were opened. Another book was opened, which is the book of life, and the dead were judged according to their works by what was written in the books. Then the sea gave up the dead that were in it, and death and Hades gave up the dead that were in them; each one was judged according to their works. Death and Hades were thrown into the lake of fire. This is the second death, the lake of fire. And anyone whose name was not found written in the book of life was thrown into the lake of fire.

—Revelation 20:11–15

Then I saw a new heaven and a new earth; for the first heaven and the first earth had passed away, and the sea was no more. I also saw the holy city, the new Jerusalem, coming down out of heaven from God, prepared like a bride adorned for her husband.

Then I heard a loud voice from the throne: Look, God's dwelling is with humanity, and he will live with them. They will be his peoples, and God himself will be with them and will be their God. He will wipe away every tear from their eyes. Death will be no more; grief, crying, and pain will be no more, because the previous things have passed away.

—Revelation 21:1–4

ONE-MINUTE MEMORY

"He will wipe away every tear from their eyes. Death will be no more; grief, crying, and pain will be no more, because the previous things have passed away" (Rv 21:4).

Related Texts: Isaiah 65:17–25; 66:22–24; Daniel 12:1–3; John 1:14–18; 2 Peter 3:1–14

Then he said to me, "These words are faithful and true. The Lord, the God of the spirits of the prophets, has sent his angel to show his servants what must soon take place."

"Look, I am coming soon! Blessed is the one who keeps the words of the prophecy of this book." . . .

"Look, I am coming soon, and my reward is with me to repay each person according to his work. I am the Alpha and the Omega, the first and the last, the beginning and the end.

"Blessed are those who wash their robes, so that they may have the right to the tree of life and may enter the city by the gates. Outside are the dogs, the sorcerers, the sexually immoral, the murderers, the idolaters, and everyone who loves and practices falsehood.

"I, Jesus, have sent my angel to attest these things to you for the churches. I am the Root and descendant of David, the bright morning star."

Both the Spirit and the bride say, "Come!" Let anyone who hears, say, "Come!" Let the one who is thirsty come. Let the one who desires take the water of life freely. . . .

He who testifies about these things says, "Yes, I am coming soon."

Amen! Come, Lord Jesus!

The grace of the Lord Jesus be with everyone. Amen.

—Revelation 22:6–7,12–17,20–21

JUST A THOUGHT

Begin your new year right by committing with faith to follow Jesus throughout the year. A year of walking with Jesus is a great year! Happy New Year!

Related Texts: Psalm 1; 37; Matthew 16:24–27; Luke 12:35–40; 1 Thessalonians 4:13–5:11; Revelation 1:1–3

TOPICAL INDEX

TOPICAL INDEX

TOPICAL INDEX

TOPICAL INDEX